Fandom and the Law

Fan Fiction, Art, Film & Cosplay

Marc H. Greenberg

AMERICAN BAR ASSOCIATION
Intellectual Property Law Section

Cover design by Amy Mandel, ABA Section of Intellectual Property Law; Jill Tedhams, ABA Design.

Cover illustration by Darick Robertson © 2021, All Rights Reserved

The materials contained herein represent the opinions of the authors and/or the editors, and should not be construed to be the views or opinions of the law firms or companies with whom such persons are in partnership with, associated with, or employed by, nor of the American Bar Association or the Section of Intellectual Property Law unless adopted pursuant to the bylaws of the Association.

Nothing contained in this book is to be considered as the rendering of legal advice for specific cases, and readers are responsible for obtaining such advice from their own legal counsel. This book is intended for educational and informational purposes only.

Printed in the United States of America.

25 24 23 22 21   5 4 3 2 1

Library of Congress Cataloging-in-Publication Data

Names: Greenberg, Marc H., author.
Title: Fandom and the law : a guide to fan fiction, art, film, and cosplay / Marc H. Greenberg.
Description: Chicago, Illinois : ABA Publishing, American Bar Association, [2021] | Includes index. | Summary: "An analysis based on the two major iterations of copyright law, the 1909 Act and the 1976 Act"—Provided by publisher.
Identifiers: LCCN 2021023094 (print) | LCCN 2021023095 (ebook) | ISBN 9781641058858 (paperback) | ISBN 9781641058865 (ebook)
Subjects: LCSH: Copyright—United States. | Copyright—Fictitious characters—United States. | United States. Copyright Act of 1909. | United States. Copyrights (1976) | Fan fiction—Law and legislation—United States. | Comic books, strips, etc.—Law and legislation—United States. | Fan films.
Classification: LCC KF3020 .G74 2021 (print) | LCC KF3020 (ebook) | DDC 346.7304/82—dc23
LC record available at https://lccn.loc.gov/2021023094
LC ebook record available at https://lccn.loc.gov/2021023095

This book is dedicated to all of the fans of popular culture and particularly to those who have been so moved and inspired by that culture that they have created new works in celebration of it—as a proud member of the acafan community, I celebrate your works.

CONTENTS

THEMATIC CONTENTS

As the preceding table of contents reflects, this book is a mixture of analysis based on the two major iterations of copyright law in the United States—the 1909 Act and the 1976 Act—discussed in detail in Section 2, Chapters 1–3, followed by a discussion of several relevant themes, including parody and satire, the transformative doctrine, and related legislation, and ending the section with brief notes on trademark law and right of publicity law.

For those readers who prefer to read the copyright sections from a thematic perspective, I offer the following table for those three copyright chapters of Section 2 to allow you to more easily find those themes in this section of the book.

ACKNOWLEDGMENTS

This book, like the first two I wrote, has been a journey. In this instance, that journey included two knee surgeries and the first eight months of a terrible health pandemic. As always, I couldn't have made it without the help of my friends, colleagues, and family. My deepest thanks go out to my research assistant Kelsey O'Rourke, who helped with the initial research; my colleague and friend Francine Ward, who helped with the original work for this project; attorney Linda Joy Kattwinkel, for our work on an early presentation of these issues at the California State Bar IP Law Section conference; my colleagues at Golden Gate University School of Law; the ever kind and patient Jeff Salyards at ABA Publishing, who never gave up hope that I would finish this manuscript; my friend and gifted artist Darick Robertson, who lent his artistic brilliance to the cover art; ABA Publishing's Amy Mandel, who shepherded the art design of the project once the manuscript was submitted; Books Board member David Rein and esteemed Harvard law professor Rebecca Tushnet, who bravely served as readers of the initial draft of the manuscript and offered critical suggestions for its improvement; and last, and by no means least, my life partner, muse, and researcher extraordinaire, my wife Kim Munson, who gets me through everything. And to those I have inadvertently omitted, my thanks to you as well—you know who you are. This is a monograph—other than quoted material, I wrote every word of this and take responsibility for all of it—the mistakes are all mine.

ABOUT THE AUTHOR

Marc H. Greenberg is a Professor of Law and the founding Director of the Intellectual Property Law Center and Program at Golden Gate University School of Law. A member of the faculty since 2000, he teaches Intellectual Property Survey, Internet and Software Law, Intellectual Property and New Technology, An Introduction to Privacy Law, and Entertainment Law in the IP curriculum. He also teaches Civil Procedure, Business Associations, Property Law, Wills and Trusts, and related courses in the general curriculum. He was the 2010–2011 Chair and is presently on the Executive Board of the Art Law Section of the American Association of Law Schools, and is a past co-chair of the Copyright Section of the San Francisco Intellectual Property Law Association. He is a member of the Books Editorial Board of the IP Law Section of the ABA.

Professor Greenberg received his A.B. degree in English Literature from the University of California, Berkeley; and his J.D. from the University of California, Hastings College of the Law. While in law school he served as an Articles Editor of the *Hastings Constitutional Law Quarterly* and published the first of his scholarly works analyzing the First Amendment cases of the Supreme Court's 1978 term.

Professor Greenberg's scholarship has focused on legal issues pertaining to comic art, content on the Internet, obscenity law in online contexts, and copyright issues both in the United States and in China. In 2014 his book *Comic Art, Creativity and the Law* was published by Edward Elgar Publishing. In 2016, his book *Copyright Termination and Recapture Laws: Policy and Practice* was published by ABA Publishing. His articles have been published in the *Berkeley Technology Law Journal, The Syracuse Journal of Law and Technology, The John Marshall Review of Intellectual Property Law,* and *The Loyola Chicago University Journal of International Law.*

Before joining the GGU faculty, Professor Greenberg practiced IP, entertainment, and business law, in both transactional work and litigation, in several firms in Northern California. He is still an active practitioner providing legal services to select clients via his firm, Law Office of Marc H. Greenberg. He can be reached at mhg@marcgreenberglaw.com or mgreenberg@ggu.edu.

INTRODUCTION

As the child of an artist (my father) and a theater-loving English literature graduate student (my mother), it is no wonder that I became first a lawyer specializing in entertainment, copyright, and pop culture, and then a law professor teaching in these areas of the law, while still maintaining (with the consent of very patient law school deans) a foothold in the practice of these areas. A lifelong collector of comic books, I have turned my love of that genre into a source of income and professional pride, representing comic book creators and historians on a diverse array of projects. I burnished my scholarship chops by writing a book about the intersection of comics and the law, which was published in 2014 under the title *Comic Art, Creativity and the Law*.[1]

A portion of the research I did for that book led me to write several chapters about cases involving comic book creators and their efforts, at times successful and in other instances not so successful, to recapture the copyright to their works from publishers under the termination and recapture rights granted by the Copyright Law of 1976.[2] This led to the authoring of my second book, *Copyright Termination and Recapture Laws: Good Intentions Gone Awry*,[3] focusing on how Congress had tried to protect content creators and how flaws in the legislation, and the determined efforts of publishers, aided by some questionable court decisions, had undermined those goals.

Before either of these books was even a glimmer in my eye, I had unwittingly begun preparation for this book. Starting in 2003, my wife and I began attending WonderCon and the San Diego Comic-Con International (SDCCI) pop culture and comic book conventions in northern and southern California. We were late to the party—SDCCI (as the largest and best-known of the conventions in the United States, it will hereinafter be referred to as Comic-Con)

---

1. Marc Greenberg, Comic Art, Creativity and the Law (Edward Elgar Publ'g 2014).
2. *See, e.g.*, 17 U.S.C. §§ 203, 304.
3. Marc Greenberg, Copyright Termination and Recapture Laws: Good Intentions Gone Awry (ABA Publ'g 2016).

began in 1970 as a small, one-day fan-based event, attended by 300 people and held in the basement of the U.S. Grant Hotel in San Diego.[4]

SDCC was not the first such convention for fans of comic books and related genres. An early iteration was the Worldcon convention for science fiction fans, launched in 1939. Initially it was not focused on comic books. The 1960 Worldcon convention in Los Angeles was one of the first to feature an emphasis on comic books. Two years later, a Worldcon convention in Chicago featured the introduction of fans dressing as comic book characters, a forerunner of today's costume play, or cosplay.[5]

Another two years later, two events brought the idea of a full-fledged comics convention to fruition: the May 1964 comics convention in Detroit and the July 1964 New York Comicon. By 1965, the scope of these conventions expanded, in the Detroit Triple Fan Fair, to include fantasy literature, films, and comic art. And so by the time SDCC launched in 1970, it billed itself as featuring comic art, films, and science fiction. In-person appearances by science-fiction writer A.E. van Vogt and Marvel graphic artist Jack Kirby made it evident that this was a convention not simply for comics fans but for a broader audience of pop-culture aficionados.[6]

Over the years, the scope of SDCC has continually expanded, and it now serves up a menu dizzying in breadth. As such, it serves as a micro view of the range of activities that attract the focus of fans of pop culture. San Diego Comic-Con, often referred to simply as "the Con," includes a significant amount of panels and programming devoted to the history of comic books and graphic novels as a media format. In addition to those programs geared to the popular history of comics, an entire conference within the Con is presented by and for academics who write scholarly treatises and articles about comics as a literary genre. This program, the Comic Arts Conference (hereinafter CAC), explores topics ranging from the psychological profile of Batman's villains (i.e., is the Joker a psychopath, or is Batman?) to the impact comics have had on traditional art.

For fans of pop culture as expressed in motion pictures and television, giant halls and auditoriums at the Con are devoted entirely to this dominant form of pop culture. The cavernous Hall H, which can seat over 6,000 people, is the site for panels and specially tailored movie trailers showcasing upcoming science-fiction, fantasy, and comics-based blockbuster movies. By bringing sneak peeks, trailers, and the casts and directors of these movies into Hall H, movie studios are hoping to build fandom buzz in support of the upcoming release of the movies and the debuts of these television shows. Those enthusiastic

---

4. Various Authors, Comic-Con: 40 Years of Artists, Writers, Fans & Friends 18 (Chronicle Books 2009).

5. *Id.* at 40–41.

6. *Id.* at 10.

six thousand fans get onto social media after the programs and spread their excitement to millions of other fans. The rebroadcast, several days later, of the highlights of those panels and trailers on social media platforms like YouTube multiplies the impact of the programs by spreading them to huge numbers of fans.

While single-story movies can develop fans, one of the characteristics of fandom is an appreciation for works that have multiple episodes, like a series of books or comics, which offer characters or narrative arcs of stories that allow fans to follow the work over periods of months or even years (as of this writing, fans are still eagerly, and somewhat impatiently, awaiting the last installment in George R.R. Martin's epic book series *A Song of Ice and Fire*, which has become a hugely popular television series entitled *Game of Thrones*). For that reason, these television series often have more die-hard and engaged fans than those of single-episode movies (I make the distinction "single-episode movies" because movie series, like the Star Wars, Star Trek, and Marvel Universe movies, contain sufficient range and character development to support a die-hard fan base).

At SDCC, three large rooms at the convention (Ballroom 20, Room 6DCEF, and the Indigo Ballroom at the Hilton Bayfront) are almost exclusively devoted to popular television shows, and the fans who attend these programs get to see and hear from the casts of the shows and the showrunners and to watch exclusive trailers for the upcoming season. I am an acafan (more about this term in Chapter 1) of a number of television shows and have attended programs full of screaming and emotional fans of these series: *Battlestar Galactica* (the reboot); *Wynonna Earp; Stargate SG1; Lost Girls; Xena, Warrior Princess; Orphan Black; Smallville; Glee; True Blood; Robot Chicken; The Umbrella Academy; The Boys;* and others. As I discuss in a number of chapters in this book, the continuity afforded by multiple seasons, over many years, of these television series allows for the development and growth of a deeply committed fan base and in many instances also supports a higher degree of interaction between those fans and the shows—with fans sometimes getting the opportunity, often through social media sites for the shows, to contribute story ideas and other elements that become a part of future episodes of the show.

Each of the four areas of fandom discussed in this book—fan fiction, fan art, fan film, and costume play (cosplay)—is the subject of a number of different platforms within comic conventions such as SDCC. The programming platform, featuring panels and individuals involved in the creation of pop-culture content, offers a dizzying array of opportunities for fans to meet writers, artists, filmmakers, and cosplayers and see and, in many cases, buy the latest works of these creators.

SDCCI provides activities for other kinds of fans, whose fandom isn't the subject of this book. Specifically, autograph collectors are often fans of particular celebrities, writers, and/or artists—and conventions allow them the previously unavailable opportunity to meet these creators in person and get a chance (sometimes requiring a payment or purchase or the opportunity cost of waiting in long lines) to spend some time with them and to obtain a valuable autograph. Because these fans generally don't create any expressive works with these autographs, they are not further discussed in this book.

Two other very significant bodies of fandom not discussed are (1) the fans of anime and manga, which are animated television and film programs and comic books and graphic novels, respectively, reflective of pop culture from Japan and other Asian countries, and (2) video and computer games, both for individuals and massive multiplayer online role-playing games (MMORPGs). In both cases, the fandom community is deep and widespread, with social mores, traditions, and a long-standing and complex culture so extensive that it merits separate books or multivolume sets. Addressing these communities calls for a level of awareness about their cultures and industries that is beyond my awareness and hence beyond the scope of this book.

As the years of attending SDCC passed, both my wife and I began to participate in the conventions at a different level. I began researching and writing about the intersection of comics and the law and, in my private practice, began representing comic artists, writers, retailers, and publishers. My wife, an art historian, focused on how comics are viewed, and exhibited, in the fine-art world.[7]

As my understanding of and participation in the comics industry grew and deepened, I became interested in the legal issues facing various stakeholders with respect to fan-created content—principally fan fiction and fan art. As I began to investigate the legal issues involving these kinds of fan-created content, I quickly realized that two other content forms were emerging and starting to occupy a significant part of the fandom landscape: fan films and cosplay. While some legal doctrines, like copyright law, applied to all of these formats, other fields of law were more specific to a particular format—the issue of consent to being touched is a significant one in cosplay that does not play a role in fan fiction, for example.

And so my path from being a fan, relatively uncurious about my role, to a professional working with creators to an acafan developed, and the impetus for writing this book arose. When I began this project, my working title was *Fandom and the Law: The Definitive Guide to Fan Film, Fan Art, Fan Fiction, and Cosplay*. As I delved further into the research and developed a greater appreciation for what a vast and complex thing fandom is, I backed off of that title, realizing that my hubris in thinking I could write "the" definitive guide was utterly

---

7. *See, e.g.*, Comic Art in Museums (Kim Munson ed., Univ. Press of Miss. 2020).

unsustainable. I considered changing the phrase "The Definitive Guide" to "A Definitive Guide." But that too, I realized, was too broad a claim—fandom is so widespread, and occupies so many different forms, that it is well-nigh impossible for anyone to validly claim to have written its definitive guide in any context short of a multivolume (or several-terabyte-long) set of books. And so I've settled on *Fandom and the Law: A Guide to Fan Fiction, Art, Film, and Cosplay.* With the title and scope of the book decided, the next threshold question was how exactly to define fan-created works.

Merriam-Webster's online dictionary defines fan fiction as "stories involving popular fictional characters that are written by fans and often posted on the Internet."[8] In an article about the growing interest in fan fiction, *New Yorker* writer Stephanie Burt, quoting from a book on the subject by Francesca Coppa, *The Fanfiction Reader,* offers the definition as "creative material featuring characters [from] works whose copyright is held by others."[9]

Word Finder defines fan art as "artworks created by fans of a work of fiction (generally visual media such as comics, movies, television shows, or video games) and derived from a character or other aspect of that work. As fan labor, fan art refers to artworks neither created nor (normally) commissioned or endorsed by the creators of the work from which the work derives."[10]

Fan film, a relatively new form of fan-created content, is defined in one popular online encyclopedia as "a film or video inspired by a film, television program, comic book or a similar source, created by fans rather than by the source's copyright holders or creators."[11]

And lastly, cosplay is defined as "the activity or practice of dressing up as a character from a work of fiction (such as a comic book, video game, or television show)."[12]

All of these definitions share certain common elements, which we can extract to aid us in defining fan-created content, which is a part of fandom, as discussed in this book. This is an important distinction to make, and it informs the definition of these kinds of work, as distinguished from fandom in general.

---

8. *Fan Fiction,* Merriam-Webster, https://www.merriam-webster.com/dictionary/fan%20fiction (last visited Jan. 14, 2021).

9. Stephanie Burt, *The Promise and Potential of Fan Fiction,* New Yorker (Aug. 23, 2017), https://www.newyorker.com/books/page-turner/the-promise-and-potential-of-fan-fiction.

10. *What Is "Fan Art",* Word Finder, https://findwords.info/term/fan%20art (last visited Jan. 14, 2021).

11. *Fan Film,* Wikipedia, https://en.wikipedia.org/wiki/Fan_film (last visited Jan. 14, 2021). While I subscribe to the general practice of writers, particularly for scholarly works, of avoiding citations to Wikipedia for the good reason that the accuracy and source of definitions found on the site are not verified, in this case the definition was consistent with my own understanding and that of similar kinds of works, and there was a paucity of other definitions available.

12. *Cosplay,* Merriam-Webster, https://www.merriam-webster.com/dictionary/cosplay (last visited Jan. 14, 2021).

The term "fandom" incorporates a much wider group of people than the creators of fan-created content. "Fandom" is defined variously as "[t]he state or condition of being a fan of someone or something" and "[t]he fans of a particular person, team, fictional series, etc. regarded collectively as a community or subculture."[13]

So fan-created content is a subset of fandom in which the fans cross the line from being excited, engaged, but essentially passive consumers of the content to people expressing their fandom by creating content that is inspired by, and usually includes elements of, the underlying content that they admire. Two important additional considerations arise from this definition.

The first is that the use of the phrase "inspired by" is limited, in defining fan-created content, to works that in some way invoke, emulate, or straight-out use the universe, story lines, and/or characters of the works the fan admires. Without this limitation, the scope of fan-created content becomes so broad that the definition becomes meaningless. So while Shakespeare may have been inspired by the works of Plutarch and Ovid, the absence of similar characters and distinctly similar story lines (as opposed to tropes like a romance or adventure story) means that his works are not fan fiction in this definition.

The second consideration is that the vast majority of fan-created content reflects a positive view of the underlying content that serves as its inspiration. While some social boundaries may be stretched in these works, such as stories that create a homoerotic relationship between *Star Trek*'s Captain Kirk and First Officer Spock, fan fiction based on *Star Trek* generally doesn't portray Kirk as a rapist or Spock as a pedophile. In general, fan-created content often is an homage to the underlying work, or an effort to take the work to a new place, that is at least to some degree consistent with the themes and tropes found in the original work.

Another important consideration is that the definition of fandom contributes to an understanding of the nature of fan-created content—that these works arise out of and become part of a dialogue within a community of like-minded creators and more passive participants (readers of fan fiction and viewers of fan art, fan films, and cosplayer performances). More about this factor later.

With these limiting principles and definitions in mind, I set about organizing how I wanted to present a discussion of the sociology of fandom, as expressed in fan-created content, and how an assortment of legal doctrines interact with and affect the creation and dissemination of fan fiction, fan art, fan film, and cosplay. As I found when I wrote *Comic Art, Creativity and the Law*, the impact the law has on this content cannot be discussed in a vacuum,

---

13. *Fandom*, Lexico, https://en.oxforddictionaries.com/definition/fandom (last visited Jan. 14, 2021).

without consideration of the underlying social drivers that motivate fan content creators.

I also had to decide who my audience was—to whom is this book addressed, and from what perspective do I offer my analysis? Answering the first question, I seek to direct this book first and foremost to attorneys and scholars who work in this particular intersection between fans and the works that inspire them—the lawyers who counsel fan content creators facing infringement claims or seeking to move from fandom to professional status, and the scholars of pop culture and fan studies who are interested in how the law affects this creative process. A second audience is those fan content creators themselves and the acafans who study pop culture and fandom. Writing for these two very different audiences is a challenge—requiring me to thread the needle between too much and too little legal analysis, pragmatic litigation-oriented advice (my 41 years of experience as a litigator shows through in many places), and a discussion of the sociology and legal theories that often drive the legal and social outcomes of the interaction between these two worlds.

And so the first section of this book focuses on *The Sociology of Fandom* and particularly that of fan content creators. There are a number of highly regarded academics writing and speaking on this subject. A term of art these academics use in describing fandom is that it is a form of participatory culture.[14] The meaning of this phrase, and the importance of this concept to fan content creators, is explored in this chapter. Fandom is a cultural phenomenon, embraced by millions of people worldwide, and its expression is the driving force for fan conventions, websites, and other forms of expression. The drivers of this movement, and the critical element of communities of fandoms, are discussed in this section as well.

The second section of the book, *The Broad Brush: Legal Doctrines Affecting All Fan-Created Works*, offers readers an in-depth historical and legal analysis of those aspects of U.S. law whose impact is felt through all fan-created creative works. We begin with a chapter on the history of copyright law, the single body of law most relevant to fan creators. Tracing the history of the law from its roots in England, and its movement across the ocean to the United States, I then focus in Chapter 3 on four key areas of copyright law embodied in the first major revision of that law in the United States: the Copyright Act of 1909.

I am mindful that many writers, particularly in the academic arena, would skip any in-depth discussion of the 1909 Act, viewing it as largely a relic of the

14. Henry Jenkins, Textual Poachers: Television Fans and Participatory Culture (Routledge updated 20th anniv. ed. 2013) (originally published in 1992 by Routledge, Chapman & Hall; an updated 20th Anniversary Edition published 2013 by Routledge. All references to this work in this book are from the 2013 edition); *see also* Henry Jenkins, Mizuko Ito & danah boyd, Participatory Culture in a Networked Era (Polity Press 2016).

past—after all, its successor, the Copyright Act of 1976, has been in effect since 1978, and most fan-created content is based on works created under that later legislation. The litigator in me, however, leads me to include the 1909 Act for several reasons—many of the provisions of the 1976 Act grew from, or are in reaction to, problems or gaps in the 1909 Act, so understanding that history has value; and in my own practice, I have encountered issues that could affect the rights of fan content creators who are creating new works based on those pre-1978 creations—recent litigation over a fan's book of Sherlock Holmes stories is one such example.

The first concept explored in my discussion of the 1909 Act is derivative works, works based on work(s) that were already in existence and form the basis of the new fan-created work. This is followed by the first of several discussions of the controversial and complex doctrine of fair use—the right of a fan creator to take portions of a previously created work and incorporate that into his or her new creation. Next, I examine the doctrine of work for hire, sometimes referred to as works made for hire, and explore those cases where employees and/or independent contractors who are fans and who create works while employed encounter the claim that the works they create are the property of their employers. This subsection on the 1909 Act concludes with a discussion of the duration of copyright protection under the Act—an area that gave rise to much conflict and that was dramatically changed in the 1976 act.

Chapter 4 moves the chronological dial forward to the Copyright Act of 1976, a huge piece of legislation that attempted to cure defects in the 1909 act, with mixed results. As this is the body of law still operative today, and as its doctrines have the greatest effect on fan creators, I take readers on a fairly deep dive into this law and its impact. The first subsection under this chapter focuses on the dramatic changes to the work-for-hire doctrine, which gained definitions it was lacking. That discussion is followed by a lengthy examination of the legal doctrine that probably has the most impact on fan creators—the growth in the application of the transformative doctrine, which opens up vast new possibilities for fan creators, with some risks, however. I explore three key cases and/or lines of cases—the Richard Prince appropriation cases, the J.K. Rowling *Lexicon* case, and the *Fox News v. TVEyes* case—to outline the contours of this doctrine.

Next up in the analysis of the Copyright Act of 1976 are the substantial changes to the duration of copyright—from the 1909 Act's "two terms of 28 years" structure to the new "life of the author plus 50 years" approach, which was then extended to life plus 70, largely at the insistence of the Disney Company, which acted to avoid Mickey Mouse falling into the public domain 50 years after the death of Walt Disney. I follow that with a deeper dive into the problem and challenge of formalities under the law. This section addresses the different approaches in U.S. and EU law about the formal requirements found in U.S. law, such as the requirement for giving notice of copyright ownership via the © symbol in the United States and the lack of that requirement under EU law. How that difference was resolved, and why it is important, are two topics discussed in this chapter.

The discussion of the 1976 act next focuses on an unusual section of the law, which Congress decided to add in an effort to solve a perennial problem for creators—how to fairly protect young creators (or simply those early in their creative career, regardless of their chronological age) from being taken advantage of by publishers and others with more economic clout who could acquire rights to those new works for less than fair prices. In the 1909 act, Congress tried the "second bite at the apple" approach by creating a two-term system of protection. A copyright creator could register his or her new work for an initial term of 28 years, and then when that term expired, he or she could renew that registration of the work for a second 28-year term. The thought was that if the work had proved popular, the creator would have leverage with the publisher in the second-term negotiation to get a better price. What Congress didn't bargain for was that publishers would react to this structure with demands that creators sign away their rights to both terms in their first contract. When publishers did exactly that, a case challenging their right to do so made its way to the Supreme Court, and the *Fisher v. Witmark* case found that the freedom of contract trumped what the Court saw as congressional paternalism and allowed the practice to take place—effectively wiping out the second bite.

So Congress fashioned a different remedy. It enacted sections 203 and 304 of the 1976 act, creating a right of termination and recapture—allowing a creator who had sold his or her rights, including copyright, in a work to recapture those rights after a designated period of years. This is a hugely significant right for fan creators to be aware of, since it can, after many years when a work has been in the hands of a major publisher, return that work to the creators or their heirs, sparking a whole new range of opportunities for the reuse and new development of an iconic work and its characters. So while it is a bit deeper in the woods than is necessary for a book about copyright law for fan creators, this discussion is added for the practitioners who may encounter this issue in the representation of their creator clients.

At this point, I shift the discussion to take on another area of vital importance to the fan-creator community: the right to express appreciation for, and sometimes to offer a critique of, works in popular culture via parody and satire—literary and artistic efforts that, through humor, either make fun of a work or use it as a base to make a humorous, and sometimes sharp, point about the events of our times. For a few years, there was a somewhat fuzzy line drawn in the law that allowed a fan to create a gentle parody of a work, so long as the work itself was the subject, but harsher critiques, and those that used the work for social commentary via satire, were not allowed—they were infringements of copyright.[15] The aforementioned transformative doctrine has had an important effect on that distinction, softening it around the edges—I examine a series of cases to show how these standards have changed and how fan creators have more freedom to use these methods to offer their viewpoints now.

This second section concludes with a focus on two key legislative developments in the post–1976 Act era, the PROTECT Act and the CASE Act, the latter of which is pending final legislative approval as of the date this book is written.

Although the approach chosen in this second section is to focus on the two copyright acts and how their provisions have changed over the years, for those readers who would rather approach this material on a thematic basis, I have included a separate table of contents that offers a thematic guide to the discussion in this section.

The third section of the book, *The Narrow Brush: Legal Doctrine Specific to Fan Fiction, Art, Film, and Cosplay*, includes chapters more narrowly focused on the interaction between the law and those specific types of fan-created works—fan fiction, fan art, fan film, and cosplay.

In the first chapter in this section, I put fan fiction under the microscope—discussing the elements of this content that make it different from the other forms discussed in this book. The examination begins by charting some of the famous authors who began their careers writing fan fiction and how the genre often serves as a gateway into professional writing. This chapter also includes a deep dive into the Organization for Transformative Works,[16] a nonprofit organization supportive of fan fiction, which not only hosts a massive archive of fan fiction but also pursues a dedicated advocacy agenda, based substantially on First Amendment jurisprudence, on behalf of fan fiction authors.

The second chapter in this section moves from the literary to the graphic as I explore the world of fan art, a rich vein of expression created by artists paying homage to, and adding their unique takes on, the subjects of many pop-culture properties. In addition to the many copyright-law issues fan art gives rise to, additional attention is focused on the intersection between fan art and trademark law and right-of-publicity law. The opportunity offered to fan artists to break into the ranks of professional artists by showing their art to publishing company artists at conventions like SDCC via the process known as portfolio review is also discussed. The pop-culture convention feature known as Artists' Alley is also noted, together with the emerging problem

15. For a discussion of this short-lived distinction, see Bruce P. Keller & Rebecca Tushnet, *Even More Parodic Than the Real Thing: Parody Lawsuits Revisited*, 94 Trademark Reporter 979 (2004).

16. Organization for Transformative Works, https://www.transformativeworks.org (last visited Jan. 14, 2021).

of fan artists purchasing tables in the Alley to sell their tributes to the artwork of professional artists and what happens when that same professional artist is selling his or her work two tables down the Alley. The deep dive in this chapter focuses on the Deviant Art website,[17] one of the best-known, and most extensive, websites featuring fan art and the legal issues it has faced in its long run.

Continuing this narrower view, the third chapter in this section focuses on fan-created films, a medium with a rich history dating back to videocassette mashups popular in the 1970s and '80s to the more recent use of digital technology to create sophisticated fan films, incorporating cutting-edge technology. The use of crowdfunding sites like Kickstarter and GoFundMe to raise the previously daunting amounts of money needed to create a feature, or even a short, film has made this medium available to fan filmmakers. A variety of legal issues arise in the fan-films context—since film is an inherently collaborative process, cocreator issues often arise, as well as licensing issues for music or other contributions. Lastly, in the wake of the recent *Paramount v. Axanar* decision, I focus on the developing trend of production companies that offer a litigation-free path for fan filmmakers, provided they comply with a detailed set of guidelines governing all aspects of their fan film.

In the fourth and final chapter in this section, I explore the newest member of the family of fan content creators—the cosplayers. Cosplay differs from the other forms discussed in that it involves the creation of makeup, costumes, and in some cases props to allow the cosplayer to "play" the character from the pop media program that he or she admires. As is the case with most live theatrical performances, cosplay is the most ephemeral of the fan content profiled here, and its creation and performances present a different set of legal issues than seen before. Since it is character driven, cosplay may involve issues relating to celebrity right of publicity (an area of focus in fan art and fan films, and less so in fan fiction), as well as issues relating to copyright and trademark law. A disturbing problem for cosplayers, primarily women, is the misinterpretation or, in more extreme cases, the outright aggressive or violent reaction some people have to cosplayers, leading conventions and other venues where cosplay is performed to launch consent protocols, making it clear that a cosplayer in a revealing or tightly fitting costume is inviting people to look at, but not touch, him or her during or after his or her performance. The role of the law in these situations shifts into interdicting criminal conduct, principally assault and/or battery.

Cosplay has become an important feature of pop-culture conventions, with players and the friends who help them creating unique and distinctive makeup (as creatures, aliens, etc.) as well as their costumes and participating

17. Deviant Art, www.deviantart.com (last visited Jan. 14, 2021).

in competitions (often called masquerade balls), which serve as an audition for professional jobs in the entertainment industry as makeup artists, fashion designers, and the like.

One last section brings the book to its conclusion. In this section, titled *Winding Up and Heading Home*, I examine the role of social media in fandom and the law and offer a few thoughts on the future of this relationship I have examined in previous chapters and sections.

In the first chapter of this section, I shift the focus from the different types of fan-created content to an examination of the legal issues arising from the huge role social media plays in fandom—it is the primary means by which fan fiction, fan art, and fan film are displayed and distributed. Cosplay too utilizes social media, with some cosplayers hosting websites that generate a phenomenal number of site visits every day and that have made some of the better-known cosplayers celebrities in their own right.

What many cosplayers don't understand is that the terms and conditions governing the many social media sites they post on often result in those sites having ownership rights over the content posted. An additional set of issues involves conflicts that sometimes arise between a creator who is posting on the site and the site operators who have the power to shut down or otherwise limit those posts if they violate the user terms and conditions that govern the site—since these are privately owned sites, the First Amendment rights of posters can be, and often are, limited.

And finally, in the last chapter, I look to the future of fan-created content and how the legal doctrines discussed in this book are likely to impact that future, in both positive and negative ways. I also examine how, in the past, production companies have chosen to respond to fan-created works based on their content and whether those reactions have changed in recent years and/or are likely to change in the future. Perhaps more so than in other areas of endeavor, fan-created content, with its inherent tension between fan creators and the original creators of the works that inspire them, turns to the law and the legal system to moderate that tension. The results, not surprisingly, are a mixed bag—offering useful and wise guidance at times and in other instances yielding results that seem perilously close to constraining free expression.

One final note before leaving this introduction—a key motivating factor for fan-created content is the element of passion and the degree to which creating art is always to some degree motivated by that powerful emotion. Fans express their passion for pop culture in a wide variety of ways. The amazing proliferation of merchandise for sale online and at fan conventions feeds the passion of many fans by giving them the opportunity to collect toys, art, games, clothing, and other goods that reflect their interests. Autograph and photo opportunities and attending panels give fans the opportunity to meet the artists and celebrities that they admire, and collectors of these items engage with other collectors on thousands of online sites. In online forums and other fan sites, fans spend hours debating the fine (and not-so-fine) points of every nuance and change in the objects of their fandom—a recent example is the pro-and-con debate that erupted among fans of the American version of the British sci-fi television show *Dr. Who* when in 2019 the program debuted a female actress (Jodie Whittaker) in the role of the Doctor.

And yet, to a certain degree, all of these expressions differ from that of fans who created content based on the programs and other original content they are inspired by, in one key element. The fans who create these works have crossed the line from passively watching the original works to adding to those works via the creation of the derivative works referred to as fan-created content. And so before examining the ways in which the law affects that creative process, it is worthwhile to begin this inquiry with an effort to understand what motivates people to become a part of fandom in the first place.

SECTION 1

The Sociology of Fandom

CHAPTER 1

A Shallow Dive into Participatory Culture Studies

Many writers describe the process of writing a book as a journey—full of side trips, dead ends, and amazing discoveries . . . a description I embrace and that I found to be true in the two books I've written before this one. For me, since I write about the intersection between law and society and more specifically elements of popular culture in society, a necessary element of the journey, which often starts in my mind as a side trip but ends up being a central core of the book, is developing an understanding of the sociology or cultural significance of the element of pop culture I am focused on.

In my first book, *Comic Art, Creativity and the Law,* I began with a detailed discussion of the neuroscience of creativity, followed by a history of comic art and an overview of the structure and common modes for comic art.[1] That discussion gave readers an understanding of the field of pop culture, in that case comic books, whose intersection with law and legal doctrine was a primary subject of the book.

As I initially thought about this book, my intent was to focus on a limited form of fandom—fans who created original content in the form of fan fiction, art, film, and cosplay, based on popular media. I was aware, of course, that this is a much smaller cohort among fandom in general and that most fans were content to enjoy popular media, sports, and other content in a mostly passive form of engagement.

---

1. Marc Greenberg, Comic Art, Creativity and the Law 7–11, 21–33 (Edward Elgar Publ'g 2014).

As the idea of this book was forming, in April 2018 I attended the ABA's annual Spring IP Law Section Conference in Washington, DC. Scanning the program for the conference, my eye was caught by a panel on the law pertaining to the creation and use of fictional characters. One of the panelists, Joshua Wattles, had been, for the previous 18 years, the in-house attorney for DeviantArt.com, one of the world's largest online repositories of fan art. The panel moderator, my longtime friend and colleague Michael Lovitz, founder of the Comic Book Law School program I participate in most years at the San Diego Comic-Con, invited me to join him and Josh for dinner after the panel, an invitation I quickly and happily accepted.

Over dinner, I described this book project to Josh, who told me, unequivocally, that if I wanted to understand fandom and fan culture, I had to familiarize myself with the works of Henry Jenkins—it was, as he put it, a must do.

A. Henry Jenkins and Fan Culture

Henry Jenkins is Provost Professor of Communication, Journalism, Cinematic Arts and Education at the University of Southern California and is the author of over a dozen books and a dizzying number of scholarly articles on the subject of fan culture and media and culture studies. He is cited in most books on the subject, and as I began to read some of his work in the field, it rapidly became obvious why he has attained such prominence.

In 1992, Professor Jenkins's seminal book on media fans, *Textual Poachers: Television Fans and Participatory Culture*, emerged as one of the leading works on fan culture. Twenty years later, he wrote an updated version of the book that, in addition to updates to the text, now led off with a conversation between Jenkins and fan culture scholar Suzanne Scott.[2]

Professor Jenkins, in the first chapter of *Textual Poachers*, begins by tracing the origin of the term "fan":

> "Fan" is an abbreviated form of the word "fanatic," which has its roots in the Latin word "fanaticus." In its most literal sense, "fanaticus" simply meant "Of or belonging to the temple, a temple servant, a devotee" but it quickly assumed more negative connotations, "Of persons inspired by orgiastic rites and enthusiastic frenzy" (*Oxford Latin Dictionary*). As it evolved, the term "fanatic" moved from a reference to certain excessive forms of religious belief and worship to any "excessive and mistaken enthusiasm," often evoked in criticism to opposing political beliefs, and

2. Henry Jenkins, Textual Poachers: Television Fans and Participatory Culture (Routledge updated 20th anniv. ed. 2013).

> then, more generally, to madness "such as might result from possession by a deity or demon" (*Oxford English Dictionary*). . . . If the term "fan" was originally evoked in a somewhat playful fashion and was often used sympathetically by sports writers, it never fully escaped its earlier connotations of religious and political zealotry, false beliefs, orgiastic excess possession, and madness, connotations that seem to be at the heart of many of the representations of fans in contemporary discourse.[3]

One doesn't have to look hard to find examples of derogatory treatment and ridiculing of fans—from the famous skit on *Saturday Night Live* that poked fun at *Star Trek* fans meeting Captain Kirk (William Shatner) at a fan convention, in which he replied to their endless questions about minutiae from the show with an exasperated cry, "Get a life, will you people? I mean, for crying out loud, it's just a TV show!," to *The Big Bang Theory*, a hugely popular television show whose central characters are stereotypical nerds or fanboys and whose episodes featured fan-culture staples such as superhero comics and, of course, the San Diego Comic-Con.

Jenkins offers a description of the breadth of fan culture, noting:

> "Fan culture is a complex, multidimensional phenomenon, inviting many forms of participation and levels of engagement.[4]

He expanded this definition in the 20th anniversary edition, adding:

> The word "fan," in popular usage, is slippery and expansive enough to include a broad range of different kinds of relationships to media, from the highly individualistic to the highly social.[5]

One of those relationships Jenkins discusses is found in the concept of the acafan—an academic who studies and writes about fan culture and is him- or herself also a fan. Jenkins, who is credited with coining the term, offers the view that academics can't really study popular culture from the outside looking in—it is necessary to our understanding that we experience fandom on an emotional level. That said, he is also critical of those who would join the fandom community only to study it—it is the combination of emotional impact and intellectual engagement that makes you an effective commentator about this cultural community.[6]

I agree with Professor Jenkins on this point. As noted in the introduction, I am an acafan. This doesn't mean that my fan status renders me incapable of being critical about fandom and its storied excesses—on the contrary, I am

---

3. *Id.* at 12.
4. *Id.* at 2.
5. *Id.* at xiv.
6. *Id.* at xii, xiv.

able to be critical from an insider's point of view, which is often more accurate and nuanced than the critique offered by those who are wholly outside of fan culture.

It is also important to note that the study of fan culture, media, and fan-created content has become a mainstream activity in academia throughout the world. The Popular Culture Association, a national organization of scholars who teach and write about pop culture, has a section specifically devoted to fan culture and theory, led by a recognized scholar in the field.[7] Members of the section present their latest scholarship at an annual conference, and there have been hundreds of books and papers presented and published at this and other pop-culture conferences all over the world.[8]

While the increased interest in fandom has led to more coverage in mainstream media of fan culture, and of the kind of fan-created content that is the focus of this book, the dark side of that coverage is the continued prevalence of sneering commentary about nerds and fanboys that marks much of that coverage. At its root, this commentary comes from sexual role stereotypes and fears about them. Much of fan activity, particularly that rooted in comic books, science fiction, fantasy, and the movies and television shows focused on these genre materials, has been characterized as the province of women and men whose high levels of intelligence are offset by weak physicality and other physically unattractive features (glasses, often held together by tape at the bridge; acne; thin hair or balding; either painfully thin or obese with big bellies and ill-fitting clothes). Pop culture–based shows like *The Big Bang Theory* and the Cartoon Channel's *Robot Chicken*, and countless Hollywood movies, particularly teen summer comedies and horror pictures, relentlessly reinforce this stereotype.

Gender also has a role to play in this stereotype—historically the fandom world was strictly segregated by gender roles. Media production companies created romance books, comic books, and movies known as rom-coms (for romantic comedies) tailored to what they understood to be an audience of girls

---

7. *Fan Culture & Theory*, Popular Culture Ass'n, https://pcaaca.org/area/fan-culture-theory (last visited Jan. 15, 2021).

8. A small and representative list of relevant works in the field includes but is by no means limited to the following, which I have used in researching this book: Henry Jenkins, Mizuko Ito & danah boyd, Participatory Culture in a Networked Era (Polity Press 2016); Henry Jenkins, Convergence Culture: Where Old and New Media Collide (N.Y. Univ. Press 2006); Fandom: Identities and Communities in a Mediated World (Jonathan Gray, Cornel Sandvoss & C. Lee Harrington eds., 2d ed. N.Y. Univ. Press 2017); Paul Booth, Playing Fans: Negotiating Fandom and the Media in the Digital Age (Univ. of Iowa Press 2015); Mel Stanfill, Exploiting Fandom: How the Media Industry Seeks to Manipulate Fans (Univ. of Iowa Press 2019); Karn Hellekson & Kristina Busse, The Fan Fiction Studies Reader (Univ. of Iowa Press 2014); Fan Phenomena: Buffy the Vampire Slayer (Jennifer K. Stuller ed., Intellect Ltd 2013); Computer Games and Immersive Entertainment: New Frontiers in Intellectual Property Law (Chrisse Scelsi & Ross A. Dannenberg eds., 2019).

and women who became fans of cute boys and good-looking men—either solo or in groups (boy bands like 'N Sync, Boyz II Men, One Direction, New Kids on the Block, and the Jonas Brothers have spanned decades in pop music, and are representative of what is popular with this audience). The only outlet for girls interested in stories other than these fan-centric works was fantasy stories, often featuring unicorns and friendly dragons.

Boys and men, on the other hand, were the sole participants in the sci-fi, war, and horror genres, as well as the comic-book world, which was so male-centric that it became a trope that women were not welcomed in comic-book stores. A featured character named Jeff Albertson, also known as Comic Book Guy in *The Simpsons* animated television show, is a perfect example of this stereotype.

So while movies like *Revenge of the Nerds* and the amazing success stories those nerds generated in the dot-com explosion, where nerdy-looking guys like Bill Gates, Mark Zuckerberg, and Jeff Bezos fostered new acceptance of the men who were otherwise classic nerds, fan culture still, Professor Jenkins notes, lagged behind on gender awareness.

Jenkins notes that while society now acknowledges, in a more favorable way, the notion of the fanboy, fandom remains slow to give equal recognition to women as fangirls. He offers an explanation for this—an explanation that reaffirms my perception of SDCCI as being a fulcrum of pop culture and fandom:

> Some of this, I think, has to do with the particular role of San Diego Comic-Con as the primary point of intersection between Hollywood and the fan community. Coming out of comics and science fiction fandom, rather than out of media fandom, Comic-Con has very much been shaped by male-centric fan traditions, norms, and assumptions, and until very recently the attendees were overwhelmingly male. So, when Hollywood went to talk to the fans, or when the news media did its annual fandom story, they mostly encountered men, and this served a particular push right now within the media industry to try to hold onto the young male demographic, which is the "lost audience segment" because they have been abandoning television for games and digital media. So, even as fan studies has suggested the centrality of women to fan culture, the media industry clings to somewhat outmoded understandings of what kind of people are fans. Over the past few years, we've seen an increase of women coming to Comic-Con (partially in response to *Twilight* and *True Blood*, but really, across the board) so there may be some hope that the industry might develop a more diverse understanding for the fan audience.[9]

9. JENKINS, TEXTUAL POACHERS, *supra* note 2, at xvii.

In the years since Jenkins wrote this in 2013, the success of Gal Gadot as Wonder Woman and Brie Larsen as Capt. Marvel and the television success of Melissa Benoist as Supergirl and Krysten Ritter as Jessica Jones, building on the history of Sarah Michelle Gellar as Buffy the Vampire Slayer and Lucy Lawless as Xena, Warrior Princess, suggests that Jenkins was right—the industry, in fits and starts, may be acknowledging the diversity of the audience.

There is, however, another social issue that fandom has been slow to acknowledge and respond to—the issue of race. Working on this book in the winter of 2020, the events of this past summer, which led to an impassioned discussion of institutional racism in the United States, a subject never before discussed in the white community with such vigor, led me to realize that I had to offer a few words about racism in fandom as part of this sociological review. I do so with some trepidation—an appropriate feeling for an old white law professor to have in venturing to write about racism.

Fortunately, I don't have to assume the role of trailblazer in this respect. There is a rich body of scholarship and some very clear and approachable work by other writers that readers of this book can discover and learn from, as I have. For example, Issue No. 29 of the journal *Transformative Works and Cultures* is devoted entirely to these issues and bears the title "Fans of Color, Fandoms of Color." Editors Abigail De Kosnik and andré carrington frame the issue of racism in fandom in a guest editorial.[10]

They begin their editorial by noting the undisputed fact that fan studies was founded, and has been dominated by, white scholars. They call for change in this situation, urging more scholars of color to write more in fandom studies about race and ethnicity. They acknowledge that fandom's claim to be a place for inclusion of traditionally marginalized, invisible communities has made strides in its representation of nonmainstream communities with respect to gender and sexuality, progress in addressing the issues and needs of people of color has lagged behind. They assert with some force that fan studies still "has much work to do" to justify its claims to be a field that challenges, rather than reproduces, oppressive social structures and conventions.[11]

For example, they note that casts of predominantly white characters in pop media programs, when they seek to add diversity, generally cast a man of color in the role of the one person of color in the cast (i.e., Geordi La Forge in *Star Trek: The Next Generation*). Why not cast a woman of color or a member of the LGBTQ community? Giving a nod to a growing awareness of this dynamic, they point to the casting of Sonequa Martin-Green and Michelle Yeoh in lead roles in *Star*

---

10. Abigail De Kosnik & andré carrington, *Fans of Color, Fandoms of Color*, 29 Transformative Works & Cultures (2019), https://doi.org/10.3983/twc.2019.1783.

11. *Id.* at 1.

Trek: Discovery, the latest iteration of the series, which finally offers female fans of color a role they can more readily identify with.[12]

De Kosnik and carrington follow this discussion with a list of over 35 scholarly works addressing racial issues in fandom, a list they note would be much longer if they were to include literary fandoms and antifandoms. They view this issue they have coedited as further contributing to the development of this vital scholarship.[13]

Another significant voice in this discussion is Dr. Rukmini Pande, author of *Squee from the Margins: Fandom and Race*.[14] In an interview in Henry Jenkins's blog, "Confessions of an Aca-Fan," Dr. Pande notes that authors of color face challenges to getting their work published that white authors don't experience to the same degree—noting that this is another product of the institutional racism that exists in the publishing industry.[15]

Dr. Pande further notes that the critique she and other scholars of color have offered to the racism in fandom has generated responses that ranged from genuine engagement to defensiveness and, in extreme cases, "outright hostility." She views it as a damning indictment of white fan-studies scholars that they require their colleagues of color to explain and define basic concepts such as institutional racism and structural whiteness. Acknowledging the fears that white scholars voice about writing about race (as I too have expressed above), Dr. Pande notes that this fear "puts the burden of doing the work of decolonization on nonwhite scholars," noting also that they too fear that they will "mess up" that critique. The result, she concludes, is that scholarship in this area remains incomplete, resulting in further entrenchment of "whiteness-as-default."[16]

Moreover, Dr. Pande argues that defensiveness and a reluctance to deal with the institutional racism in fandom studies are contrary to the very nature of academia—which is to be self-critical. Her challenge seems a fair one, which fandom-studies scholars should embrace.

And the responsibility for addressing issues of institutional racism in fandom and fandom studies doesn't stop with just members of the fan communities and the scholars that study them. Lawyers and courts, presented with claims of racial discrimination and other racially influenced conduct in the negotiation of contracts, the decision to license or decline to license work, and decisions by litigators and courts, are likely all, in one way or another, subject to and influenced by the structural racism and institutional racism that

12. *Id.* at 2.

13. *Id.* at 3.

14. Rukmini Pande, Squee from the Margins: Fandom and Race (Univ. of Iowa Press 2018).

15. Henry Jenkins, *Squee from the Margins: Interview with Rukmini Pande (Part III)*, Confessions of an Aca-Fan 2–3 (June 21, 2019), http://henryjenkins.org/blog/2019/6/1/interview-with-rukmini-pande-part-iii-b9c92.

16. *Id.* at 5.

is endemic in U.S. society. It is our job, as officers of that legal system, to be similarly aware of and to make efforts to confront and change those behaviors as well.

B. A Breakout Moment: How Does Studying the Sociology of Fandom Help Us Understand the Legal Issues Affecting This Culture?

At this point in this book, many readers may be wondering why I felt it necessary to dive into this sociological analysis before getting to the discussion of how the law interacts with, at times helps, and at other times hinders the success or results of that interaction. The answer is simple. With few exceptions, fan-created content is not driven by a financial profit motive, and most of these works never earn back their cost of creation or any money at all. So if economic incentive is not a motivating factor for most of this work, several leverage points the law deploys to affect social behavior, like buying off competition or imposing steep fines against infringers, are unavailable or are of limited benefit. Since it is almost never the case that a fan-created work causes economic loss to the owner/producer, damage awards in infringement cases are limited to statutory damages, and the optics of a major production company suing fans for art they created about their favorite television show, which they posted on a website but otherwise didn't profit from, is a bad look for the production company.

Nonetheless, before the transformative doctrine began to lessen the likelihood of being successfully sued for infringement (more about this later), most fan creators knew, albeit imperfectly, that what they were doing violated some aspect of ownership law—and many knew in particular that their works violated copyright law. So why do this?

Professor Jenkins offers a valuable insight into the soul of these fans. He shares his awareness that the daily life of many fans is beset by the failures endemic to contemporary life—traditions are evaporating, marriages frequently end in divorce, friendships don't last and are annoyingly superficial, and emotional and social life is dominated by materialism. Fans, he notes, are often stuck in unrewarding jobs, which fail to allow them to use their education and are intellectually unchallenging. Is it any wonder then that these fans choose to participate in what he calls a "weekend-only world" rich with creativity, social awareness, and a concern for humanity?

Jenkins is not Pollyannish here—he acknowledges that fandom communities don't always succeed in offering a more intelligent and humane experience. There are petty feuds and personality conflicts—some participants are rude, selfish, and greedy. Yet Jenkins is convinced that, unlike daily life in the real world, fandom remains, on balance, a place where there is overall a commitment to more democratic values. He points to the negative reaction fan communities generally have to noncommunal behavior—which is more often than not responded to with outrage in the community.

He also acknowledges that people cannot live their lives entirely in this self-curated world. Yet it is in those few short hours or days spent in this milieu that members of this community find the strength and will to return to that less-than-ideal world after the weekend is over.[17]

It is a disabling mistake for those who engage, in one way or another, with the fan community of content creators to fail to understand the deep levels of satisfaction these creators have in offering their work to their fan community. This community nurtures the work through online forums and other exchanges, in addition to providing access to an unlimited audience. That fan support, if it manifests in large enough numbers, can shape the reaction of a production company or other content owner to what might otherwise be an unquestionable infringement warranting a judicial response. And so throughout this book, we will see ways in which awareness of the nature and enduring strength of fandom and fan culture affects the manner in which it is received and responded to by the producers of pop-culture content.

C. From *Textual Poachers* to *Participatory Culture*

In titling his early work *Textual Poachers*, Jenkins was referring to fans, mostly female, who took the text of their favorite television shows and movies and used that appropriated, or "poached," text to weave their own stories about the characters and settings of these shows—with fan fiction as the outcome of that effort. When he revisited his work 20 years later, he offered a different label for these works—he used the term "participatory culture," which he found more useful for describing the various relationships that exist between the producers of pop-culture content and their consumers. He notes that fandom is a specific form of participatory culture with its own history and rituals and contrasts those with the Web 2.0 business model, which he asserts tries to capitalize on and commodify participatory culture.

He finds "participatory culture" a more apt description of the changing nature of the relationship between producers and fans—a change facilitated by the ability of fans, using digital tools, to create a more active "participation" level of engagement with the objects of their fandom. Production companies

17. Jenkins, Textual Poachers, *supra* note 2, at 282–83.

can't ignore that participation, and so they now have to embrace a new, more complex and nuanced, relationship with their fans. He notes the question now relevant is "Who is (and who is not) participating?"

And even more relevantly for our purposes, what factors enhance or limit and constrain that participation—are there legal restrictions that affect that participation? Are there technological constraints? Educational limitations resulting from unequal access to education and tech? Are there economic and social limitations, as the rising number of fan-studies scholars of color assert?

Jenkins concludes this assessment as follows:

> The reality is that the "digital revolution" has resulted in real, demonstrable shifts in media power, expanding the capacity of various subcultures and communities to access the means of media production and circulation.[18]

Jenkins's point here warrants reemphasizing and expanding. Fandom, in some form or other, has existed probably for as long as humans have formed and existed in social groups. And in various limited contexts, fan-created content in the forms of fan fiction and fan art have been created for many years as well (fan film and cosplay are primarily digital-age fan-created content).

It is, however, the digital revolution that has both broadened and focused the widespread growth and impact of fan-created content. There were very few forums in which fan art could be displayed and viewed in the predigital era; fan-fiction magazines were marginalized, not available on newsstands or in stores; and fan-fiction writers had to create their works, submit them to fanzines, and hope they would be accepted, then wait months for the issue in which their work appeared to come out, and then wait another month or two to see if any readers would offer a review or comment.

Our postdigital world offers a vastly different environment for fan-created work. Today fan-art creators can paint a picture, either digitally or in physical format (using paint, canvas, brushes, etc.), scan and post a copy of the graphic on a public website like deviantart.com, repost the work on their own website, make prints in a variety of formats, and sell or trade their works at hundreds of pop-culture conventions across the country and the world. Authors of fan fiction have hundreds of websites devoted to the distribution of fan works available to them, as well as the opportunity to distribute their work via their own websites and to meet with members of their fan community at pop-culture conventions.

Citing Catherine Tosenberger, Jenkins notes that she has suggested that what is powerful about fan fiction is that it is "unpublishable"—that is, that it

---

18. *Id.* at xxi–xxiii.

"is not bound by the constraints that shape commercial media production."[19] He questions that assumption, noting that "the bounds of what is and is not publishable are constantly shifting"—a shift that has had an important impact.

Jenkins asserts that as production companies reappraise the nature and scope of fan engagement, they have become less likely to engage in knee-jerk reactions to fan works—less likely to file an infringement suit and more likely instead to start looking for ways to engage with those fans—offering them the opportunity through fan forums and program websites to suggest story and character lines; developing more character backstories to give fans more content to engage with; and in general looking to do anything that will lead to a larger and more "fanatic" fan base.[20]

With respect to fan-created content, and the reaction of the owners of the underlying works, Jenkins acknowledges the range of reactions encountered. He notes that some companies view fan-created works as a threat to their own control over the content and that there is a tension between the companies, which want to control how fans express themselves and consume their products, and the fandom communities, which push back against such control.[21]

As I noted in the introduction, Section 4 addresses the issue of how production companies and creators of underlying works respond to fan-created works. The responses range from acceptance and encouragement and active engagement with their fan communities to the routine generation of cease-and-desist letters and even infringement litigation. To a great degree, to the extent there is tension between these players, it is reflective of the different perspectives they bring to the work. For virtually all production companies, while they usually start out of a love of the content, over time the necessity of making a profit and growing their companies adds a layer of commercial motivation to their efforts—by contrast with the vast majority of fan creators, who are creating both for the sheer fun of it for themselves and to be a contributing member of their fan community, whose unwritten codes of conduct often reject the commercialization of fan works.

Jenkins also comments on the interplay between fans who create content for nonpecuniary reasons and the original content creators or corporate owners, for whom the economic value is a, if not the, primary driver of their activity. In so doing, he also gives a nod to the Organization for Transformative Works (OTW)—a nonprofit organization devoted to the promotion and protection of fan-created works, with a particular focus on fan fiction. Characterizing the

---

19. *Id.* at xv (citing Catherine Tosenberger, *Gender and Fan Studies (Round Five, Part One): Geoffrey Long and Catherine Tosenberger*, CONFESSIONS OF AN ACA-FAN (June 28, 2007), http://henryjenkins.org/blog/2007/06/gender_and_fan_studies_round_f_1.html).

20. *Id.*

21. *Id.* at xxvi.

members as "fan activists," Jenkins lauds the work of the OTW, which he sees as providing the valuable service of advocacy for fan creators so that they can reap the nonprofit, community-based benefits of their activities, rather than allowing the production companies the opportunity to monetize those works. He views fan cultural production as a form of gift economy, motivated more often by social reciprocity, friendship, and good feelings than by the profit motive.[22]

Jenkins offers a description of the breadth of fan culture, noting, "Fan culture is a complex, multidimensional phenomenon, inviting many forms of participation and levels of engagement."[23]

Addressing the effect of fan-created content, Jenkins notes that once a television show or character becomes widely known and a part of our social fabric, they he or she "belongs" to their audience—a claim that goes beyond the ownership rights of their original creators. He points out that fan art is created by artists to share with their other fan friends, via a system of distribution that rejects monetary gain and instead encourages widespread access to its expression of creativity.[24]

Echoing Wikipedia's assertion that everyone is an expert, Jenkins addresses the blurring of lines between creator and reader/viewer, noting that fandom doesn't acknowledge the line between artist and consumer, positing that all fans are potential writers, whose contributions, even if modest in nature, still enhance and benefit the greater community.[25]

The digital revolution led to a change in the role fan creations play in popular media. Works that were once relegated to little-seen fanzines and local art galleries now occupy center stage in an array of contexts, and production companies ignore these works at their peril. Rather than go down that path, contemporary original creators and production companies now devise strategies for dealing with these creations—strategies that often involve co-opting these creators and their creations, which gives rise to the question posed in this next section.

D. Who's Exploiting Whom? Fandom and Media Companies

The recognition that fan-created works specifically, and fandom generally, should no longer be thought of solely as irrelevant expressions of fan approval

22. *Id.* at xxx.
23. *Id.* at 2.
24. *Id.* at 279–80.
25. *Id.* at 280.

but rather as works that contain the seeds of possible changes in the original content to meet fan expectations and that can be a source of discovery of new writers, artists, costume designers, or even filmmakers has led many companies to seek to exploit that fan interest for their own benefit. Unpacking how this interaction works requires us to delve into the sometimes murky waters of economic analysis. Two scholars, in recent works, have addressed this change.

Paul Booth, in the introduction of his book *Playing Fans: Negotiating Fandom and the Media in the Digital Age*,[26] citing an article by Swinburne University Professor Dr. Bertha Chin and Professor Jenkins, offers a cogent explanation of how these two forces (fandom and media companies) have come to recognize the extent to which they feed each other and the impact social media has on that interaction. Booth attributes to Dr. Chin the view that among other factors, it is the fragmentation of the media environment that has stimulated the media companies to engage with their fandoms in a more creative way in order to keep their loyalty to the companies' products. In this way, Dr. Chin asserts, the two groups can exist in the same space, at least on a symbolic level.

Dr. Jenkins adds to this discussion, noting that convergence is a street with lanes in each direction—operating both as a top-down production-company process and as one driven by consumers as a bottom-up process.[27]

As an example of that top-down, production-company-driven form of engagement with their fandoms, Jenkins cites the work of Suzanne Scott, who points to how production companies have commercialized fan "gifting" by creating, on the companies' websites, opportunities like SyFy's Battlestar Galactica Video Maker Tool Kit, which allows fans of the television show to create their own fan videos using actual material from the production company—a great opportunity until the fan creator realizes that only authorized film clips can be used and that SyFy promotional tags must also be used in the videos. I discuss this trend in fan films in greater detail in Section 3 of this book. Scott also argues that this format is male-oriented, leaving the female fan-film creators marginalized once again.[28]

Booth concludes with this thought: "Monetary recompense for fan work is often touted as one way for this merger to occur, and examples such as Fanlib, Amazon Kindle Worlds, and *Fifty Shades of Grey* complicate this nuance. As Abigail De Kosnik notes, much of what fans have done already online could

26. Paul Booth, Playing Fans: Negotiating Fandom and the Media in the Digital Age (Univ. of Iowa Press 2015).

27. *Id.* at 5–6 (citing Bertha Chin, *The Fan-Media Producer Collaboration: How Fan Relationships Are Managed in a Post-Series X-Files Fandom*, 1 Sci. Fiction Film & Television 6 (2013); Jenkins, Convergence Culture, *supra* note 8, at 18; Henry Jenkins, Sam Ford & Joshua Green, Spreadable Media: Creating Value and Meaning in a Networked Culture 1 (N.Y. Univ. Press 2013)).

28. Booth, *supra* note 26 at 9 (citing Suzanne Scott, *Repackaging Fan Culture: The Regifting Economy of Ancillary Content Models*, 3 Transformative Works & Cultures ¶¶ 1.6, 3.3 (2009)).

be considered a type of labor and thus 'should be valued as a new form of publicity and advertising . . . that corporations badly need in an era of market fragmentation.'"[29]

What market fragmentation? In the 1950s, the media business was conducted by an array of companies, each primarily operating in its own respective silo, with little crossover, either in technology or in content. For consumers, the mass-market entertainment choices were movies, shown in stand-alone single-theater movie houses; black-and-white television on small box-shaped sets with monaural sound systems (new color sets were just being introduced); sound recordings (records played at 33 1/3 or 45 rpm) played on a single integrated system or a component system; and radio, also played on a separate player. Urban consumers also had varying levels of access to live performances via theater, symphony, pop-music concerts, and sports events. These last options were generally not available in suburban and rural communities.

Moreover, the output of content for use by these separate devices was much less than today. The studio system and the remnants of vertically integrated delivery systems meant that fewer movies were being released annually, and independent movie studios had a much-reduced market share. There were no ancillary markets for rerelease of movies, and foreign movies were seen only in major urban markets in the United States.

Television was dominated by three networks: ABC, NBC, and CBS. Independent local networks were limited by available technology and weren't able to produce much original programming. In most markets, only a dozen or so channels were available. The record business was similarly dominated by a few companies, and distribution channels were limited to hardcopy polyvinyl chloride discs and airplay on radio.

And in key contexts, these forms of entertainment did not compete with each other. Movies, with rare exceptions, were not shown on television. After a movie ended its run in commercial theaters, it wasn't seen again.

Fast-forward to the contemporary era, in a postdigital world, and the market has become saturated with content, available on incredibly powerful and portable devices, on a 24-hour program cycle. Movies now are released to theaters, then to other formats, ranging from streaming online versions to DVDs and cable-television programming. Television now offers hundreds of channels, available in broadcast, streaming, and other digital formats, with entire seasons of shows available for binge-watching on specialty platforms like Netflix, Hulu, Amazon, etc. Today's television viewer buys a huge screen (some screens are over 80 inches!) and then pays monthly subscriptions for content

---

29. *Id.* (citing Abigail De Kosnik, *Fandom as Free Labor, in* Digital Labor: The Internet as Playground and Factory 99 (Trebor Schultz ed., Routledge 2013)).

spanning a massive array of programming and pays again for "premium" channels like HBO, Showtime, and Starz.

The record business and radio have similarly experienced substantial growth and increased costs for consumers—who, if they are willing to pay subscription rates, can hear music via streaming channels and can purchase an endless number of sound recordings via digital downloads, ranging from albums to collections of songs they curate themselves.

All of this seemingly unlimited choice in entertainment comes at a cost—a real dollar cost that has made the entertainment business more competitive than ever, with all of these industries battling to capture the scarce dollars of consumers for their product. That market fragmentation and the need to have your product jump out to attract those buyers have made it critical for media companies to capitalize on the loyalty of fans to both buy and, through their fan activities, promote the products of these companies.

So can media companies gather that attention by providing monetary incentives to those fans? Professor Booth notes that monetary incentives don't always work, as they sometimes violate community norms. It is not hard for a production company to cross the line with fan communities into a realm where the engagement of fans with a work begins to feel like they are exploited labor.

Professor Booth offers the oft-cited example of fan-fiction author E.L. James, whose fan-fiction story, *Master of the Universe*, was initially written as *Twilight* fan fiction (based on the popular series of books and movies featuring a love triangle between a mortal human young woman, a vampire, and a werewolf). Booth cites articles by Bethan Jones and others who assert that James's fan fiction was aided by many contributions from its hundreds of thousands of readers and that many of those contributions went unrecognized and unattributed when James morphed her story into a series of new mainstream books, the incredibly popular and successful *Fifty Shades of Grey* series.

Fans felt that their many suggestions for improvement to *Master of the Universe*, including plot development ideas and even new dialogue for characters, were repurposed and used in the *Fifty Shades* text without attribution. Many fans felt this to be a misappropriation that violated the fan-fiction community's values and norms.[30]

So while it may have been uncomfortable for James to face the criticism that she appropriated the contributions of fans in her work and failed to give them

---

30. *Id.* at 9–10 (citing Bethan Jones, *Fifty Shades of Exploitation: Fan Labor and "Fifty Shades of Grey"*, TRANSFORMATIVE WORKS & CULTURE 15 (2015); Anne Jamison, *Full Exchange with Jason Boog for NPR .org Piece*, FIFTY SHADES OF POP CULTURE THEORY (Mar. 26, 2012); Jason Boog, *The Lost History of Fifty Shades of Grey*, GALLEYCAT (Nov. 21, 2012); Jane Litte, *Masters of the Universe versus Fifty Shades by E.L. James Comparison*, DEARAUTHOR.COM (Mar. 13, 2012)).

attribution, the real-world question is whether what she did was illegal. The next two chapters offer an explanation and answer to that question.

The other question worth investigating, before we move to discuss the legal doctrines that affect fandom and fan-created works, is this idea that the contributions of fans are a form of labor. It's a valid question and one not susceptible of an easy answer.

On the one hand, fan-created content, as well as fan commentary on blogs, websites, and other online forums, takes effort and, in some instances, involves hours of time and the investment of hard cash on various tools and supplies needed to create these works. Those factors make the "it's labor" argument an easy one to make. On the other hand, though, this effort is largely unpaid and unsolicited, often amateurish in execution, and, as noted previously, largely unpublishable.

In *Exploiting Fandom: How the Media Industry Seeks to Manipulate Fans,*[31] author Mel Stanfill outlines how media companies have come to see fan engagement and participation as having more value to them than in the past and offers a Marxist analysis that concludes that fans are exploited by this involvement. She argues that fan production has become normalized and promoted as evidence of the collapse of the distinction between producers and consumers. She points to the changes in technology, such as the growth of the Internet and the availability of cheap computing power, that mean that everyday people, previously relegated to the pure consumer role, now have the power to produce and, more importantly, to distribute their own media products.

Jenkins sees this normalizing of access to the means of production as enabling fans to demand a more active role as participants in the creation process within the culture—and as a battle the fans are winning.[32]

Having cited Jenkins's view that fan power has grown, Professor Stanfill offers a Marxian analysis to suggest the contrary:

> These fan activities look different viewed as labor. Seeing participation as inherently good short-circuits analysis. There is nothing else to say. The lens of labor, however, opens up the question of what fan productive activity means. If fans are a vital part of the new economy, then it is important to take the economy part as seriously as the vital part. A labor framework lets us ask who benefits from these fan activities, and in what ways. Importantly, even the most pro-industry discussions of fan participation acknowledge that it produces value for media companies.

---

31. MEL STANFILL, EXPLOITING FANDOM: HOW THE MEDIA INDUSTRY SEEKS TO MANIPULATE FANS (Univ. of Iowa Press 2019).

32. *Id.* at 130–31 (citing JENKINS, CONVERGENCE CULTURE, *supra* note 8, at 157–58).

> This chapter takes the following simple premises. First, fan activity adds value to the media object it works on. Second, fans do this work without receiving equivalent monetary value in return, producing a net benefit to industry. Third, this means fan activity produces what Marxist theory calls surplus value and therefore it makes sense to view the recruitment of fan work as incitement to exploitive labor.[33]

Professor Stanfill goes on to explain that she uses a classic Marxian definition for "exploitive labor"—it is "extracting surplus value from workers—making more money from their labor than you pay them . . . ."[34] Of course this isn't a compellingly new insight—capitalism as an economic system is built on the premise that profit can be obtained by producing and selling goods for more than their cost of production. Power, under a Marxist analysis, belongs to those who control the means of production. Professor Stanfill notes that ownership of those means of production is **not** something fans have—pointing out that having access to the means of production is not the same thing as owning those means. That said, she adds that a difference in this interaction in the pop-culture space is that the owners of those means of production are now giving consumers/fans that access and encouraging and recognizing fan efforts to capture that value.[35]

As we move now from this shallow introductory dive into how sociology approaches fandom to the primary focus of this book, which is how fandom intersects with the law, keep in mind the importance of community to fans as a forum for sharing their fan-created content; as arbiters of the values of the members of the community; and as occasional, weekend resistance fighters against commercialization. Remember, it is these same fans who often at the same time are the willing recipients of the efforts of media producers to solicit, engage, and at times exploit their contributions. These themes will echo throughout the remainder of this book.

For now, though, these themes take a back seat as we begin to explore the key legal doctrines that are at the forefront of the intersection between fandom and the law.

---

33. *Id.* at 131 (citations omitted).
34. *Id.*
35. *Id.* at 133.

SECTION 2

The Broad Brush: Legal Doctrines Affecting All Fan-Created Works

CHAPTER 2

Initial Sources of Copyright Law

Intellectual property (IP) law covers a wide range of topics, from patent law to trade secrets law and beyond. For our purposes, the IP law relevant to fandom is primarily copyright law and, to a lesser degree but no less important, trademark law and right-of-publicity law.

Article I, Section 8 of the Constitution of the United States granted to Congress the power to create laws pertaining to IP rights. This fundamental grant reads:

> The Congress shall have Power to promote the Progress of Science and useful Arts, by securing for limited Times to Authors and Inventors the exclusive Right to their respective Writings and Discoveries.[1]

This chapter focuses first on copyright law and begins with the two most important versions of U.S. copyright law: the Copyright Act of 1909 and the Copyright Act of 1976. Since most fandom arose under the 1976 act and the provisions of that act address a number of issues relevant to fan-created content, a considerable amount of attention is focused on that act.

Fan-created content also often ventures into the legally murky areas of parody and satire—areas where the law has changed dramatically in recent years, warranting special attention. The ability of fan-created content to poke fun at pop-culture works has both expanded and been more curtailed by recent decisions by an array of courts.

1. U.S. Const., art. I, § 8, https://www.usconstitution.net/xconst_A1Sec8.html (last visited Jan. 18, 2021).

Which leads us, in this chapter, to move from the discussion of copyright law to the distinct but related legal doctrines regarding the creation of fan works that parody existing works or use existing works as the basis for making a satirical commentary on unrelated topics. The law of parody is messy—it is difficult to come up with a uniform explanation for what a court will find is a permissible parody—and after many years of studying the topic, the only unqualified statement I used to be able to offer, somewhat in jest, is that it wasn't a good idea to make fun of Disney characters—the company historically took a dim view of that kind of humor and was quick to sue offenders—but even that certainty has changed over time and is no longer uniformly the case.

The *Air Pirates* case is one of a number of key cases discussed in this chapter. This is a limited view of key cases that impact fan-created content—a review of all copyright cases is far beyond the scope of this book.

Copyright law is not the only statute that impacts fandom. Two other statutes, the PROTECT Act and the CASE Act, the latter of which is still working its way through the legislative process at this writing, also have important implications and limitations for fan creators.

Chapter 6, sub-section C, addresses two other statutory rights that impact fandom—trademark law (both state and federal) and right-of-publicity law adopted by many states (but not by the federal government). These rights are involved in instances where fan-created content uses, usually without advance permission, the registered and often well-known trademarks of a company or individual or when the fan work includes an appropriation of the name, image, likeness, and/or elements of identifiability that give rise to a right-of-publicity violation claim.

For practitioners experienced in copyright law particularly, and IP law in general, much of this chapter will be a basic review; for readers lacking that level of experience, some of this may be tough sledding. For all readers, however, understanding this material is essential to understanding the subsequent chapters, which focus on how these legal doctrines specifically affect our given areas of focus on fan fiction, art, film, and cosplay.

And so we begin, in the early 18th century, with the adoption of the first copyright law in the world.

A. The Statute of Anne and Its Migration to the United States

Copyright law traces its origins to the Statute of Anne, an act of the British Parliament enacted on April 10, 1710. Prior to its enactment, copyright in Britain had been administered and controlled by either a "printing patent" or what was known as the "stationer's copyright." The latter of these started as a grant of control via the 1557 Charter, a grant of national monopoly over the power to print books in the country. This power was bestowed by the Crown on the leading printing company in the country, the Stationer's Company. Both of these rights were granted for the publishers of books and offered little or no protection to the authors.[2]

The Statute of Anne sought to change that balance of power and control to shift those qualities to the authors of the books it protected. For many, but not all, legal scholars, the opening recital makes this shift eloquently clear:

> Whereas printers, booksellers, and other persons have of late frequently taken the liberty of printing, reprinting, and publishing, or causing to be printed, reprinted, and published, books and other writings, without the consent of the authors or proprietors of such books and writings, to their very great detriment, and too often to the ruin of them and their families: for preventing therefore such practices for the future, and for the encouragement of learned men to compose and write useful books: may it please your majesty, that it may be enacted, and be it enacted by the Queen's most excellent majesty, by and with the advice and consent of the lords spiritual and temporal, and commons, in the present parliament assembled, and by the authority of the same . . . .[3]

Although this language makes it clear that the rights of publishers in the books they publish are also to be protected, it seems clear, particularly with the reference to incentivizing "learned men to compose and write useful books," that a central purpose of the statute was to protect author rights. When the British colonists crossed the ocean and settled in what became the original colonies of America, they brought this interpretation of copyright law with them.

The first U.S. law that addressed copyright was the Copyright Act of 1790, an act that was heavily influenced by the Statute of Anne. The initial recitals in the 1790 Act closely parallel those of their British predecessor:

> **Section 1.**
>
> Be it enacted by the Senate and House of Representatives of the United States of America in Congress assembled, That from and after the passing of this act, ***the author and authors of any map, chart, book or books already printed within these United States,*** being a citizen or citizens thereof, or resident within the same, his or their executors, administrators

---

2. Oren Bracha, *The Adventures of the Statute of Anne in the Land of Unlimited Possibilities: The Life of a Legal Transplant*, 25 BERKELEY TECH. L.J. 1432–35 (Summer 2010).

3. The Statute of Anne, 8 Anne, c. 19 (1710), last viewed at https://avalon.law.yale.edu/18th_century/anne_1710.asp.

> or assigns, who halt or have not transferred to any other person the copyright of such map, chart, book or books, share or shares thereof; and any other person or persons, being a citizen or citizens of these United States, or residents therein, his or their executors, administrators or assigns, ***who halt or have purchased or legally acquired the copyright of any such map, chart, book or books, in order to print, reprint, publish or vend the same, shall have the sole right and liberty of printing, reprinting, publishing and vending such map, chart, book or books, for the term of fourteen years from the recording the title thereof in the clerk's office, as is herein after directed:*** And that the author and authors of any map, chart, book or books already made and composed, and not printed or published, or that shall hereafter be made and composed, being a citizen or citizens of these United States, or resident therein, and his or their executors, administrators or assigns, shall have the sole right and liberty of printing, reprinting, publishing and vending such map, chart, book or books, for the like term of fourteen years from the time of recording the title thereof in the clerk's office as aforesaid. ***And if, at the expiration of the said term, the author or authors, or any of them, be living, and a citizen or citizens of these United States, or resident therein, the same exclusive right shall be continued to him or them, his or their executors, administrators or assigns, for the further term of fourteen years;*** Provided, He or they shall cause the title thereof to be a second time recorded and published in the same manner as is herein after directed, and that within six months before the expiration of the first term of fourteen years aforesaid.[4]

Parliament's intent to protect British authors' copyright in their works is carried across the ocean in the 1790 act, which also copied the 14-year term of copyright duration. In the years that followed, Congress passed other changes to the copyright law, including in 1831, when it expanded the term of protection from 14 to 28 years, and importantly in 1870, when it gave copyright owners the exclusive right to create and own derivative works, being works that were based on a previously created original work (i.e., a theatrical play based on a previously written book is a derivative work).[5]

In 1897, Congress established the Copyright Office and appointed the first Register of Copyright, an administrative appointment of an individual (Thorvald Solberg) to run the Copyright Office, which was made a part of the

---

4. Copyright Act of 1790, § 1, https://www.copyright.gov/about/1790-copyright-act.html (last visited Jan. 18, 2021).

5. The Copyright Office website offers a comprehensive timeline of developments in copyright law at https://www.copyright.gov/timeline.

Library of Congress.[6] As the country moved into the 20th century, Congress completed its third general revision of copyright law with the passage of the Copyright Act of 1909, one of the most influential copyright laws in our history, and one that still has an effect on fan-created works made today, since many incorporate characters and storylines that were created under that act.

6. *Id.*

CHAPTER 3

The Copyright Act of 1909

On March 4, 1909, President Theodore Roosevelt signed the 1909 Copyright Act into law. This third general revision of U.S. copyright law contained a number of important provisions and also left out some elements that would create significant problems over the next 67 years, that Congress would spend over a decade trying to rectify, and that would form the basis for the next major revision of the law, in 1976.

The 1909 Act is important both for what it provided in its terms and for what was not provided. For creators of fan works, some of the important provisions included the following.

A. Derivative Works under the 1909 Act

A derivative work under copyright law is a work that is based on an underlying or previously existing work. Since fan-created content is in virtually all cases work that builds upon, and in some way references, previously existing work, pretty much all fan-created content is derivative work. As such, it is vitally important to understand that fan-created works, to avoid being subject to suit for violating the copyright of the original work they are based on, must either be created with the consent of the creator of that original work or fall into one of a series of exceptions to that underlying right.

The 1909 Act grants exclusive control over "derivative works," without directly using that term, in subsection (b) of the Act, which provides that creators

> shall have the exclusive right: (b) To translate the copyrighted work into other languages or dialects, or make any other version thereof, if it be a literary work to dramatize it if it be a nondramatic work to convert it into a novel or other nondramatic work if it be a drama; to arrange or adapt it if it be a musical work; to complete, execute, and finish it if it be a model or design for a work of art . . . .[1]

So if original creators retain exclusive control over the right to create derivative works based on their original works, does this mean that a third party seeking to create a derivative work must get permission to do so? Does it mean that fan creators must get permission? That critics of the work must get permission to write a critique? One would think so; however, a key contemporary doctrine, known as "fair use" and explicitly defined in the Copyright Act of 1909, allows a limited un-consented-to use to be made of works, without incurring liability for copyright infringement.

B. Fair Use under the 1909 Act

What is the purpose of a fair-use policy? Essentially, it is to allow certain uses of a copyright-protected work to be made without the consent of the original creator, in contexts that generally do not affect the economic value of the work or the attribution and integrity rights of the original creator. Good examples of when this policy is necessary include allowing critics to write reviews of creative works so that they can quote from, or show pictures from, a work they are reviewing, without facing a copyright infringement claim for that use. Similarly, for a teacher who wants to allow students to see portions of a work so they can study it in their class, fair-use policy allows the teacher to make and distribute multiple copies of the work without being sued for infringement.

It's quite a stretch to argue that these kinds of uses aren't "fair" to the owners of the underlying work—principles of free speech and the educational purpose of using works in the classroom seem inherently fair and justify these kinds of uses. However, the tough issues in the law never come from the easy examples—it's the hard cases that test the limits of the policy.

In the fair-use context, the uses that have spurred the most contentious debate are uses that fall under the realm of "derivative works." In such uses, a creator or distributor takes an existing work, incorporates it in some fashion in a new work, and publishes and distributes the new work without the consent

1. Copyright Act of 1909, https://law.scu.edu/wp-content/uploads/hightech/1909%20Act%20as%20enacted.pdf (last visited Jan. 18, 2021).

of the original creator, often without giving attribution to that creator and, not surprisingly, also without compensating the original creator for the use.

Two competing policy viewpoints are at play in this dispute. On the one hand, many (but not all) creators argue passionately that their works should not be available for use by others without attribution or payment and should not be subject to alteration by third parties that damages either the integrity of the work or the context in which it appears.

On the other hand, advocates for expanded rights to use these original works argue with equal force that the creative process has always involved new uses of preexisting works and that imposing financial or other costs on those kinds of uses discourages such creativity, in violation of the Article I, Section 8 constitutional goal of stimulating and incentivizing new works of creative expression.

This is a tough battle, with merit to be found on both sides of the argument. An added complication is the historic social battle over the value of art and artists. A recent survey puts the average salary of an artist in the United States at $14.02 per hour—which, when you consider that the current push for an increased minimum wage in the United States would set that wage at $15 per hour, gives a sense that artist pay is at the bottom of the scale.[2]

So the relevant question is whether the fair-use doctrine applied to works created under the 1909 Act. And the answer is that since the 1909 Act doesn't include, in the statute, a clear definition of the nature and limits of fair use, parties claiming fair use of works created before the 1976 Act must support their claims under case law from that time—and case law didn't always paint a clear picture of how the doctrine should be applied. The vagueness and uncertainty of the application of fair-use doctrine to works created under the 1909 Act was well summarized in a Copyright Office study on fair use done in 1960. The author of this study No. 14 was Alan Latman, formerly Special Advisor to the Copyright Office. After summarizing an array of cases that had discussed the ambiguities in the doctrine, Mr. Latman offered two conclusions:

> The cases examined above support the conclusion that fair use is not a predicable area of copyright law. One writer has characterized this situation as follows:
>
>> There is one proposition about fair use about which there is widespread agreement: it is not easy to decide what is and what is not a fair use.[3]

---

2. *Artist Salaries*, Indeed, https://www.indeed.com/salaries/Artist-Salaries (last visited Jan. 18, 2021).

3. Studies Prepared for the Subcommittee on Patents, Trademarks, and Copyrights of the Senate Committee on the Judiciary, 86th Cong., Studies 14–16, at 14 (Comm. Print 1960), https://

In his second conclusion, Latman notes that the decision to not add a statutory definition or criteria for the application of the fair-use doctrine to the 1909 Act was intentional—the legislators felt this was a matter for the courts to handle, without legislative guidance. He wrote in his report:

> The silence of the 1909 act on the question of fair use is consistent with prior history. There has apparently never been any specific statutory provision dealing with the question in the copyright law of the United States.[4]

He later offers an explanation for the omission, citing several sources. He notes that the failure to make specific mention of fair use in the 1909 Act was not an accident. Rather, Congress intentionally decided to omit a definition of the term, leaving it instead for the courts to define. This decision echoed one made by the Senate Committee on Patents, which decided in 1907 to leave the definition to the courts.[5]

Which leads, of course, first to the question of whether, over time, this proved to be a wise approach. Latman's report looks at cases prior to the date it was written, in 1960, in an effort to discern what the criteria are for finding that a given work's use of preexisting material is a fair use. He cites cases where the following eight uses were found to be fair use: 1. Incidental Use; 2. Reviews and Criticism; 3. Parody and Burlesque; 4. Scholarly Works and Compilations; 5. Personal or Private Use; 6. News; 7. Use in Litigation; and 8. Use for Non-Profit or Governmental Purposes.[6]

As to each of these categories, the next question is what elements the courts looked to in order to make a determination of fair use. Once again, ambiguity is a problem, with different courts and commentators applying different criteria—an outcome guaranteed to happen in these pre–1976 Act cases because of the absence of a uniform statutory guideline.

So what does all of this uncertainty and ambiguity in application of the fair-use doctrine mean for fan content creators? It means that if you are creating a fan work based on an original work created before January 1, 1978, the date the 1976 Copyright Act went into effect, you will have to rely on case law, rather than a clearly articulated statute, for your definition of the doctrine and its elements. Works created under the 1909 Act are still judged according to that case law, even in cases brought now. And the lesson learned from the

---

www.copyright.gov/history/studies/study14.pdf (citing Cohen, *Fair Use in the Law of Copyright*, ASCAP, Copyright Law Symposium, No. 6, at 52 (1955)).

4. *Id.* at 6.

5. *Id.* at 18 (citing *Hearings before Committee on Patents on S. 6330 and H.R. 19853*, 59th Cong., 1st Sess., at 15 (June 1906); S. Rep. No. 6187, 59th Cong., 2d Sess. (1907)).

6. *Id.* at 8–18 (citing numerous cases).

Copyright Office's own 1960 report is that certainty is sorely lacking as to the applicability of the fair-use doctrine in any given case.

C. Work for Hire under the 1909 Act

The basic concept and policy underlying the work-for-hire doctrine are straightforward ones. If a person creates a work subject to copyright and does so within the course and scope of his or her role as an employee, using the tools provided by his or her employer, the law presumes that the work so created is the property of the employer—that the work was created for the benefit and use of the employer. The effect of the application of the doctrine is that the employee has no ownership interest in the work.

Just as we've seen with the fair-use doctrine, the Copyright Act of 1909 contains virtually no discussion of the work-for-hire doctrine, except for the following brief reference found in the definitions section of the Act:

> § 26. Terms defined
>
> In the interpretation and construction of this title "the date of publication" shall in the case of a work of which copies are reproduced for sale or distribution be held to be the earliest date when copies of the first authorized edition were placed on sale, sold, or publicly distributed by the proprietor of the copyright or under his authority, *and the word "author" shall include an employer in the case of works made for hire.*[7]

Congress apparently felt that there was no need to further define "works made for hire." This was a mistake similar to the failure to add a legislative definition and set of criteria for fair use. While the question of whether a particular work was a "work made for hire" was an easy determination to make in a classic employer/employee relationship, it was a much more complex question when the work was created by an independent contractor.

Independent contractors use their own tools and often create work on their own schedule and in their own work space. How then is a court, or a creator, able to determine if the work of an independent contractor belongs to the contracting party or to the artist?

Since Congress failed to provide guidance on this issue in the 1909 Act, courts felt compelled to fill in this gap, via the creation of a judicial test known as the instance-and-expense doctrine. U.S. District Court Judge Roderic McKelvie, in his opinion finding that comic-book characters initially created by

7. Copyright Act of 1909, § 26 (emphasis added), http://www.kasunic.com/1909_act.htm#a26 (last visited Jan. 18, 2021).

artist Marv Wolfman became works for hire when he enhanced them for Marvel Comics, summarized this doctrine as follows: "If the employer can meet its burden to show some credible evidence that an employee worked at the 'instance and expense' of the employer, then the court will presume that the employer holds the copyright to the material produced."[8]

What is meant by "instance and expense"? Courts have explained this as the situation when the "motivating factor in producing the work was the employer who induced the creation"[9] and "whether the employer had the right to direct and supervise the manner in which the work was being performed. Actual exercise of that right is not controlling, and copyright is vested in the employer who has no intention of overseeing the detailed activity of any employee hired for the very purpose of producing the material."[10] These are hardly clear definitions and have generated much uncertainty in the cases where the application of the test is at issue.

Looking first to the issue of whether a work is produced at the expense of the employer, the court in the *In re Marvel Entertainment* case finds that regardless of whether the work was produced by an employee or an independent contractor, it is done at the "expense" of the employer if the payment is a sum certain, rather than a royalty, citing *Playboy Enterprises, Inc. v. Dumas*.[11]

While the *Playboy* case established the rule that payment by the employer is sufficient to meet the expense portion of the test, the court's decision in that case also reveals the shaky foundation of the more difficult portion of the test, the instance component. The court noted that until the mid-1960s, "federal courts applied the work-for-hire doctrine only to cases in which a traditional employer/employee relationship existed between the hiring party and the creator of the work."[12] The court notes that the Ninth Circuit expanded the definition of "work for hire" in *Lin-Brook Builders Hardware v. Gertier*[13] to include independent contractors under this instance-and-expense test. While this is an accurate statement of the rule in the *Lin-Brook* case, what is missing in the court's analysis is any examination as to the merits of the conclusion that work for hire should be extended to independent contractors.

This is not a minor point of concern. The interpretation of work for hire that prevailed prior to these mid-1960s cases was an easy one to apply—if the

---

8. *In re Marvel Ent. Grp., Inc. et al.*, Civil Action no. 97-638-RRM, at 23 (Nov. 6, 2000) (op. of U.S. Dist. Ct. Judge McKelvie, citing Dolman v. Agee, 157 F.3d 708, 712 (9th Cir. 1998); Siegel v. Nat'l Periodical Publ'ns, Inc., 508 F.2d 909, 914 (2d Cir. 1974); Brattleboro Publ'g Co. v. Winmill Publ'g Corp., 369 F.2d 565, 567 (2d Cir. 1966)).

9. *Siegel*, 508 F.2d at 914.

10. *Id.*

11. Playboy Enters., Inc. v. Dumas, 53 F.3d 549 (2d Cir. 1995).

12. *Id.* at 554.

13. Lin-Brook Builders Hardware v. Gertier, 352 F.2d 298, 300 (9th Cir. 1965).

relationship was a traditional employer/employee one, marked by the payment of a wage to the employee and the works being done using the employer's tools and at the employer's place of business, ownership of the resulting work by the employer was logical and easily explained. In the independent-contractor situation, where the work was done by the contractor using his or her own tools, on the contractor's schedule, and with the work entirely under the contractor's control, it seems an unwarranted extension of the doctrine to say that this was a work for hire. It also invites controversy and uncertain results in judicial decision, because there is no clear standard to apply as to the instance component of the test.

So how is this important for creators of fan fiction, art, film, and cosplay? It is important for several reasons.

First, for creators who wish to create derivative works based on works originally created during, and subject to, the 1909 Copyright Act, it means that in attempting to obtain a license for the use of those underlying works, if you seek the license from the known creator of the works, you may be talking to the wrong person—someone who never owned the rights to the work because it is a work for hire that belongs to his or her employer—so not only does the creator not have the rights to license, but relying on his or her approval of the right to use the work may also be evidence that you knew you needed permission and are liable for failing to find out the right person or entity to obtain it from.

Second, in evaluating whether you want to make a derivative use or even what you view as a transformative use (more about this doctrine in the next section), you may underestimate the risk you are taking if you think any claim might come from the estate of a long-dead creator, as opposed to the entertainment division of a huge, multinational corporation with a fleet of in-house attorneys charged with the duty of protecting the companies' brands. And by the same token, you will also not know who is entitled to negotiate those license deals if you don't know who actually owns the rights to the work you are hoping to adapt.

Lastly, because Congress did not establish a statutory framework to guide prospective creators as to whether a given work was created as a work for hire or remained the property of the original creator, the courts attempted to fill the gap by issuing decisions in cases where disputes over ownership reached them for resolution. This good intention resulted in a patchwork of cases with different standards coming out of different regions of the country—a situation that created more confusion than clarity.

So bottom line for creators of fan fiction, art, film, or cosplay—if you are dealing with an original work created and published before January 1, 1978, it is governed by the 1909 Copyright Act, which does not give you clear guidelines as to what is a work for hire. Determining who actually owns, rather than who created, the work may require some research, or using a rights clearance service, to answer the question. And you need to know who the true owner is if you are either going to try to obtain a license to use the work or assessing the likelihood of getting into a rights dispute with a multinational corporation or a solo owner. That said, if you are solely creating fan fiction, art, movies, or cosplay based entirely on characters and stories that only include material originally created after January 1, 1978, you need not be concerned with the 1909 Act and the application of the instance-and-expense test.

D. Duration (Term) of Copyright under the 1909 Act

As noted previously, the term, or length, of copyright protection under the 1909 Act was initially 28 years, renewable for an additional 28 years for a total span of 56 years of protection. As we will see shortly, when the copyright law was revised in the 1976 Act, a new period, being the life of the author plus 50 years, was substituted for the 56-year period. To make things more complicated, the 1976 Act also increased the length of the second renewal term to 67 years, making the total amount of years covered by a properly renewed 1909 Act copyright now 95 years, rather than 56 years. For creators hoping that the pre-1978 work they want to use is in the public domain, this significant extension of the copyright duration means that very few pre-1978 works are now in the public domain.[14]

Calculating the duration of a copyright can be a tricky business, particularly if the work is a "bundled" one—a work that incorporates a variety of copyright-protected works (for example, a film). Movies are bundled works, often including sound recordings, underlying musical compositions, a script (a literary work), costume design, choreography, production artwork, and the motion picture that combines all of those elements. Here again, there are multiple potential traps for the unwary creator, and engaging the services of a clearance company and competent counsel may be the best way to avoid an unpleasant surprise like a cease-and-desist letter right before or shortly after release of the finished work.

By the mid-1960s, Congress realized that the patchwork quilt of more than nine different limited efforts to revise the 1909 Act to keep up with the fast-moving and ever-changing pace of technology aiding the delivery of creative content was not effective and that a top-to-bottom revision of the copyright law was needed.

---

14. *Duration of Copyright*, U.S. Copyright Off. Circular 15A (reviewed Aug. 2011), https://www.copyright.gov/circs/circ15a.pdf.

CHAPTER 4

The Copyright Act of 1976

The revision process began on August 18, 1965, when the Subcommittee on Patents, Trademarks, and Copyrights of the Senate Judiciary Committee commenced a series of hearings on Senate Bill 597, a revision of federal copyright law. It was the beginning of what would be a process encompassing more than 11 years of work, finally resulting in the Copyright Law of 1976—adopted by Congress in September 1976 and signed by President Gerald Ford on October 19, 1976.

The legislative history and the discussion of the 1976 Act by an array of academic and practitioner commentators offer a rich collection of information about Congress's intentions in adopting these features. For our purposes, let's focus on those changes that most impact fan-created works.

A. Work for Hire under the 1976 Act

In the 1976 Act, Congress attempted to remedy the lack of statutory clarity that gave birth to the instance-and-expense test for determining if a given work fell under the work-for-hire doctrine. For the first time, Congress defined the phrase; section 101 of the Act added a definition of works made for hire. The definition, still valid law, is as follows:

> A "work made for hire" is—
>
> (1) a work prepared by an employee within the scope of his or her employment; or

> (2) a work specially ordered or commissioned for use as a contribution to a collective work, as a part of a motion picture or other audiovisual work, as a translation, as a supplementary work, as a compilation, as an instructional text, as a test, as answer material for a test, or as an atlas, if the parties expressly agree in a written instrument signed by them that the work shall be considered a work made for hire. For the purpose of the foregoing sentence, a "supplementary work" is a work prepared for publication as a secondary adjunct to a work by another author for the purpose of introducing, concluding, illustrating, explaining, revising, commenting upon, or assisting in the use of the other work, such as forewords, afterwords, pictorial illustrations, maps, charts, tables, editorial notes, musical arrangements, answer material for tests, bibliographies, appendixes, and indexes, and an "instructional text" is a literary, pictorial, or graphic work prepared for publication and with the purpose of use in systematic instructional activities.
>
> In determining whether any work is eligible to be considered a work made for hire under paragraph (2), neither the amendment contained in section 1011(d) of the Intellectual Property and Communications Omnibus Reform Act of 1999, as enacted by section 1000(a)(9) of Public Law 106-113, nor the deletion of the words added by that amendment—
>
> (A) shall be considered or otherwise given any legal significance, or
>
> (B) shall be interpreted to indicate congressional approval or disapproval of, or acquiescence in, any judicial determination, by the courts or the Copyright Office. Paragraph (2) shall be interpreted as if both section 2(a)(1)of the Work Made for Hire and Copyright Corrections Act of 2000 and section 1011(d) of the Intellectual Property and Communications Omnibus Reform Act of 1999, as enacted by section 1000(a)(9) of Public Law 106-113, were never enacted, and without regard to any inaction or awareness by the Congress at any time of any judicial determinations. The terms "WTO Agreement" and "WTO member country" have the meanings given those terms in paragraphs (9) and (10), respectively, of section 2 of the Uruguay Round Agreements Act.[1]

While this new definition offers much more clarity about the meaning of "work made for hire" than was found in the 1909 Act, it remains far from a model of clear and easily understandable legislation. The two subsections, while not identified as such, appear to embody the distinction between works

1. Copyright Act of 1976, § 101 (Definitions), http://copyright.gov/title17/92chap1.pdf (last visited Jan. 19, 2021). For reasons not entirely clear, Congress decided not to number the numerous terms defined in section 101, preferring instead to list them in alphabetical order—an understandable approach, particularly if Congress thought it likely that new terms might be added in the future; however, this structure makes citing to the definitions somewhat of an inexact science.

created by employees and those created by independent contractors or any other third parties. That said, there are numerous terms within these subsections that are not explained or further defined and that, as a consequence, provide openings for widely differing understandings and interpretations.

Beginning with the definition in subsection 1, Congress offers no definition for the terms "prepared," "employee," and "within the scope of his or her employment." The failure to define these terms makes it difficult for all stakeholders to determine if a given work is a work made for hire.

Starting with the first undefined term, how is one to determine if a work is "prepared" by an employee? Is a work "prepared" by an employee if the employee outlines the idea for a work and an independent contractor executes the creation of it? Is a work edited by an employee after the first draft or rough cut is created by an outside contractor a work "prepared" by the employee? What is the treatment of works created jointly by teams of employees working for different companies—who "prepared" that work? In sum, the absence of a definition for what "prepared" means leaves all parties uncertain regarding ownership of the resulting work.

The next definition problem lies with the term "employee." In 1909, and perhaps even in 1976, the majority of workers toiled for employers, did their work on premises controlled by the employer, and received a paycheck twice monthly. They used the tools provided to them by their employer and followed the instructions given them by their employer as to how to do their work and what the ultimate product of that labor would be.

The world of work has changed greatly since those times. A significant amount of contemporary work is done in a wide array of different work contexts. Independent contractors, part-time workers in the shared or gig economy, and outsourced work done by workers in other countries have made the definition of "employee" much more fluid. Again, Congress has not revisited the meaning of "employee" since 1976—and the resultant lack of clarity presents opportunities for all parties to contest whether a given work was created by an "employee" and is therefore not a work made for hire.

Lastly, the limitation that a work is not a work made for hire unless it was done by the employee "within the scope of his or her employment" offers a veritable minefield of uncertainty. What is the "scope" of a given employee's employment? In many occupations, employees aren't given a written contract of employment at all, let alone one that defines the scope of their employment. And even in instances where such a contract term is provided, the language used is generally so vague that the scope can be altered to fit the employer's interest at any time and in any context.

By way of example, I was once asked to advise some clients who worked as animators for a major motion-picture company. The company was known for its family-friendly fare, and all of their assigned work was done in that genre.

On their own, they had developed a cast of animated characters whose appearance and actions had a more adult-oriented and sexually explicit approach. They asked me to review their employment contract to see if, in my opinion, the terms of that agreement meant that the company would own these new characters if they published them or tried in any other way to commercially exploit them.

The language of their contract with the company was so broad that it was clear that these new characters, although very different from the usual fare the company produced, were nonetheless the property of the company and would be deemed works made for hire. Given the uncertainties that persist in determining if a work is a work made for hire, the advice given to those artists was that the only safe approach they could take would be to leave their present employment and to attempt to market characters they created only after their employment ended to eliminate any possibility that their employer could claim ownership of their creations.

B. Fair Use and the Transformative Doctrine under the 1976 Act

1. The Richard Prince Appropriation Cases

The uncertainty that has marked the struggle to consistently and coherently define "work-for-hire" is matched, if not exceeded, by the uncertainty of when a work can be deemed to have been sufficiently "transformed" that it becomes a noninfringing fair-use work, despite substantial use of an underlying work. So how has this ill-defined doctrine developed and been applied?

The answer, unfortunately, is that the doctrine has been interpreted in a somewhat haphazard way, creating great uncertainty for lawyers and creatives as to whether they can successfully respond to an infringement claim with a transformative fair-use defense. Prior to the 1976 Copyright Act, most of this uncertainty can be attributed to the absence of a statutory guideline—fair use in that era was judge-made law, and courts and their decisions in cases came up with different approaches. The basic outline of the doctrine comes from Justice Story's distillation in the decision in *Folsom v. Marsh*.[2] He advised counsel to "look to the nature and objects of the selections made, the quantity and value of the materials used, and the degree in which the use may prejudice the sale, or diminish the profits, or supersede the objects, of the original work."[3]

2. Folsom v. Marsh, 9 F. Cas. 342 (No. 4,901) (C.C.D. Mass. 1841).
3. *Id.* at 348.

Justice Story's formula served as the basis for Congress's adoption of section 107 of the Copyright Act of 1976, which includes a predicate section and a four-factor test for determining whether a given use was deemed a fair use and therefore not an infringement of copyright. Look at the language of the statute—you can see where it has adopted Justice Story's formula and where it has branched out from that structure:

> Notwithstanding the provisions of sections 106 and 106A, the fair use of a copyrighted work, including such use by reproduction in copies or phonorecords or by any other means specified by that section, for purposes such as criticism, comment, news reporting, teaching (including multiple copies for classroom use), scholarship, or research, is not an infringement of copyright. In determining whether the use made of a work in any particular case is a fair use the factors to be considered shall include—
>
> **(1)** the purpose and character of the use, including whether such use is of a commercial nature or is for nonprofit educational purposes;
>
> **(2)** the nature of the copyrighted work;
>
> **(3)** the amount and substantiality of the portion used in relation to the copyrighted work as a whole; and
>
> **(4)** the effect of the use upon the potential market for or value of the copyrighted work.
>
> The fact that a work is unpublished shall not itself bar a finding of fair use if such finding is made upon consideration of all the above factors.[4]

The principal difference between Justice Story's formula and the statute is the addition of the prefatory comments, offering examples of categories of use that are likely fair, and the addition of the first of the four factors—regarding the purpose and character of the use, including whether it is of a commercial nature or is for nonprofit educational purposes.

In the first decade following adoption, as of January 1, 1978, of the Copyright Act of 1976, courts and counsel using the fair-use defense viewed the first factor as being primarily focused on whether the use made by the defendant was a commercial or a nonprofit use. If the use was a commercial one, most courts viewed that as a disqualifying factor and found no fair use.

Judge Pierre Leval, in an article, *Toward a Fair Use Standard,*[5] asserted that this first element of the four-part test should be viewed as requiring a showing of whether the alleged infringing work adds something new, with a further purpose or different character, that alters the original work with new expression, meaning, or message—in other words, is it transformative? If so,

---

4. 17 U.S.C. § 107.
5. Pierre N. Leval, *Toward a Fair Use Standard,* 103 HARV. L. REV. 1105 (1990).

he reasons, this kind of transformation is at the heart of copyright law in that it furthers the promotion of science and the arts.[6]

Judge Leval's article laid the groundwork for a new interpretation of this first section of the fair-use test—an interpretation that would become the heart of a key decision by the U.S. Supreme Court that has become the cornerstone of what is generally referred to as the transformative doctrine, a standard that plays a huge role in expanding the rights of fan creators to use preexisting works in their creations.

The seminal case that is generally acknowledged as having launched the mainstream application of the doctrine is *Campbell v. Acuff-Rose.*[7] The case focuses on whether *Pretty Woman,* a parody song written by the rap group 2 Live Crew that pokes fun at Roy Orbison's classic rock ballad *Oh Pretty Woman,* was a copyright infringement or a protected fair use of the original song.

The district court made short work of the case, granting summary judgment for 2 Live Crew, finding that the song was a parody that made fair use of the original song. Acuff-Rose, owners of the song, won an appeal before the U.S. Court of Appeals for the Sixth Circuit. The Court of Appeals, using the then-common approach to fair-use analysis that found any commercial use to presumptively not be a fair use, found that 2 Live Crew's use was of a commercial nature and, based solely on that determination, found it was not a fair use.

On appeal to the U.S. Supreme Court, Justice Souter, writing for the majority of the Court (Justice Kennedy wrote a concurring opinion—there were no dissenting opinions), held that all four of the fair-use factors had to be considered in applying the law and that it was an error for the Sixth Circuit to decide the case solely based on whether the use was a commercial one.

Justice Souter also addressed, for the first time, the question of whether a parody could be a transformative fair use, as that concept had been explored in Judge Leval's article. He concludes:

> Suffice it to say now that parody has an obvious claim to transformative value, as Acuff-Rose itself does not deny. Like less ostensibly humorous forms of criticism, it can provide social benefit, by shedding light on an earlier work, and in the process, creating a new one. We thus line up with the courts that have held that parody, like other comment or criticism, may claim fair use under §107.[8]

The decision in *Campbell,* and its application of the transformative doctrine, became the guiding principle in a number of subsequent cases, expanding the doctrine from music to art, to literary works, and to other contexts.

---

6. *Id.* at 1111.
7. Campbell v. Acuff-Rose, 510 U.S. 569 (1994).
8. *Id.* at 579.

One case that caused huge ripples in the art world, and that brought the application of the transformativeness doctrine to public attention, was *Cariou v. Prince*.[9] This case focused on the action of self-titled "appropriation artist" Richard Prince, who took a coffee table–style book of Cariou's photos of Rasta men in Jamaica, entitled *Yes, Rasta*; removed photos from the book; scanned them into a much larger size (as tall as six feet in some instances); and added elements to them. In one instance, he pasted a picture of a guitar into one Rasta's hands; in another, he painted blue circles (what the Court referred to as "lozenges") over the Rasta's eyes and mouth. The resulting works were sold to Prince's high-society clients (read Beyoncé, Robert De Niro, and others) for prices in excess of $150,000 each. No credit or attribution was made identifying Cariou as the creator of the underlying photographs, nor was Cariou paid any share of the sales price for the works. A side-by-side comparison of one of the images at issue follows—the image on the left is Cariou's original photograph, followed on the right by Prince's version of the work, in which he has painted lozenges over the eyes and mouth of the Rasta and added a photo of a white hand and an electric guitar as if the Rasta is playing it.

[10]

9. Cariou v. Prince, 714 F.3d 694 (2d Cir. 2013).

10. Patrick Cariou, photograph of a Rasta, *in* PATRICK CARIOU, YES RASTA (Powerhouse Books 2000) (left image); Richard Prince, altered photograph of a Rasta, *in* RICHARD PRINCE, CANAL ZONE (Rizzoli 2008) (right image). These images were submitted in evidence in the case and were attached as exhibits to the Court's decision.

Cariou understandably sued Prince and the New York Gagosian Gallery, which sold the works, for copyright infringement. The District Court agreed that the works were infringing and awarded damages to Cariou. The Court based its rejection of Prince's "transformative" defense on the ground that his version of Cariou's works did not comment on, relate to the historical context of, or critically refer back to the original works.[11] On appeal, the Second Circuit reversed, accepting the argument made by Prince's counsel that the photos at issue were transformative and therefore not infringing. The Court rejected the argument that a transformative work had to make some comment on the original work. All that was necessary, said the Court, citing *Campbell*, was that the new work must alter the original with "new expression, meaning or message; or must create new information, aesthetics, insight or understandings."[12]

The Court found that Prince's alterations of Cariou's photos created a new aesthetic—admittedly a crude and jarring one, in contrast to Cariou's serene and beautiful works. The Court noted also that Prince added color and greater size to Prince's photos, finding that his composition, color palette, and media were fundamentally different from Cariou's work.[13]

A disturbing aspect of this part of the decision is the extent to which the Court is engaging in art criticism and analysis. It seems a fair question to ask whether the members of the Court are qualified to engage in this level of assessment and critique of Prince's appropriation art.

The Court continued in this vein by noting that Prince, in his deposition testimony, acknowledged that he had no interest in what Cariou's intent was in creating the original photos—rather, he claimed that he was "trying to make a kind of fantastic, absolutely hip, up to date, contemporary take on the music scene." The Court concluded, based on Prince's testimony, that he was, in his adaptation of Cariou's work, relating to a "post-apocalyptic screenplay" Prince had planned and "emphasiz[ing] themes [of Prince's planned screenplay] of equality of the sexes; highlight[ing] 'the three relationships in the world, which are men and women, men and men, and women and women'; and portray[ing] a contemporary take on the music scene."[14]

The District Court viewed Prince's deposition testimony as evidence that the work was not transformative because the artist didn't really have a message and was not trying to create anything with new meaning or a new message—which seems to track the descriptions of both Justice Story and the Court in *Campbell* of what was needed to make the work transformative. The Second

11. *Cariou*, 714 F.3d at ¶ 34, https://cyber.harvard.edu/people/tfisher/cx/2013_Cariou.pdf (last visited Jan. 19, 2021).

12. *Campbell*, 510 U.S. at 579.

13. *Cariou*, 714 F.3d at ¶¶ 52–53.

14. *Id.* at ¶ 54.

Circuit rejected that argument, holding that "no such rule exists" and that they would not analyze satire or parody differently from other transformative uses.[15]

Given the Court's prior citation to the *Campbell* case to the effect that "to qualify as a fair use, a new work generally must alter the original with 'new expression, meaning, or message,'"[16] it seems disingenuous of the Second Circuit to disregard Prince's admission that in appropriating Cariou's work, he was not offering any new meaning or message. Why doesn't that admission lead to a rejection of his claim that his work is transformative? The Court doesn't explain this glaring contradiction. Instead, the decision explains that while it is helpful to a transformative defense if the artist can provide an explanation for his or her use of the underlying work, the failure to do so is not dispositive. The Court finds that it is how the work is perceived by the "reasonable observer" that is important to a finding that the work is transformative. The test, argues the Court, is how the works may "reasonably be perceived" in order to assess their transformative nature—citing *Campbell* as support.[17] Based on this standard, the Court finds 25 of the Prince works to be transformative as a matter of law. They assert that these works are transformative because they give Cariou's photos a "new expression and employ new aesthetics."[18]

The Court offers a disclaimer as well—asserting that its decision should not be read as meaning that any cosmetic changes to a photograph would automatically mean it was fair use. A modified work would not be transformative, they note, if it merely presents the same material but in a new form, such as a book of synopses of televisions shows.[19]

The Court, in this decision, offers little guidance for fan creators who are trying to determine when their works would be found to be transformative and therefore not infringing—and by the same token provides no guidelines for the creators of original works to know when their works can lawfully be used by others in new works. The only example it offers where a third party's work would not be found to be transformative is a "work that merely presents the same material but in a new form, such as a book of synopses of televisions [sic] shows."[20] This definition is closer to the ban on literal copying, which often forms the basis for copyright infringement claims—a copying of the "same material." It leaves open for use any new work that, in the perception of the viewer or reader, is perceived to offer a new expression or aesthetic, regardless of whether the artist intended that perception to be made. So a creator can

15. *Id.* at ¶¶ 54–55.
16. *Id.* at ¶ 52.
17. *Id.* at ¶ 56.
18. *Id.* at ¶ 58.
19. *Id.* at ¶ 58.
20. *Id.*

make a transformative work without intending to do so and without offering any comment about the underlying work. This broad interpretation leaves many legal scholars asking what is left of the right to control derivative works found in section 104 of the 1976 Act? The answer is "not much."

As disheartening as this decision is to advocates for stronger protection of the rights of creators to control the creation of derivative works based on their original work, it offers significant support for fans creating fan art, film, fiction, and cosplay—so long as their works offer a new interpretation of the underlying work or present a new aesthetic, it is likely that they will be found to be transformative and therefore not infringing.

However, as is often the case in the law, several other decisions in cases have muddied the waters, leaving everyone in a state of uncertainty about whether the transformative defense is available to them. A look at these cases illustrates the difficulty of relying on a transformative fair-use argument in response to a copyright infringement claim.

In a case similar to the *Cariou* litigation, in 2014, photographer Donald Graham's photo entitled *Rastafarian Smoking a Joint* was appropriated by Prince, who uploaded and copied an Instagram post of the photo, adding only a caption of his own and blowing up the original post to a large size and offering it, along with other works taken from other Instagram posts, for prices in excess of $100,000 per work. As he did in the *Cariou* case, Prince did not identify the photo as Graham's work, nor did he share any of the sales proceeds with Graham.

In response, Graham sued Prince in the U.S. District Court in New York City, alleging copyright infringement of *Rastafarian Smoking a Joint*, seeking "declaratory relief; injunctive relief including orders of seizure, forfeiture, and destruction of the various works at issue; statutory or actual damages; and attorneys' fees and costs."[21] Secure in his assumption that this case would go the same way as the *Cariou* case, Prince, through his counsel, filed a motion to dismiss the lawsuit on the grounds that his use of Graham's photo was a transformative use and therefore was not an infringing one. To his surprise, the District Court disagreed and denied the motion. As of this writing, the case is still pending, but the outlook doesn't look good for Prince.

In his July 17, 2017, Decision and Order denying Prince's Motion to Dismiss, Judge Sidney H. Stein begins his analysis by citing the Court in the *Cariou* decision for the rule that "[t]he determination of fair use is a 'mixed question of fact

21. Donald Graham v. Richard Prince, Op. and Order, Case No. 15cv-10160(SHS), at 10 (U.S. Dist. Ct. S.D.N.Y. July 18, 2017).

and law,' which necessitates 'an open-ended and context-sensitive inquiry.'"[22] With that precedent in mind, Judge Stein reviews the four-factor fair-use test elements that led the Second Circuit to find in the *Cariou* case that 25 of the 30 Prince works at issue were transformative and that caused them to send five works back for further review by the District Court.

Judge Stein makes it abundantly clear that, in *Cariou*, once the Second Circuit found that the works were transformative and that Prince's work didn't likely appeal to, and therefore didn't detract from, the market for Cariou's work, the remaining elements of the test were not a sufficient basis to overrule the finding that the transformative nature of the work removed it from a successful infringement finding. He then turns to the case at hand to see if the outcome in *Cariou* compelled a similar result in Graham's case.

Judge Stein finds that none of the four factors in the fair-use test supported Prince's argument that his use of Graham's photograph was a fair one. For the purpose of this discussion of the transformative doctrine in fair-use cases, the clarity of language in Judge Stein's decision on this issue is worth repeating.

Judge Stein evaluates the claim that Prince's version is transformative, distinguishing in many respects the facts of the *Graham* case from the *Cariou* decision. He begins by citing the defendant's argument that Prince used Graham's photo of a Rastafarian smoking a joint as "raw material" to convey an array of messages, any of which were new and distinct from Graham's effort to honor and capture the spirit of the Rastafarian people. Defendants claim that Prince's messages in the work included a critique of the power of social media and the power of that media platform to generate discussion of art.

Judge Stein notes Graham's response as well—that Prince's placement of Graham's photo in a social media frame and the addition of what Prince himself called "gobblygook" words below the photo could not be a transformative use. Graham argued that the predominant feature of Prince's work was still Graham's black-and-white photo of the Rasta man and that Prince was simply exploiting the creative strength of Graham's original photo.

And then, as happened in the *Cariou* case, Judge Stein enters into the world of the art critic. He notes that if viewers were to conduct a side-by-side comparison of the two works, they too would see ("it is evident," he writes) that Prince's work cannot join the ranks of secondary works that are so aesthetically different that they would pass the Second Circuit's reasonable-viewer test laid out in the *Cariou* decision. Unlike Prince's additions to Cariou's photos, Judge Stein characterizes the additions to Graham's photo as failing to materially alter or heavily obscure the underlying work—he characterizes the result

22. *Id.* at 11 (citing Cariou v. Prince, 714 F.3d 694, 704–05 (2d Cir. 2013)).

of Prince's alteration of Cariou's photos as so significant that the resulting work was "barely recognizable" compared to the original photo. Rather, he notes, Prince's reframing of Graham's photo does not alter the content of the photo itself in any way.[23]

Judge Stein, in the conclusion of his opinion, offers a bit more of an explanation for why he did not find Prince's *Untitled* to be transformative:

> Because Prince has reproduced Graham's portrait without significant aesthetic alterations, *Untitled* is not transformative as a matter of law. Moreover, *Untitled* is a work made with a distinctly commercial purpose; Graham's original *Rastafarian Smoking a Joint* is, without question, expressive and creative in nature; Prince's use of the entirety of Graham's photograph weighs against a finding of fair use; and the Complaint adequately alleges usurpation of the primary market for *Untitled.* Accordingly, Prince's motion to dismiss the Complaint is denied.[24]

So does this mean that Judge Stein, in his *Graham* decision, has overruled the much-criticized decision in the *Cariou* case? In a word, no, and for several reasons. First, Judge Graham's decision was made in response to Prince's motion to deny Graham's suit at the early stage of the proceedings—the decision simply means that Graham can go forward with his case. It doesn't guarantee that the ultimate decision in the case will echo this first decision—however, Judge Graham has made a pretty strong argument against the transformative claim, one that will be hard for Prince to overcome.

Second, Judge Stein's decision is rendered at the trial-court level, in the district court, and the *Cariou* decision comes from the Second Circuit Court of Appeals, a higher court than the district court. It will take a higher-court decision to challenge the *Cariou* decision—and unless that higher court is the U.S. Supreme Court, the decision of the Second Circuit cannot be overturned even by a decision of another court of appeal—a conflict of appellate decisions is often what leads the Supreme Court to take up a case so as to resolve that conflict and issue a decision that will be binding on all federal court districts.

23. *Id.* at 24.
24. *Id.* at 32.

2. The J.K. Rowling *Lexicon* Case

An earlier case where the court grappled with the application of the transformative doctrine—the 2008 decision in the case of *Warner Bros. v. RDR Books*[25]—resulted in a determination that while the work at issue was somewhat transformative, it wasn't transformative **enough**. Although the case focuses on a guidebook written by a fan, which cannot be characterized as traditional fan fiction, since it involves a work written by a fan, this *Harry Potter Lexicon* case offers another good example of the difficulty courts and creators face in determining when a work crosses the line and is not found sufficiently transformative to escape an infringement claim.

David Kluft, writing in the Trademark and Copyright Law blog hosted by law firm Foley Hoag LLP, offers the following cogent summary of the case:

> This is probably the most famous lawsuit ever brought by an author against a fan, and it serves as an example of what can happen when fan work starts to become independently profitable. The defendant was a super fan of JK Rowling who created an online guide to the *Harry Potter* universe, called the *Harry Potter Lexicon*. The *Lexicon* was so good that Rowling herself was said to have used it as a reference. However, when the super fan was about to ink a deal for a book version of the *Lexicon*, things went haywire. The *Lexicon* book was going to be a *Harry Potter* encyclopedia, each entry recounting some element of Rowling's work: dialogue, plot summaries, characters, etc. Was the book or website critical of Rowling? No, so in order to qualify for the fair use defense, he would have to have shown that the rearrangement of all of these fictional elements in encyclopedia format was somehow otherwise transformative. With the *Carol Publishing* cases already on the books, this was an uphill battle, and the Court found that the *Lexicon* was not fair use. Moreover, Rowling herself was planning her own *Harry Potter* encyclopedia, with which the *Lexicon* would compete for readers, thus having an effect on Rowling's market for her product. Copyright law will permit fans to do a lot of things, but it wasn't going to allow a fan to compete with J.K. Rowling in the market for *Harry Potter*-related derivative works.[26]

A deeper dive into the analysis and decision in this case illustrates how even at this earlier stage of analysis of transformative doctrine, courts were struggling to define the parameters of how the doctrine should be applied.

---

25. Warner Bros. v. RDR Books, 575 F. Supp. 2d 513 (S.D.N.Y. 2008).

26. David Kluft, *10 Copyright Cases Every Fan Fiction Writer Should Know About*, Trademark & Copyright Law (Oct. 18, 2016), https://www.trademarkandcopyrightlawblog.com/2016/10/10-copyright-cases-every-fan-fiction-writer-should-know-about/.

As Kluft notes, the *Harry Potter Lexicon*, created and maintained by superfan Steven Vander Ark, was such a well-regarded website resource for all things Harry Potter, even series author J.K. Rowling was said to have consulted its archives and was certainly aware of its content. However, in a scenario common to fan-created content, what is initially viewed benignly takes on a different aspect when the fan creator wants to move the project to another, usually more highly visible, arena. In this case, it was Vander Ark's stated decision to, through RDR Books, publish a hardcopy book, an encyclopedia of Harry Potter data. A quote from Rowling attesting to the value of the website was used as a back-cover blurb of the book. When Rowling's representatives read about the forthcoming book, they sent a cease-and-desist letter to RDR, threatening a copyright infringement suit if RDR published the book.

At an earlier point in time, Vander Ark had publicly written that publishing a book of the *Lexicon* would violate Rowling's IP rights and that he would do so only if he got Rowling's express permission. He changed his mind after hearing the case for publication made by Roger Rapoport, owner of RDR Books, which wanted to publish this book. Rapoport argued that publishing the *Lexicon* was allowable fair use, and contrary to industry standard practice, not only did he not require that Vander Ark warrant that the publication would not violate any laws, but he also offered to indemnify and hold Vander Ark harmless if Rowling did sue him.[27] Which she did.

The procedural history, detailing when the case was filed, the nature of the claims and counterclaims, and how the parties came to present their evidence in a bench trial (meaning a trial before a judge, rather than a jury), was summarized by Judge Robert P. Patterson, Jr., in the first pages of his decision. He notes that plaintiff Warner Bros. Entertainment and J.K. Rowling filed the action on October 31, 2007 (with no indication whether filing on Halloween was intentional), against defendant RDR Books, seeking damages for copyright infringement as well as a series of other state and federal law claims. In addition to money damages, Warner also sought an injunction to stop sales of the *Lexicon*. After a series of pretrial motions, the parties narrowed the case into one focused on Warner's statutory and common-law infringement claims and RDR's fair-use defense and its affirmative defense that Warner and Rowling brought the case with "unclean hands"—an equitable defense. The more narrowly focused case was then tried before a judge (no jury) over three days in April 2008.[28]

So what this tells us is that concurrent with the filing of their lawsuit, plaintiffs Rowling and Warner Bros. set a hearing with the court, seeking a

27. *Warner Bros.*, 575 F. Supp. 2d at 521–23.
28. *Id.* at 517–18.

preliminary injunction—a court order—directing RDR to cease any effort to publish or sell the *Lexicon*. This kind of motion, for a preliminary injunction, is a common tactic used by plaintiffs in copyright infringement cases. It makes sense to seek this kind of relief, since if the publication of the book at issue is a violation of plaintiff's copyright, the plaintiff does not want the defendant to be able to continue selling the book during the time the lawsuit is moving through the court process—because it sometimes takes years before a case comes to trial, and by then, plaintiff could have lost substantial amounts of money due to the infringing sales.

There is, however, a risk in seeking a preliminary injunction in these cases—if the plaintiff loses the motion, it usually means that the likelihood of plaintiff winning the subsequent trial is not very good. So in many copyright infringement cases, the outcome of these early motions for a preliminary injunction ends up bringing the case to a quick resolution via settlement after the motion is resolved.

Perhaps mindful of that likely outcome and aware that in a preliminary injunction hearing, the parties, just as they would do in the trial of the case, must present evidence in support of, and in opposition of, the motion, Judge Robertson ordered the preliminary injunction hearing consolidated with the trial of the case and moved up the trial date so that the entire case could be resolved in that preliminary hearing. And so this lawsuit, filed in October 2007, came to trial in April 2008.[29] For a case to go from lawsuit to trial in six months is rare—and may have also happened because the judge felt that the issues would be pretty easy to resolve.

The judge began his analysis by characterizing the *Lexicon* as fitting in the "narrow genre of non-fiction reference guides to fictional works," noting that such guides are often created for literary series of books that encompass "an elaborate imaginary world over thousands of pages."[30] The decision then devotes eight pages to summarizing the many elements of the *Harry Potter* universe that are copied verbatim or extensively discussed in the *Lexicon*.

Turning to conclusions of law based on that summary, the Court begins with the question of whether Rowling established a prima facie case of copyright infringement. Citing the classic *Feist* case,[31] the Court noted that the claimant must show (1) that he or she is the valid owner of the copyright and (2) that there has been a copying of the constituent elements of the work that are original.[32]

29. *Id.*
30. *Id.* at 526.
31. Feist v. Rural Tel. Serv. Co., 499 U.S. 340 (1991).
32. *Id.* at 361.

The first element, ownership of the work, was not really in dispute—a point likely to be true in virtually all fan-created content cases, since this kind of fandom expression depends on the existence of a pop-culture work that has engendered fan interest. The real battle in the case was over the second element.

The copying element of the second test is divided into two kinds of cases, the first involving literal copying, which are pretty easy to prove by simply comparing the two works side by side or by overlaying a transparent sheet with the alleged infringing work on top of the original (or, in this case, the underlying work) to observe the degree to which an exact copy has been made.[33] The second kind of copying, known as nonliteral copying, generally looks to see if there is "substantial similarity" between the works involved.

And this is where things get complicated. In a 2013 essay entitled *A Fresh Look at Tests for Nonliteral Copyright Infringement,* Berkeley law professor and noted copyright scholar Pamela Samuelson identifies and examines five different conventional tests used for judging nonliteral infringement and offered seven ways to improve upon them.[34] While it is beyond the scope of this book to delve into the details of these tests, suffice it to say that conducting this substantial-similarity test is a complex process, with different courts choosing from an array of accepted approaches, all of which, as Professor Samuelson demonstrates convincingly in her article, have their flaws.

Defendant RDR Books admits that it copied significant amounts of invented facts from the *Harry Potter* novels, which was necessary in creating a guidebook to those novels. It argues, however, that this copying did not reach the level of substantial similarity with the original works because the fictional facts it copied were not used, as they were in the original, for the purpose of advancing the fictional story.

Judge Patterson makes short shrift of that argument, holding that "[r]eproducing original expression in fragments or in a different order, however, does not preclude a finding of substantial similarity. . . . Here, the Lexicon's rearrangement of Rowling's fictional facts does not alter the protected expression such that the Lexicon ceases to be substantially similar to the original works."[35] Based on these findings, the Court held that Rowling had established a prima facie case of infringement.

After finding that the *Lexicon* is not a derivative work because it does not fall under any of the categories of such works, the Court turns to the key issue in the case: is the *Lexicon*'s use of *Harry Potter* fictional facts a fair use under

33. The overlay method is often used in art and music composition infringement cases.

34. Pamela Samuelson, *Essay: A Fresh Look at Tests for Nonliteral Copyright Infringement,* 107:4 Nw. U. L. Rev. 1821 (2013).

35. Warner Bros. v. RDR Books, 575 F. Supp. 2d 513, 537 (S.D.N.Y. 2008).

copyright law and therefore noninfringing? It is this section of the decision that addresses the applicability of the transformative doctrine as a defense in the case.

Judge Patterson begins by characterizing the fair-use doctrine as the mediator between the

> [p]roperty rights [that copyright law] establishes in creative works, which must be protected up to a point, and the ability of authors, artists, and the rest of us to express them or ourselves by reference to the works of others, which must be protected up to a point. The fair-use doctrine mediates between the two sets of interests, determining where each set of interests ceases to control.[36]

Citing the language of section 107 of the 1976 Copyright Act, which defined the fair-use doctrine, Judge Patterson lists the four elements of the test, which are

> (1) the purpose and character of the use, including whether such use is of a commercial nature or is for nonprofit educational purposes;
> (2) the nature of the copyrighted work;
> (3) the amount and substantiality of the portion used in relation to the copyrighted work as a whole; and
> (4) the effect of the use upon the potential market for or value of the copyrighted work.[37]

Judge Patterson identifies the two interests at stake in the *Lexicon* case and gives a nod to Judge Pierre Leval, credited as the leading scholar on the transformative doctrine, as follows:

> At stake in this case are the incentive to create original works which copyright protection fosters and the freedom to produce secondary works which monopoly protection of copyright stifles—both interests benefit the public. *See* Pierre N. Leval, *Toward a Fair Use Standard,* 103 Harv. L. Rev. 1105, 1109 (1990) (noting that on one hand "[t]he monopoly created by copyright . . . rewards the individual author in order to benefit the public," and on the other "[m]onopoly protection of intellectual property that impeded referential analysis and the development of new ideas out of old would strangle the creative process").[38]

---

36. *Id.* at 540.
37. 17 U.S.C. § 107.
38. *Warner Bros.*, 375 F. Supp. 2d at 540.

With these twin and sometimes competing interests in mind, Judge Patterson delves into the four fair-use factors, analyzing each in turn. He begins with the first factor, the purpose and character of Vander Ark's use of the *Harry Potter* novels in the *Lexicon*. His findings are a mixed bag.

Pointing out that the purpose of the *Harry Potter* series was to tell "an entertaining and thought-provoking story centered on the character Harry Potter and set in a magical world,"[39] he contrasts that with the purpose of the *Lexicon*, which is to make that world readily accessible to readers in a reference guide format. He concludes that the *Lexicon* is a transformative work—it serves a different purpose.

Judge Patterson finds the *Lexicon*'s transformative argument less compelling with respect to its use of material taken from J.K. Rowling's two companion books to the *Potter* series—*Fantastic Beasts* and *Quidditch through the Ages*. Since these two books are also reference guides to elements found in the *Potter* series, and since Vander Ark quotes from them both extensively and verbatim, the Court finds these usages to be "transformative to a much lesser extent."[40]

It is in how the *Lexicon* uses materials from the *Potter* series that Judge Patterson finds the most support for the transformative fair-use argument. Its use as a reference guide is undisputed—Rowling herself acknowledges using its online version as a resource. Moreover, while the adding of significant analysis or commentary is not the focus of the *Lexicon*, the Court rejects the argument that the *Lexicon* offers no such analysis while at the same time acknowledging that doing so is not its principal purpose.

At this point in the decision, we see the first crack appear in the otherwise bulletproof transformative defense of RDR. Judge Patterson notes that the *Lexicon* makes frequent and extensive use of direct quotes of words, phrases, and other elements of the underlying *Potter* books "in excess of what is reasonably necessary" and that it failed to limit those quotations in ways that would limit the taking of the "expressive value" of the original version. Judge Patterson speculates that perhaps Vander Ark is such a *Potter* fan that he was incapable of exercising necessary restraint in using Rowling's original expression for "its inherent entertainment value."[41]

This is a key holding of the *Lexicon* case. It injects a new criterion for proponents of a transformative defense—that while a work may be transformative, the defense will be weakened if that transformative use is not consistently present throughout the work. This raises the possibility that, in essence, a work may be found to be transformative, but the use of that as a defense to copyright

39. *Id.* at 541.
40. *Id.*
41. *Id.* at 544.

infringement may fail if it is not transformative **enough**. For the secondary user, like a fan creator who uses too much of the original work in his or her secondary work, the risk this analysis carries is that if you use too much of the entertainment-value elements of the original work, you raise the possibility that the inconsistently transformative argument can swamp your defense.

A similar problem, overuse of the original work, resulted in the *Lexicon* case in a finding against Vander Ark and RDR on the third fair-use factor, the amount and substantiality of the portion used in relation to the copyrighted work as a whole.[42] Here the Court finds that in many instances, verbatim copying of the vivid descriptions of characters or other items listed in the *Lexicon* took far more original content than was necessary for the purpose of a description in a reference guide.[43]

The Court offers an example of this taking that exceeds necessity, as follows:

> Other times, however, the Lexicon disturbs the balance and takes more than is reasonably necessary to create a reference guide. In these instances, the Lexicon appears to retell parts of the storyline rather than report fictional facts and where to find them. For example, the Lexicon entry for "Trelawney, Sibyll Patricia" not only copies exactly the Divination professor's prophecies about the fates of Voldemort, Harry Potter, and Peter Pettigrew, it then tells how the prophecies are fulfilled, including events that do not involve Trelawney. (*Compare also* Pl. Ex. 10 at 714-720, *with* Pl. Ex. 1, entry for "Deathly Hallows, The," ¶ 5 (retelling the story that Dumbledore tells Harry about his own quest for the Hallows with Grindelwald in Chapter 35 of the seventh novel).) While it is difficult to draw the line at each entry that takes more than is reasonably necessary from the *Harry Potter* series to serve its purposes, there are a number of places where the Lexicon engages in the same sort of extensive borrowing that might be expected of a copyright owner, not a third party author.[44]

With respect to the copying of excerpts from the *Potter* companion books, the Court finds even less justification for the large amount of original material taken and concludes that this taking also was not a fair use:

> The Lexicon's use of copyrighted expression from Rowling's two companion books presents an easier determination. The Lexicon takes

42. The Court also found, in a brief and unremarkable aspect of its decision, that the second fair-use factor, the nature of the copyrighted work, also favored Rowling, since the *Harry Potter* novels, as fictional works, "are generally more deserving of protection than factual works." *Id.* at 549.

43. *Id.* at 544.

44. *Id.* at 548 (citations omitted).

> wholesale from these short books. *See supra* Findings of Fact. Depending on the purpose, using a substantial portion of a work, or even the whole thing, may be permissible. *See, e.g., Perfect 10,* 508 F.3d at 1167-68; *Bill Graham Archives,* 448 F.3d at 613; *Nunez v. Caribbean Int'l News Corp.,* 235 F.3d 18, 24 (1st Cir.2000). In this case, however, the Lexicon's purpose is only slightly transformative of the companion books' original purpose. As a result, the amount and substantiality of the portion copied from the companion books weighs more heavily against a finding of fair use.[45]

Here the Court offers a useful reminder and lesson. This third factor, the amount and substantiality of the portion used compared to the work as a whole, has often been overlooked in the growth of importance attached to the transformative use of a work. This element remains a critical part of the fair-use analysis. It stands as a warning for fan creators that taking too much of an underlying work, or taking the essence of that work, may provide substantial support to an attack on any fair-use defense offered in an infringement case.

Judge Patterson, after briefly noting that the fictional nature of the *Harry Potter* series makes it easy to determine that the second fair-use analysis factor, the nature of the copyrighted work, favored the plaintiffs,[46] then turns his attention to the last fair-use factor—the extent of provable market harm caused by the alleged infringement. He begins by noting that the market harm can be either to the original work or to the right of the original author to create derivative works based on that underlying work.

That broader scope doesn't help Rowling on this point, as the Court notes that the *Lexicon* isn't really a derivative work—as a reference guide, it exists for a different purpose than the fictional *Potter* novels, and as such, "[r]eference guides to the Harry Potter works [are] not exclusively hers (Rowling's) to exploit or license . . . ."[47] The Court notes that this difference in the nature of the works also supports a finding that the *Lexicon* offers no threat of market harm to the *Potter* novels, and presumably no direct evidence of such harm was offered at trial.

Judge Patterson does note, however, that the same analysis does not apply to the *Potter* companion books Rowling authored. Here, the wholesale copying of excerpts from the *Potter* novels, a fact the Court noted made the *Lexicon*'s use of those companion books "only marginally transformative,"[48] led to the conclusion that the *Lexicon* was likely to supplant the market for the companion

45. *Id.* at 549.
46. *Id.*
47. *Id.* at 550.
48. *Id.*

books. For that reason, the Court concludes that the fourth factor also tips in favor of plaintiffs.

Based on this analysis, Judge Patterson finds that the plaintiffs had established copyright infringement of the *Harry Potter* novels and the companion books and that RDR and Vander Ark had failed to establish the affirmative defense of fair use. Defendant's publication of the *Lexicon* was permanently enjoined, and plaintiffs were awarded statutory damages of $6,750.[49]

3. *Fox News v. TVEyes*: A Contemporary Case Critical of the Transformative Doctrine

After the *Cariou v. Prince* decision came down, copyright experts warned that the derivative-rights doctrine was dead and that the transformative doctrine would become the exception that ate the rule—copyright owners could no longer control any unauthorized use of their work because by waving the "transformative" wand, infringers would escape all liability. That decision, coming out of the powerful Second Circuit Court of Appeals, led many attorneys representing original creators to fear the worst for their clients.

However, the always amazing resiliency and flexibility of the U.S. legal system came to the fore, and the direction of the law bounced back—first with the *Prince v. Graham* case and then with the *Fox News v. TVEyes* case.[50]

TVEyes, the defendant in the case, was a media company that continuously recorded the audiovisual content of over 1,400 television and radio channels, which it deposited in a database it made available to its clients, who in turn could e-mail clips, download, and archive, all for a $500 monthly fee. Clips included closed captioned text, making them searchable by clients as well. Plaintiff Fox News Network sued TVEyes in Federal Court in the Southern District of New York, alleging copyright infringement—and TVEyes responded with a fair-use defense, which the district accepted. Fox appealed, and the Second Circuit reversed.[51]

The Second Circuit decision analyzes TVEyes's use of Fox News programming and concludes that the redistributive use is transformative but also finds that the amount of Fox content TVEyes used was too much to avoid an infringement finding. The TVEyes use was transformative, the Court finds, because it enabled its clients to isolate from the huge amount of Fox programming just

49. *Id.* at 554. The Court explained that because the *Lexicon* had not yet been published when the suit was filed, the statutory damage amount was based on the lowest amount allowed under the law, $750 per infringing act, which in this case was multiplied by the seven *Potter* books and the two companion works to yield the $6,750 total.

50. Fox News Network, LLC, v. TVEyes, Inc., 883 F.3d 169 (2d Cir. 2018).

51. *Id.* at 170.

that material they were looking for and to access that material in a manner responsive to their interests.

However, the Court points out that in order to provide that full range of choices to their clients, TVEyes copied and made available the entire catalog of Fox's programming and, in so doing, copied far more than was needed for fair use. TVEyes also deprived Fox of any revenue from the licensing of its content—content it owned and was now being deprived of revenue from.[52]

Turning to the copying of Fox content, the Court finds that the program used by TVEyes to aid viewers in easily finding content that meets their needs from the vast trove of material in Fox's archives is a transformative use. The Court cites the decision in the *Sony Betamax* case for the transformative nature of a program that allows a viewer to choose the time and place when they view content. This analysis suggests that the Court is going to find that TVEyes's use is a fair one because of this transformative purpose. Here is how the Court summarizes it:

> TVEyes's copying of Fox's content for use in the Watch function is similarly transformative insofar as it enables users to isolate, from an ocean of programming, material that is responsive to their interests and needs, and to access that material with targeted precision. It enables nearly instant access to a subset of material—and to information about the material—that would otherwise be irretrievable, or else retrievable only through prohibitively inconvenient or inefficient means.
>
> . . . .
>
> The Watch function certainly qualifies as technology that achieves the transformative purpose of enhancing efficiency: it enables TVEyes's clients to view all of the Fox programming that (over the prior thirty-two days) discussed a particular topic of interest to them, without having to monitor thirty-two days of programming in order to catch each relevant discussion; and it eliminates the clients' need even to view entire programs, because the ten most relevant minutes are presented to them. Much like the television customer in Sony, TVEyes clients can view the Fox programming they want at a time and place that is convenient to them, rather than at the time and place of broadcast. For these reasons, TVEyes's Watch function is at least somewhat transformative.[53]

But then the Court continues the fair-use analysis, turning to the third and fourth factors, and the direction of the decision begins to shift, something not usually seen in fair-use analysis in this era. In most cases applying the

52. *Id.* at 176.
53. *Id.* at 182–83.

transformative doctrine, once a court finds that, under the first factor, the use is transformative, that finding overwhelms other factors that might favor the original creator. Not so in this case. In assessing the third factor, the amount and substantiality of the portion used in relation to the copyrighted work as a whole, the Court notes that the relevant consideration is not how much of the protected material was used by the copier but how much of that material was "made available to the public." And based on that criterion, the Court finds that this third factor clearly favors Fox because TVEyes makes available "virtually the entirety of the Fox programming," noting that this amount of copying doesn't automatically negate a fair-use finding, but it certainly makes a finding of fair use "less likely," and that this amount of copying is dissimilar to the copying in the *Google Books* case, which was found to be fair.[54]

And finally, the Court reaches the fourth factor in its analysis. In the era before the transformative doctrine came into prominence, this fourth factor, the effect the new work has on the market for the underlying work, was always the key element in fair-use analysis. If the allegedly infringing work didn't harm the market for the underlying work, courts generally found the use to be fair . . . and if there was a market effect, the work would not be found to be a fair use. Under the transformative doctrine, this fourth factor seemed to have lost much of its impact—after all, if the new use was transformative, it was entitled to make its creator a lot of money, irrespective of its impact on the underlying work—as Patrick Cariou saw when Richard Prince's slightly altered versions of Cariou's photos brought in hundreds of thousands of dollars, none of which went to Cariou.

And yet the Second Circuit, without overruling *Cariou*, seems here to reassert the importance of the fourth factor in fair-use analysis with this language:

> This factor is "undoubtedly the single most important element of fair use." Harper & Row Publishers, Inc. v. Nation Enters., 471 U.S. 539, 566 (1985). It "focuses on whether the copy brings to the marketplace a competing substitute for the original, or its derivative, so as to deprive the rights holder of significant revenues because of the likelihood that potential purchasers may opt to acquire the copy in preference to the original." Google Books, 804 F.3d at 223. (internal quotation marks and alteration omitted).[55]
>
> . . . .
>
> Consequently, there is a plausibly exploitable market for such access to televised content, and it is proper to consider whether TVEyes

54. *Id.* at 184–85.
55. *Id.*

displaces potential Fox revenues when TVEyes allows its clients to watch Fox's copyrighted content without Fox's permission.

The Court answers its question in the affirmative. It finds that since the distribution of Fox's content generates revenue for TVEyes, it should be willing to pay Fox something for that content. By refraining from paying for that content, TVEyes is depriving Fox of licensing revenues it gets and cuts Fox out of the market of providing a similar service of its own. TVEyes has thus usurped a market that belongs to Fox. As the Court concludes:

> In short, by selling access to Fox's audiovisual content without a license, TVEyes deprives Fox of revenues to which Fox is entitled as the copyright holder. Therefore, the fourth factor favors Fox.[56]
>
> . . . .
>
> At bottom, TVEyes is unlawfully profiting off the work of others by commercially re-distributing all of that work that a viewer wishes to use, without payment or license. Having weighed the required factors, we conclude that the balance strongly favors Fox and defeats the defense of fair use.[57]

Judge Lewis Kaplan went even further, rejecting the transformative argument in its entirety in his dissenting opinion:

> Even on the majority's view that TVEyes' Watch function substantially improves the efficiency with which TVEyes customers can access Fox copyrighted broadcasts of possible interest, it does no more than repackage and deliver the original works. It adds no new information, no new aesthetics, and no new insights or understandings. I therefore doubt that it is transformative. Indeed, I regard *Infinity Broadcast Corp. v. Kirkwood* as having settled the question whether a use is transformative simply because it is more efficient or convenient than what preceded it.[58]

So what can lawyers and fan creators reading this section take away about the impact this transformative doctrine has on fan-created works? First, that the law is in flux about the scope of the reach of this doctrine, meaning that it is risky to proceed with a project on the assumption that if you are sued for copyright infringement, the transformative nature of the project will protect you. It might, and then again, it might not.

Moreover, it is a mistake to assume that the doctrine has taken over and largely eliminated the right of the original creator of the copyrighted work to

56. *Id.* at 186–87.
57. *Id.*
58. *Id.* at 193.

control who can create a derivative work based on the original. All four of the fair-use factors continue to be important, and a fair-use analysis of a project still requires assessing all of them—even where, as was the case in the *TVEyes* case, it appears that the use is transformative.

And from the *TVEyes* case, we can also take away the revival of the fourth fair-use factor, the effect of the use on the market for the original work, as still being a critical component of the analysis, and if the taking is excessive, even a transformative work can still be found to be infringing. Like so many elements of the law, the details count, and a case-by-case analysis is necessary.

We will return to the application of this doctrine in the coming chapters, which delve more deeply into the four kinds of fan-created works addressed in this book, but for now, we move to consideration of another important statutory set of rules that affect fan-created works—the duration of copyright's protection of original works under the 1976 Act.

C. Duration under the 1976 Act

As noted previously, when Congress began its consideration, in March 1967, of whether to retain the two terms of 28 years for copyright's duration, the legislators ultimately decided to shift to a single term of the life of the author plus 50 years as the applicable term. The decision was in part fueled by a concern that copyright holders were losing their rights through the expiration, often inadvertently, of those rights as a result of a failure to renew after the end of the first term.[59]

This change affords a mixed bag of benefits and problems for fan creators. On the one hand, it gives them the benefit of a much longer preparation and use period for their fan fiction, art, film, and cosplay. Coupled with the elimination of the registration and notice requirements, discussed in the next section, this change makes it easier for fan creators to obtain decades-long protection for their works.

On the other hand, this extended duration of protection and the elimination of the two-term protection structure mean that virtually all original works created post-1978 are still under copyright protection and will likely remain so until at least the middle of this century, if not for an even longer period. This increases the need for policies like the transformative doctrine, and fair use in general, to protect those fan-created works from infringement actions filed by original creators.

---

59. *See generally* Marc Greenberg, Copyright Termination and Recapture Laws: Good Intentions Gone Awry 25–27 (ABA Publ'g 2016).

D. Formalities under the 1976 Act

The process for securing and protecting a copyright in a creative work under the 1909 Copyright Act required the creator to take several mandatory steps. Once a work was created, copyright protection was not automatically granted. The creator was required to register the work with the U.S. Copyright Office in order to take advantage of the protections afforded under the law. Moreover, each published copy of the work had to bear a copyright notice, comprised of the circle "c" symbol, ©, and the name of the author and the date the work was created.

These requirements were referred to as copyright formalities. The failure to comply with these formalities could have dire consequences. An unregistered work was not allowed any of the benefits of the statute. A work published without a notice, unless the creator could prove the error was inadvertent and made a good-faith effort to correct the error upon discovery of it, would result in the work being deemed to be in the public domain, free to be used by anyone without restriction.

When Congress began deliberating the revisions to copyright law that ultimately led to the Copyright Act of 1976, an important item on their agenda was addressing the problems these formalities had created for copyright holders and their heirs. In too many cases, works were not registered at all, or the creators might have died during the first term and their heirs didn't know they had to renew the works, or they were published without notice or with defective notice (using the word "copyright" instead of the international symbol © or abbreviations like "copyr" were found to be insufficient notice). The result was the loss of valuable rights and a windfall for unscrupulous publishers or infringers.

Noted underground cartoonist Robert Crumb almost lost the rights to his iconic cartoon panel featuring a repeating image of a big-footed man in a zoot suit, striding out under the title "Keep on Truckin'," due to a failure to post a copyright notice on all published copies of it. He had allowed a friend to use the image on business cards, and the friend had failed to include the copyright notice. This gave defendant A.A. Sales the opportunity to make use of the image and, at least initially in the trial court, to prevail against Crumb's infringement suit. On appeal to the Ninth Circuit, Crumb got lucky when the Court determined that there was an issue of fact regarding whether Crumb had actually authorized his friend's use of the image on the business cards, and they reversed and remanded the case back to the District Court. A.A. Sales subsequently settled with Crumb, who was thus able to retain his copyright in the image, but it was nearly a loss of this historic image.[60]

60. Ilona Bray, Richard Stim & the Editors of Nolo, The Judge Who Hated Red Nail Polish & Other Crazy but True Stories of Law & Lawyers 192–95 (Nolo Press 2010).

Robert Crumb's iconic "Keep on Truckin'" cartoon, first published in Zap Comics, 1968. Copyright © 1968 by R. Crumb, all rights reserved.

So Congress, in the Copyright Act of 1976, began the process of unwinding those formalities to allow creators greater ease in obtaining the benefits of the law and in prosecuting claims of infringement. The first step in this direction dealt with the registration requirement. The new Act did away with the requirement that a work had to be registered in order for it to be protected by copyright law. Now as soon as a work was rendered in a tangible form (i.e., it no longer solely existed in its creator's mind but could now be perceived in some manner), the right of that work to copyright protection vested automatically.

It remains a good idea, even though it is no longer required, to register works with the Copyright Office. The main reason for this is that a creator cannot sue an infringer for copyright infringement under the statute until the work has been registered. So while you automatically have almost all of the rights of copyright as soon as the tangible work exists, the key right to be able to sue for damages under the copyright law still requires registration.

A similar situation applies to the other formality, the giving of notice of one's claim to copyright in a work via the use of the © symbol on all copies. In 1988, Congress did away with this formality as part of the agreement by which the United States signed the Berne Convention, an international copyright treaty. So it is no longer necessary to place a copyright notice on a published work—if you have registered the work, you can still sue for statutory copyright infringement even if the work is published without notice.

But here's the catch. There are two kinds of copyright infringement—innocent and willful infringement. And the statutory damages for these two kinds of infringement differ substantially. Willful infringement carries a statutory penalty of up to $150,000 per infringing act, whereas innocent infringement has a maximum penalty of $30,000—quite a big difference.

A work that is published with the copyright notice displayed on every copy is entitled to a presumption in an infringement claim that the infringement was willful. Which makes sense, since the infringer would have to have seen that the owner was claiming copyright in the work before it was infringed.

So again, similar to the registration process, giving notice may not be necessary, but doing so carries great benefits at a tiny cost, and there is no good reason why both registration and notice should not be given. And so even while Congress did away with these formalities in order to prevent the loss of the copyright for those who did not comply with them, strong incentives for compliance remain, and attorneys and fan content creators are advised to make sure they comply with these formalities to obtain the maximum benefits allowed under the law.

E. Termination and Recapture under the 1976 Act

If you haven't already concluded that U.S. copyright law is an arcane brew of difficult-to-understand concepts and principles, this next discussion topic will likely lead you to, or confirm, that conclusion. Throughout its history, Congress has been concerned that creators of copyright-protected works often get a bad deal in their initial publishing contracts because as young artists with little or no reputation, they lack the bargaining power to insist on better terms. Those initial bad deals can have long-lasting impact, since the deals often involve an outright transfer of, or a decades-long license of, their work to a publisher.

So why, in a book about fan-created content, should we focus on the rights original creators have when they create their works and how they may, or may not, recapture those rights many years later if they initially transferred their rights in the early years of their career? There are several reasons. In evaluating whether to create a new work based on an original piece, fan creators should research who owns the rights to the original work to get a sense of how their adaptation or other use of that work will be received. As I discuss in later chapters, there is a wide range of responses of original owners to fan-created works, and the more you know about the attitudes of owners to these adaptations, the more likely you are to be able to avoid a litigation situation.

Knowing the history of the ownership of a work may also help you to assess the likely reaction to your adaptation in another sense. An original owner who has had to fight a lengthy, bitter battle to recapture his or her rights may have a less tolerant view toward adaptations than those creators who either never lost the rights to their works or were able to recapture them with little or no conflict.

Additionally, as I discuss in *Copyright Termination and Recapture Laws,* it often happens that the settlement of a termination and recapture case leaves both the original creator and the publisher who acquired, and then lost, those rights in a situation where they are joint owners of the derivative works created from the original work (for example, the heirs of the creators and transferors of the Superman character—originally transferred in 1938—ended up in a co-ownership status with DC Comics for the version of Superman that was in use in 2013 when the Ninth Circuit finally decided that termination case).

For these reasons and more, understanding how and why the termination and recapture laws were developed and implemented as part of the 1976 Copyright Act is important for fan creators and those interested in, or representing parties involved in, those works to be aware of how and why these laws were developed and are implemented.

So in the discussions leading to the 1976 Act, Congress looked for ways to lessen the negative impact that unequal bargaining power had on the careers of artists. In the 1909 Act, when Congress was debating how long a copyright registration would last, one idea they discussed was to make the length of protection last for the life of the author plus an additional 50 years. But, they reasoned, doing that would be bad for young creators, because their first deals, made when they lacked leverage, would leave them tied to that bad deal for the rest of their lives and another 50 years on top of that! Too long to be stuck in a bad deal, they reasoned.

Congress, aware of these concerns, took a different approach. Rather than one copyright term, they considered creating two terms, each 28 years in length. The reasoning behind this approach was that any license granted by the author during the first term would end at the expiration of that term, and the author, who in the intervening 28 years would hopefully have gone on to build up his or her reputation (and concurrently, the asking price for his or her work), would then be free to go into a negotiation with that producer for a new contract, presumably at a higher rate for the author.

So by creating a second term, Congress believed it was giving those authors the proverbial second bite at the apple. The subtitle of my book on copyright termination reveals the outcome of this approach: *Good Intentions Gone Awry.* It was a truly well-meaning, well-intentioned approach. But it was undone with the stroke of a pen in a court case, *Fisher v. Witmark.*[61]

---

61. M. Witmark & Sons v. Fred Fisher Music Co., Inc., 125 F.2d 949 (1942), *aff'd,* Fred Fisher Music Co., Inc., v. M. Witmark & Sons, 316 U.S. 643 (1943).

1. *Fisher v. Witmark*: Undoing the Second Bite

The facts in the case paint a familiar picture: in 1912, Ernest R. Ball, Chauncey Olcott, and George Graff Jr. wrote a song entitled *When Irish Eyes Are Smiling*, the rights to which were transferred by each of them to their music publisher, M. Witmark and Sons. The transfer was done per the terms of a contract between Witmark and the writers that allowed the publisher to register, in its name, the copyright in the work for the first term of copyright—which, under the then–recently enacted 1909 Act, was for 28 years.

Five years later, at a point in his life when he had very little money, George Graff Jr. entered into a second contract with Witmark regarding the song, as well as 69 others he had previously written. In this 1917 contract, in exchange for a $1,600 payment, Graff agreed that Witmark would receive a conveyance of "all copyrights and renewals of copyrights and the right to secure all copyrights and renewals of copyrights in the [songs], and any and all rights therein that I or my heirs, executors, administrators or next of kin may at any time be entitled to."

Witmark received an irrevocable power of attorney to execute, in Graff's name, all documents "necessary to secure to Witmark the renewals and extensions of the copyrights in said compositions and all rights therein for the terms of such renewals and extensions" and, "upon the expiration of the first term of any copyright," Graff would execute and deliver to Witmark "all papers necessary in order to secure to it the renewals and extensions of all copyrights in said compositions and all rights therein for the terms of such renewals and extensions."[62]

The terms of this agreement are different from those found in the later well-known *Rear Window* movie rights case, *Stewart v. Abend*,[63] in one very significant detail—rather than promising to renew and transfer rights back to the production company when the second term arose, which the Court found in *Abend* created a mere expectancy, in this instance Graff transferred a current right to the renewal terms to Witmark and promised to sign and deliver any papers Witmark might need to secure those now-transferred rights to the renewal term.

Per these terms, on August 12, 1939, which was the first day of the 28th year of the first term of copyright protection for *When Irish Eyes Are Smiling* and therefore the first day when it was possible to apply for renewal rights for a second term, Witmark applied for and registered the copyright for the renewal term. Simultaneously, per the terms of the 1917 contract, Witmark used its power of attorney to assign to itself Graff's interest in the renewal. So far,

62. *M. Witmark & Sons*, 125 F.2d at 949–50.
63. Stewart v. Abend, 495 U.S. 207 (1990).

so good for Witmark, which then assumed it had properly secured the rights granted to it in the 1917 contract.

What they didn't know was that Graff had other plans for the rights to the renewal term of the song. Eleven days after Witmark's registration, Graff filed an application for and registered the song in his own name. Two months later, on October 24, 1939, Graff assigned his interest in the renewal term to another music publishing firm, Fred Fisher Music, Inc.

And so Graff engaged in the kind of conduct seen in the motion picture *The Producers*—he apparently sold the same renewal rights to *When Irish Eyes Were Smiling* to two entirely different music publishers. Shortly thereafter, Fisher published and sold copies of the song, representing that it was the lawful owner of the rights. The good folks at Witmark weren't smiling—they filed suit against Fisher alleging copyright infringement, based on the 1917 contract. Witmark sought an injunction against Fisher based on Witmark's superior claim to ownership of the song. Fisher's defense was that Graff had no rights to grant any transfers of the rights in the song until the renewal period began and that the 1917 renewal and transfer agreement was therefore void and unenforceable.

And so the issue was teed up nicely for the courts—since the 1909 Act provides for two terms of copyright protection, and since section 42 of the Act allows copyrights to be assigned in writing, does the Act prevent the author from assigning his or her interest in the renewal copyright before securing it?

The case proceeded in the U.S. District Court for the Southern District of New York. That court granted Witmark's application for an injunction, finding that the terms of the 1917 contract were valid and binding and that Fisher could not acquire from Graff copyright rights that Graff had already sold to Witmark. Given that this ruling was dispositive of the ultimate issues to be resolved in the case, Fisher was entitled to file what is called an interlocutory appeal (a form of interim appeal) of the District Court's decision, and that sent the case up to the Circuit Court of Appeals for the Second Circuit. Following briefing and oral argument, the Court rendered its decision on February 11, 1942.

Judge Charles E. Clark wrote the majority opinion, which was joined by Judge Augustus N. Hand.[64] Judge Clark, in affirming the injunction, begins by noting that the issue in the case was one of statutory construction that had never arisen before.

He then moves to a statutory analysis focused on section 23 of the 1909 Act. He notes that the statute only creates an expectancy of an ownership right in a renewal term, an expectancy that may not rise to fruition if the renewal is not timely applied for within one year of the expiration of the first term.

64. M. Witmark Sons v. Fred Fisher Music Co., 125 F.2d 949 (2d Cir. 1942), https://casetext.com/case/m-witmark-sons-v-fred-fisher-music-co (last visited Jan. 19, 2021).

Judge Clark makes the point that the statute does not forbid assignment of the renewal term interest.

The opinion next turns to an analysis of statutory history. While he acknowledges that the reference to "assigns" found in the 1790 Act was eliminated in the 1831 amendment, he doesn't read that as a sign of congressional intent to forbid assignments. He supports his view by noting that the words "executors, administrators" were also removed and posits that this change was made to make sure that only heirs would be entitled to seek a renewal. He notes further that the 1831 amendment does not express "a public policy against disposal of the possibility of renewal."[65]

What is missing from this analysis is any consideration of the reasons Congress considered in seeking to protect the interests of the creators of these kinds of works—specifically their relative lack of leverage in negotiating the terms of their transfer of rights. As we will see, this omission forms the basis for the strong dissent this majority opinion gave rise to.

Judge Clark next points out that the 1909 Act does not bar assignment of the renewal term and cites the legislative history of section 23. Here is where things get interesting in this opinion.

Citing the Congressional Report on the Act of March 4, 1909, he quotes the text of the Committee Report on this subject as follows:

> More to the point is the Congressional Report on the Act of March 4, 1909, which is the present statute, 17 U.S.C.A. § 23—except for a slight textual change of 1940, here immaterial. The committee was supporting the decision to extend the right of renewal another fourteen years to make a total renewal period of twenty-eight years, and it stated its preference for this arrangement, ***rather than a single and longer term as for life or fifty years.*** So it said,
>
>> Your committee, after full consideration, decided that it was distinctly to the advantage of the author to preserve the renewal period. It not infrequently happens that the author sells his copyright outright to a publisher for a comparatively small sum. If the work proves to be a great success and lives beyond the term of twenty-eight years, your committee felt that it should be the exclusive right of the author to take the renewal term, and the law should be framed as is the existing law, so that he could not be deprived of that right.
>>
>> The present term of twenty-eight years, with the right of renewal for fourteen years, in many cases is insufficient. The terms, taken together, ought to be long enough to give the author the exclusive

65. *Id.* at 951.

> right to his work for such a period that there would be no probability of its being taken away from him in his old age, when, perhaps, he needs it the most.[66]

Judge Clark asserts that "defendants' case substantially depends on this quotation, as expressing a clear intent as to the statutory meaning and one to which we should give effect."[67] He continues this assessment by arguing that the comments of the committee, like the statute itself, are not clear but rather are ambiguous and therefore don't provide the support Fisher hoped for.

He notes first that the purpose of the language in the comment is to explain why Congress chose to continue the two-term approach rather than move to a single long term of protection—which Clark claims is evidence that prohibiting transfers of rights in the second term was not the point of the comment. He offers the classic argument—that if Congress had wanted to write in a prohibition, it could have done so in express terms, so since it didn't, it must mean that Congress did not intend to make that change. The weakness of this oft-used argument is that there is no basis to believe, here and in other instances, that Congress knew or could foresee how its words would be interpreted by the courts and by litigants.

Congress, in this regard, failed to consider that outside of the bubble of the legislative process are hordes of smart industry lawyers looking for ways to work around restrictions imposed by new legislation via creative interpretation and wordsmithing. Moreover, the legislative process also fails to consider how courts will interpret its efforts, and often the process produces vaguely worded laws in need of judicial interpretation.

Moving to the clause that states that the committee felt that the author should retain exclusive rights to the renewal term, so that "he could not be deprived of that right," Judge Clark argues that if this means the right isn't assignable, it in fact does deprive the author—of the right of alienation of his renewal right. He then makes short work of the committee's concern that the combined term is necessary for authors to avoid the "probability of its being taken away from him in his old age"—asserting that it is just "a repetition of the same thought, and suffers from the same ambiguity."[68]

Having dismissed Fisher's interpretation of the statute and the committee's commentary, Judge Clark finds further support for the majority's decision in the absence of any supportive interpretation from any other branches of the government. He notes further that four treatises published before 1909 stated unequivocally that an author could validly assign his or her expectancy

66. *Id.* (citing H.R. Rep. No. 2220, 60th Cong., 2d Sess., at 14).

67. *Id.* at 951.

68. *Id.* at 951–52.

of renewal and that the Court found no treatises taking the opposite view. He acknowledges that after the passage of the 1909 Act, commentators were less definite, and at least one denies assignability.[69] Continuing this analysis, Judge Clark notes that in the 33 years since the 1909 Act, a number of congressional amendments to the law chose not to address this ambiguity, further supporting his claim that first-term assignment of the renewal term was not intended to be prohibited.[70]

Judge Clark concludes his analysis by the somewhat dubious assertion that authors and their heirs, far from being harmed by an allowance of first-term renewal transfers, are actually more likely to be benefited by this practice:

> Notwithstanding this history, we might well be moved by a demonstration that only by holding all assignments void could we further the policy of the act. But even this seems to us quite doubtful. True, it would be nice for an author to look forward to more money when the renewal time comes. But he can do that by not assigning. What we would be saying is that all authors who have already assigned can eat their cake and have it too. Only in the future would such a ruling be fair all around. Furthermore, it is not clear that authors wish to be deprived of the privilege of obtaining more money now, or that a widow whose husband dies penniless wishes to be deprived of the privilege of anticipating on her statutory renewal right. We are, in effect, asked to impose forced saving on authors and widows by requiring them to forego for twenty-eight years whatever additional money they could obtain by assignment of their expectancies. It should require more than an ambiguous committee report on an ambiguous statutory provision to produce such a drastic restriction on free assignability.[71]

And so, with this majority opinion, the carefully considered effort of Congress in the 1909 Copyright Act to create a second bite of the apple for creators went badly awry. But it didn't happen without reaction.

Judge Jerome Frank wrote a stinging dissent in this case. He argued that the injunction order should be reversed. His argument begins with the notation that given that Graff was paid $1,600 for the initial period rights and the renewal rights to 70 songs, the amount paid per song was tiny. Assuming that the entire payment was to be allocated solely to the renewal rights, it still meant that Witmark paid about $23 for what became an extremely valuable right of renewal—worth far in excess of the amount paid for it.[72] Why make this argu-

69. AM. JUR. *Copyright Law and Practice* 532–38, 540–41 (1936).

70. M. Witmark Sons v. Fred Fisher Music Co., 125 F.2d 949, 952–53 (2d Cir. 1942).

71. *Id.* at 953.

72. *Id.* at 955.

ment? Because Judge Frank was able to thus begin his dissent by highlighting how Congress's intent in establishing two terms of copyright protection—which was to enable creators to get a second bite at the apple once their works achieved commercial stature—would now be frustrated by the majority decision, anchoring that argument with this analysis of the real-dollar value of the work in that renewal period. The majority decision gave Witmark a huge windfall and left Graff's heirs in a much-weakened financial state.

Acknowledging that this case is one that arises in equity, Judge Frank then offers an argument that isn't likely to warm the hearts of many artists but that has an element of unfortunate truth to it—that artists in general lack sufficient business acumen to avoid getting cheated in business deals. It is an argument that may apply with equal force to fan creators who are not deeply immersed in, and knowledgeable about, the intricacies of copyright law. He argues:

> We need only take judicial notice of that which every schoolboy knows—that, usually, with a few notable exceptions (such as W. Shakespeare and G. B. Shaw), authors are hopelessly inept in business transactions and that lyricists, like the defendant Graff, often sell their songs "for a song."
>
> Here, then, is a case where (a) the defendant was an author, one of a class of persons notoriously inexperienced in business, and the particular author was actually, at the time, in desperate financial straits, while the plaintiff was a successful and experienced publisher; (b) the property contracted for was of such a character that, when the contract was made, "neither party could know even approximately the value," so that "it was a bargain made in the dark"; and (c) the consideration was a very small sum.
>
> That is not the kind of contract which equity will specifically enforce.[73]

In addition to the logical inconsistency inherent in the overbroad generalization that almost all artists are "hopelessly inept in business transactions" and are "a class of persons notoriously inexperienced in business," there is an untenable oversimplification in this argument. What is missing is any acknowledgment of the relative bargaining power of the parties to these transactions. The author with a genius IQ and no bargaining power will still sign away his or her rights for a relative pittance in order to feed the family and keep a roof over their heads. So whether it is or isn't true that artists, or by extension to today, fan creators, lack business skills and abilities, it remains true that their lack of bargaining power renders them incapable of resisting one-sided deals.

---

73. *Id.* at 955–56.

This, then, is at the heart of Congress's intent in adopting a two-term copyright protection structure. It is the hope that by the time the renewal term arrives, the author may have achieved sufficient recognition and professional stature, and possibly some greater financial stability, to negotiate terms of a license for the second term that will afford a higher return. This is far from a perfect solution to the relative bargaining power problem—there will still likely be many authors who will not have achieved a sufficient increase in their bargaining power to obtain a better deal—but at least those that have will have a mechanism in place to allow them to reap some benefits from their improved status.

Judge Frank next argues that an agreement transferring renewal rights in the first term should not be enforceable, because at the time it was made, the author was unable him- or herself to exercise that option. The option granted is thus of no value at that time—and the purchaser of it takes the risk that if the author dies intestate before the renewal period arrives, the option is worthless because the 1909 Act limited renewal rights to the author.[74] The previously discussed decision in *Stewart v. Abend*[75] offers an example of this outcome.

Returning to the 1909 Act committee report cited by the majority opinion,[76] Judge Frank rejects the majority opinion's dismissal of the committee's desire to help authors obtain better contract terms via renegotiation in the renewal period, noting that if this wasn't a real concern of Congress, why not simply adopt a single term of 56 years for copyright protection? The majority's interpretation, he argues, expressly frustrates that intention.

Judge Frank, in rejecting the argument that creators should have the freedom of contract to transfer their renewal term rights at any time during the first term, notes that if this was Congress's intent, it would make more sense to have a single long term for copyright so that the term being sold would have more value. After all, since only the original author and his or her heirs held the right to renew the work for the second term under the statute, the production company that bought those second-term rights was taking a risk—if the creator died before the renewal term came due, the rights to that term would die with him or her.[77]

Judge Frank completes this argument with a compelling analysis of why the majority's interpretation of the 1909 Act is contrary to Congress's intent to protect creator interests:

> The statute as interpreted by the majority means merely this: An author cannot make a direct "outright" sale before the twenty-eighth year. But,

74. *Id.* at 957.
75. Stewart v. Abend, 495 U.S. 207 (1990).
76. Quoted and discussed herein *supra* note 66 and accompanying text.
77. M. Witmark Sons v. Fred Fisher Music Co., 125 F.2d 949, 958–59 (2d Cir. 1942).

> say my colleagues, he can do so by indirection—by making (twenty-two years earlier as here) a specifically enforceable agreement, absolutely binding on him, to have it assigned in his name as soon as the twenty-eighth year arrives. The majority opinion admits that the difference between such a transaction and the forbidden direct "outright" sale is of the tweedledum-and-dee variety. The hocus-pocus employed by the plaintiff makes clear the artificial character of the distinction: The plaintiff, M. Witmark & Sons, relies for its title to the song on an assignment executed in 1939 "to M. Witmark & Sons," signed by George Graff "by M. Witmark & Sons" as George Graff's "appointed attorney." Congress could not have intended that its admitted purpose—to prevent a direct sale prior to the twenty-eighth year—should be so easily circumvented. If it had intended that an anticipatory assignment should be valid, it is strange that in the course of a century, since 1831, it has provided no machinery by which the assignee might perfect the renewal in his own right and in his own behalf and without resort to such hocus-pocus.[78]

Despite the sound reasoning of his dissent, Judge Frank's views did not carry the day. Fisher appealed the Second Circuit decision to the U.S. Supreme Court—and lost again. The Supreme Court, in a 5–1–3 decision, accepted the freedom-of-contract argument and rejected the idea that authors needed a bar to first-term assignments of their renewal interests in order to obtain some leverage in an otherwise highly unequal bargaining power context. Witmark's counsel managed to convince Justices Black, Douglas, and Murphey, who expressly endorsed Judge Frank's analysis, but that simply wasn't enough votes. Justice Frankfurter, writing for the majority, explained why the court rejected Judge Frank's view:

> It is not for courts to judge whether the interests of authors clearly lie upon one side of this question rather than the other. If an author cannot make an effective assignment of his renewal, it may be worthless to him when he is most in need. Nobody would pay an author for something he cannot sell. We cannot draw a principle of law from the familiar stories of garret-poverty of some men of literary genius. Even if we could do so, we cannot say that such men would regard with favor a rule of law preventing them from realizing on their assets when they are most in need of funds. Nor can we be unmindful of the fact that authors have themselves devised means of safeguarding their interests. We do not have such assured knowledge about authorship, and particularly about song writing, or the psychology of gifted writers and composers, as to

78. *Id.* at 959. Readers unfamiliar with the reference to Tweedledum and Tweedledee are referred to Lewis Carroll's *Through the Looking-Glass and What Alice Found There* (1871).

> justify us as judges in importing into Congressional legislation a denial to authors of the freedom to dispose of their property possessed by others. While authors may have habits making for intermittent want, they may have no less a spirit of independence which would resent treatment of them as wards under guardianship of the law.
>
> We conclude, therefore, that the Copyright Act of 1909 does not nullify agreements by authors to assign their renewal interests.[79]

And so, with these words, the Supreme Court unraveled Congress's plan to protect authors by giving them a second bite at the apple via an exclusive right to control the renewal period for copyright registration. The Court's majority was convinced that Congress did not intend to limit the alienability of copyright interests and that it held freedom of contract to be more important than engaging in what the Court saw as unnecessary paternalism.

2. Congress Responds: The Termination and Recapture Laws

Twenty-three years later, as Congress in 1966 began discussions about the scope of revisions to the copyright law that would result in the 1976 Act, one of their foremost concerns was to return to the issue of giving creators a second bite at the apple. Recognizing that the *Witmark* decision decimated that attempt, and desiring to find another route to that goal, the idea of a right to terminate copyright grants, even after the passage of many years, was explored. After ten years of discussion and hearings, Congress settled on the approach found in sections 304 (for pre-1978 works) and 203 (for post-1978 works).[80]

So let's take a look at what these sections provide, beginning with section 304, which deals with those works subject to the 1909 Copyright Act.

a. Section 304 Terminations

The Copyright Office staff briefing memos prepared for the 1974–75 congressional hearings specifically addressed the purpose of sections 304 and 203. With respect to section 304, the memo notes that it serves two different purposes—it explains how works in their first term, with a right to a renewal term, would now be treated under the law, and it explains when and how the termination and recapture process would operate for these pre-1978 works. Here is their analysis:

> Section 304 is a transitional provision, but an important one. It deals with two types of subsisting copyrights: (1) those in their first twenty-eight

79. Fred Fisher Music Co. et al. v. M. Witmark & Sons, 318 U.S. 643, 657–58 (1943).

80. The legislative history of the adoption of these sections is detailed in Chapter 4 of my book Copyright Termination and Recapture Laws: Good Intentions Gone Awry 23–41 (2016).

year term, and (2) those already in their second, renewal term, including some copyrights whose renewal terms have been extended.

With respect to the first type, section 304 provides that any copyright subsisting in its first term on the effective date will continue to have a first term of 28 years from the date it was originally secured, with a right to a renewal term of 47 years, thus extending the total potential copyright term to 75 years. As under the present renewal system, application for the renewal term must be submitted within one year before expiration of the original term of copyright by the same specified renewal claimants. The reason for retaining the renewal provisions of the present law during this transitional period is that many of the present expectancies in these cases are the subject of existing contracts, and it would be unfair and confusing to cut off or alter these interests.

In the case of subsisting copyrights already in their renewal term when the new law comes into force, the term is automatically extended to a total of 75 years from the date when copyright was originally secured.

For both types of subsisting copyrights (those in their first 28-year term and those in their second, extended renewal term), section 304 sets out detailed provisions governing the termination of grants conveying future interests in the extended terms. The approach is closely patterned on the reversion provision of section 203. The objective is to permit the author or his or her statutory beneficiaries to receive the real benefit of the extended term. For this reason, they are given termination rights under specific conditions, including timely notice to the assignee. A five-year period is provided for effecting a termination, but it does not begin until 56 years have passed from the date copyright was originally secured. In this way, the contracts entered into on the basis of the present law remain unimpaired, but the assignee does not get a windfall through the extension of the term.[81]

This explanation reflects the compromises the Copyright Office and Congress made in drafting the revised act. Works in their first 28-year term when the new act would go into place could have simply been relegated to the term provided under the 1909 Actso that when their first term was up, they were entitled to a renewal term of another 28 years—meaning that the new term under the new act would not be available to them. Alternatively, those works in their first term when the law changed could have had their term extended to life plus 50 years, which would have given them a much longer term than the creators expected to receive when they created the work. Each of these alternatives creates problems of fairness and offers opportunities to game the system. In an effort to moderate those possible problems, the drafters of the Act

81. *Copyright Law Revision: Hearings before the Subcomm. on Courts, Civil Liberties, and the Admin. of Justice of the Comm. on the Judiciary*, 94th Congress 2083 (1975).

came up with a compromise—grant all copyright holders under the 1909 Act a 75-year term, which represents a 19-year extension over the two 28-year terms they originally were entitled to.

And with every new solution comes new problems. By extending the term of these copyright holders to 75 years, the drafters of the Act created a new issue—if those copyrights were the subject of prior grants to third parties, who would be entitled to the benefit of the added 19 years? Should this benefit go to the transferees, or should it revert back to the original grantor? As the briefing memo notes, the decision was made to allow a reversion, via section 304's termination and recapture process, for those grantors whose works still retained enough value to make it worthwhile to go through the process of getting the rights back.

Copyright Office Register Barbara Ringer offered, in her 1975 testimony before Congress, a cogent summary of the extensive, and exhaustive, discussions that focused on refining section 203. She noted that the formulation proposed in 1965 had survived the legislative process virtually unchanged. She also advanced her view that the result of this process would be beneficial to authors in the future and was a vast improvement over the 1909 Act:

> Almost every provision in chapter 2 represents a compromise of one sort or another. And those involving works made for hire and termination of transfers were extraordinarily difficult to achieve.
>
> However, by the time the bill reached the stage of hearings before your subcommittee in 1965, most of the disagreements were either resolved or on the way to being resolved. After painstakingly reviewing chapter 2, particularly the labyrinthine provisions of section 203, and after adopting some amendments, the subcommittee produced a chapter on copyright ownership and transfer together with a definitive legislative report that have remained unchanged and virtually unchallenged for nearly 10 years. I guess I should say virtually unchanged and virtually unchallenged; there has been one minor change.
>
> There were some tradeoffs, particularly on the reversion in section 203, but I would say that essentially the author gets a better shake in almost every respect under chapter 2 than he does under the present bill. I may be challenged on this, but this is my own opinion.[82]

It's telling that Ringer would characterize the provisions of section 203 as "labyrinthine"—the infuriatingly complex requirements of section 203 present very real and serious obstacles to authors' ability to claim the right to terminate their grants and recapture their copyrights. If this complexity is the result of

---

82. *Id.* at 1889.

the compromises needed to gain acceptance of the bill from publishers and other industry representatives, it raises the question of whether the purpose of injecting this complexity into the bill was to make it harder for authors to exercise the rights granted thereunder. Whether intentionally done or simply the result of a failure to consider the consequences of creating this labyrinthine process, the result was the same—a right whose exercise is rife with traps for the unwary.

b. Section 203 Terminations

Under section 203, grants may be terminated within a five-year period that starts in the last five years of a 35-year grant—***which is not limited to any particular grant.*** In other words, a grantor under section 203 has the right, prior to the expiration of any 35-year period, to negotiate for a new grant period—**and at the 35-year mark of that extended period once again has an inalienable right to terminate the grant.**

While there are many similarities in the prosecution of termination and recapture claims under section 203 with the process under section 304, there are also significant differences between the two statutes that practitioners need to be aware of. In short, the persons eligible to file claims are different, the relevant limitations periods are different, the work-for-hire analysis is different, and the meaning of "notwithstanding any agreement to the contrary" language is interpreted differently. I will examine each of these differences separately in this chapter.

i. Persons Eligible to File Claims under Section 203

Eligibility to file claims to terminate grants of works executed by the author on or after January 1, 1978, under section 203 is limited to the author of the work, and if there is more than one author, to those who "are entitled to exercise a total of more than one-half of that author's termination interest"; if the author is dead, the claim may be filed by the widow or widower (and if there are heirs, the widow must own at least one-half of the author's interest). If there is no surviving spouse or children or grandchildren, the author's executor, administrator, personal representative, or trustee will own the author's entire termination interest.[83]

This approach differs from that found in section 304. In that section, claimants for termination can also include corporate bodies and employers for whom the work was made as a work for hire, as well as the author's next of kin. Consequently, practitioners doing their initial evaluation of the viability of a section 203 claim may not rely on the broader group of eligible claimants found

---

83. 17 U.S.C. § 203(a)(1)(2).

in section 304 and need to be mindful of the more limited group of eligible claimants for these later-created works.

ii. Limitations Periods under Section 203

One of the more significant differences between these two sections, referred to previously, is the relevant limitations periods. Section 203(3) provides, in pertinent part, the following:

> (3) Termination of the grant may be effected at any time during a period of five years beginning at the end of thirty-five years from the date of execution of the grant; or, if the grant covers the right of publication of the work, the period begins at the end of thirty-five years from the date of publication of the work under the grant or at the end of forty years from the date of execution of the grant, whichever term ends earlier.[84]

This subsection offers grantors and their heirs a very different opportunity than is found in the analogous subsection 304(c)(3). In that subsection, termination may be effected only on one discrete occasion—during a period of five years beginning at the end of 56 years from the date copyright was initially secured or beginning on January 1, 1978, whichever is later. In the case of a section 203 grant, the termination may be effected during a period of five years beginning at the end of 35 years after execution of a grant—**but there is no limitation on the number of grants that a grantor may offer to third parties.** In short, this subsection allows a grantor to offer a grantee more than one grant for varying time periods—subject to the limitation that any grantee takes the grant with the understanding that eligible parties will have the right to terminate it after 35 years.

For the practitioner evaluating the viability of a claim, this means that a determination will need to be made as to when the initial grant was effected and whether any subsequent grants were made—with the calculation of the relevant 35-year period to be based not on the first grant but on the last one. This information may not be as easy to come by as it would be in section 304 cases, since verifying the date of registration of the work won't necessarily aid this determination, and in some cases, heirs may not be aware of the extension of any grant.

As a consequence, it may be necessary to the evaluation of the claim to obtain verification of the existence of any grant from any grantee then utilizing the work. A polite request for verification of the basis for that grantees exercise of rights to the work should bring a prompt response—if the request is met

84. *Id.* § 203(a)(3).

with silence or resistance, it may be helpful to remind the grantee or his or her counsel that the information can always be obtained in litigation discovery and that courts won't view favorably a defendant who could have avoided litigation by providing this information.

As has been discussed previously, the fact that section 203 contemplates that grantors or their heirs might execute more than one grant without waiving their ultimate right to terminate any of those grants, and that this is a right that doesn't exist under the section 304 structure, means that the interpretation of the "notwithstanding any agreement to the contrary" language in this section is different from the meaning of that language under section 304.

iii. Work-for-Hire Analysis under Section 203

Section 203 mirrors section 304 in its carve-out of an exception to the right to terminate grants if the work in question was a work made for hire. However, the meaning of "work made for hire" and the manner in which that classification is determined have both changed under the 1976 Act, necessitating a very different approach and analysis by practitioners developing a claim under section 203.

As has been noted previously, the 1976 Act contains a specific and detailed discussion of what makes a work a "work made for hire" and includes a list of the kind of works that qualify for that characterization. For a work prepared by an employee to qualify for the category, it must have been prepared within the scope of the employee's employment, terms I have noted are vague and undefined.

With respect to works created by persons other than employees, the definition notes that only works "specially ordered or commissioned" will qualify. Again, the terms are not defined, so what constitutes a specially ordered or commissioned work is unclear and presumably was left purposely unclear in order to give courts and parties an opportunity to tailor the meaning to a wide array of circumstances.

Of equal importance is that the definition includes a list of works that will qualify for "work made for hire" categorization, a list limited to "a contribution to a collective work, as a part of a motion picture or other audiovisual work, as a translation, as a supplementary work, as a compilation, as an instructional text, as a test, as answer material for a test, or as an atlas . . . ."[85]

The list is not presented as a representative list, and there is no "including but not limited to" or "for example," references that would allow one to argue

85. 17 U.S.C. § 101 (Definitions).

that the list is greater than the items listed. The only two terms in the list that get a further explanation are "supplementary work" and "instructional text."

"Supplementary work" is defined as

> [a] work prepared for publication as a secondary adjunct to a work by another author for the purpose of introducing, concluding, illustrating, explaining, revising, commenting upon, or assisting in the use of the other work, such as forewords, afterwords, pictorial illustrations, maps, charts, tables, editorial notes, musical arrangements, answer material for tests, bibliographies, appendixes, and indexes . . . .

And "instructional text" is defined as "[a] literary, pictorial, or graphic work prepared for publication and with the purpose of use in systematic instructional activities."

The limitations in this list would suggest that a novel written for popular consumption and not intentionally for use in classrooms (this limitation seems to encompass textbooks rather than novels that might end up on a literature class's reading list) and a song and its sound recording would not qualify as a work for hire if created by a nonemployee. However, even that determination may depend on whether any agreement purporting to characterize these kinds of works as works for hire would be enforceable or would be prohibited under section 203(A)(5)'s "notwithstanding any agreement to the contrary" language.

This "work made for hire" definition in section 101 of the 1976 Copyright Act also adds another important limitation. After the list of the categories of works subject to the definition, the following additional qualifier appears: "If the parties expressly agree in a written instrument signed by them that the work shall be considered a work made for hire . . . ."[86]

The popular interpretation of this language is that in order for a work created by an independent contractor to be deemed a work for hire belonging to the employer, there must be an express written agreement between the contractor and the employer effecting the transfer of copyright ownership in the work. That would seem to be what Congress intended for this language to mean—but as we have seen previously in this context, what Congress giveth, the courts taketh away.

3. How to Use the Termination and Recapture Process

One of the first determinations to be made is whether the claim should be brought under the terms of section 304 or 203. Section 304 applies to copyrights in their first or second term under the 1909 Act. Specifically, section 304 (c) provides:

86. *Id.*

(c) Termination of Transfers and Licenses Covering Extended Renewal Term.—*In the case of any copyright subsisting in either its first or renewal term on January 1, 1978,* other than a copyright in a work made for hire, the exclusive or nonexclusive grant of a transfer or license of the renewal copyright or any right under it, executed before January 1, 1978, by any of the persons designated by subsection (a)(1)(C) of this section, otherwise than by will, is subject to termination under the following conditions . . . .[87]

So it is important to remember that although the revised Act is referred to as the Copyright Act of 1976, its terms did not become effective until January 1, 1978. In simplest terms, this means that any work created before that date is covered by section 304, regardless of when, or even whether, it has been registered.

The next consideration is whether the work in question is a work made for hire. If it is, then the section does not apply and your client may not terminate any grant previously made. As the discussion in the work-for-hire section of Chapter 3 detailed, answering the question of whether a work was one made for hire in the pre–1976 Act era may sometimes pose significant challenges.

Practitioners will need to evaluate all of the circumstances under which the work was created, as well as the nature of the work and the nature of the employment relationship, in order to determine if the doctrine applies. Particular attention must be paid to independent-contractor relationships where there was no written contract transferring ownership of the work created. In such instances, the practitioner may have to investigate whether the claim, and ultimately any litigation, will need to be brought either in a federal court district that is supportive of the broad application of the instance-and-expense test, as appears to be the situation in cases filed with the Second Circuit, or in other jurisdictions that might take a different view.

Often the initial investigation into a client's prospective claim will not yield easy or clear answers to these questions. For the practitioner, this uncertainty creates several problems, mostly in the area of managing client expectations. Clients will need to understand that the use of the work-for-hire exception is a primary defense position for most publishers and that the battle over this issue will likely dominate the litigation of the case. The problem of finding evidence in support of either side of this dispute is often made more acute due to the age of the properties at issue. Properties created in the late 1930s to the 1960s may yield little in the way of documentary evidence, and many relevant witnesses may have died or no longer remember key events.

87. *Id.* § 304(c) (emphasis added).

These evidentiary problems fall primarily on the plaintiffs in these cases, due to their obligation to carry the burdens of persuasion and proof.

An added concern is the relative bargaining power of the parties, a factor that often presents a "damned if you do, damned if you don't" dilemma for plaintiffs. If the publisher/defendant is a well-established and well-funded company (e.g., Marvel Comics (owned by the Disney Company), DC Comics (owned by Warner), or Random House) and the property itself is a valuable one, plaintiffs should prepare themselves for a difficult, hard-fought, and expensive battle. Practitioners representing plaintiffs on a contingency basis in these cases need to be sufficiently well funded to withstand several years of intense, full-court litigation.

Conversely, if the publisher/defendant is not well established or well funded, either it will fight just as hard in the case if the work at issue is considered a key asset for the business or the work itself may no longer be of much value in the marketplace due to a variety of factors, rendering the cost of litigation versus the value to be received if the claim is successful not a wise use of resources.

One potential risk in this context is unreasonable client expectations. Many plaintiffs in these section 304 cases are the heirs of the original creators. These people may not have ever worked in the creative sectors of the film, television, publishing, or music businesses. Their lack of experience may leave them vulnerable to predators (with which the entertainment business is rife) who have filled their heads with dreams of vast fortunes they can make if they can recapture the properties their parents or grandparents created decades ago.

A related problem in this context is that these same heirs and relatives may demonstrate fierce protectiveness toward the works they seek to recapture, and once they become aware that there is a possibility that they could gain control over the works, they become inflexible in their approach to any dispute-resolution discussion. This presents counsel with a real problem of client management, since for a variety of reasons, copyright termination and recapture cases, like most civil litigation matters, are often ultimately resolved via a settlement between the parties. Settlements are often more beneficial to all parties if they involve a compromise of wishes—a result that isn't likely if the copyright recapture claimants and/or their counsel have taken a no-compromise position.

A corollary problem with these kinds of expectations is what can be done with works whose characters have been significantly changed via derivative works created by the original grantees or their successors. This is a problem that, had their cases not settled or been otherwise resolved, the heirs of the creators of Superman and the characters in the Marvel universe would have faced. In each of those instances, the termination claims applied to the characters as they appeared in the late 1930s (Superman) or the mid-1960s (most of Kirby's characters that appeared in Marvel comics). In the decades that followed these initial appearances, DC and Marvel made substantial and significant changes to the characters. All of these changes were derivative works, based on the original character. Since these changes weren't done by the original creators, copyright ownership of these changes remains with DC and Marvel.

Ultimately, this means that even if the creators or their heirs had succeeded in fully recapturing the rights to these iconic characters, if they wanted to further exploit the contemporary versions of the characters, they would have had to do so via some form of collaboration agreement with those publishers. This same issue will apply in any of these section 304 termination cases, and even possibly in some section 203 cases, where the works that are the subject of the termination claim have undergone substantial changes by the grantees.

At first blush, one might think that this is a limited concern, applicable only in the instance where the work involved characters, such as comic-book characters, whose portrayal has changed dramatically over the decades since they first were published. This might have been true 30 years ago, but it isn't anymore. Pre-1976 works like films and television shows have largely been digitally remastered and/or updated (i.e., *Hawaii Five-O, Star Trek, Dr. Who* (the American version), etc.).

In the majority of these instances, the revised work has been done by the grantee of the copyright. As such, ownership of these derivative, updated, and revised works is in the hands of those grantees or their assigns. Terminating the grant of the original underlying work results only in the return of rights to that original version to the creators or their heirs. Subsection 6(A) of section 304(c) addresses the treatment of derivative works created by grantees during the term of their grant:

> (A) A derivative work prepared under authority of the grant before its termination may continue to be utilized under the terms of the grant after its termination, but this privilege does not extend to the preparation after the termination of other derivative works based upon the copyrighted work covered by the terminated grant.

So this means that to the extent derivative versions of a work have been created by the grantee and are still in circulation at the time the underlying grant is terminated, those works can continue to be sold and otherwise distributed, and the grantee is only obligated to continue to pay royalties to the creator and/or heirs at the same rates and under the same terms as were originally negotiated for the work—which in many cases means very low royalties due to the lack of bargaining power the creators usually had at the earlier stages of their careers.

An additional limit to the benefits accruing to the creator or heirs that terminate a copyright grant is that sections 304 and 203 only apply to copyright grants and only apply to those grants as they are exploited in the United States.

So trademark and/or patent rights that may have been transferred are not subject to the right of recapture. Similarly, any of these rights, and even copyright grants, are not subject to recapture to the extent that the work is being sold or otherwise exploited in markets foreign to the United States.

Beginning with the statute, section 302(c)(4) provides that "[t]he termination shall be effected by serving an advance notice in writing upon the grantee or the grantee's successor in title." If the grant was signed by someone other than the author, then the notice of termination must be signed by all of those entitled to terminate the grant. Where there is more than one creator of a work (such as cowritten books or other literary works, or artists and writers for illustrated books), a termination notice can be prepared and served just as to that author's contribution, or all of the creators can jointly prepare and serve the notice.[88]

In subsection 304(c)(4)(A), we find the first two traps for the unwary or careless practitioner. This subsection provides:

> (A) The notice shall state the effective date of the termination, which shall fall within the five-year period specified by clause (3) of this subsection, or, in the case of a termination under subsection (d), within the five-year period specified by subsection (d)(2), and ***the notice shall be served not less than two or more than ten years before that date. A copy of the notice shall be recorded in the Copyright Office*** before the effective date of termination, as a condition to its taking effect.[89]

So while subsection 3 of this section provided that termination of the grant can be ***effected*** "at any time during a period of 5 years," if the notice is not served "not less than two" years before the five-year period runs, it is not timely notice and the claim will be disallowed. Practitioners representing claimants must, therefore, make sure that in advising clients and in calendaring limitations periods for the filing of claims, they have accurately calculated the last day for timely service.

Whew. I know this is some heavy lifting, particularly for readers without a legal background—hang in there—we don't have too much more of this to complete this section!

The other trap here is the requirement that the notice be recorded with the Copyright Office. This is not a courtesy filing—it is jurisdictional; the notice does not take effect if it is not filed with the Copyright Office. And again, the

88. As a side note, this aspect of the termination law is another reason why coauthors should have written agreements with each other that detail their respective contributions to their works and should make sure that any copyright registrations filed, either by them or by their publishers, accurately identify the nature of their respective contributions. Bitter disputes frequently arise over who did what on cocreated works, and preparing a valid notice of termination is made much more difficult if contributions are not clearly defined and agreed upon.

89. 17 U.S.C. § 304(c)(4)(A) (emphasis added).

notice filed with that office must also comply with the same time-of-service requirements.

Subsection (4)(B) requires that the notice filed comply, "in form, content, and manner of service, with requirements that the Register of Copyrights shall prescribe by regulation." At this point, practitioners must refer to 37 C.F.R. section 201, and in particular to subsection 201.10, for the requirements prescribed by the Copyright Office for notices of termination.

Upon review of this section, the first somewhat unhelpful piece of news is that the "Office does not provide printed forms for the use of persons serving notices of termination." While this doesn't absolutely preclude lay persons from serving notice, it makes it less easy for them to do so, particularly given that the multiple required elements the section enumerates must be included in the notice. In this way, the termination process differs significantly from the copyright registration process—the Copyright Office uses easy-to-read forms for registration and provides extensive, clear, and easy-to-understand instructions for how to register. In contrast, the only discussion of the requirements for a notice of termination found in Copyright Office circulars is in Circular 15T, which only provides a general comment that "[i]t can be exercised only by certain persons (the author, or specified heirs of the author), and it must be exercised in accordance with prescribed conditions and within strict time limits."[90]

Given the complexity of the requirements necessary for a successful claim, this is not very helpful. The message ultimately is clear—preparing, serving, and filing a claim for copyright termination is not an easy process, and it is unlikely that a claimant can successfully navigate this process without the aid of experienced counsel.

Returning to the requirements found in 37 C.F.R. section 201.10, subsection (b) offers a list of the contents required for the notice. Claimants must identify if the termination is made under section 304(c) or (d) (the difference being if the claim is for a work whose underlying term expired or will expire before or after the implementation of the Sonny Bono Copyright Term Extension Act (the CTEA), which extended the term to life plus 70 years); the name and address of the grantee or its successor in title, for purposes of service of the notice; the title of the work to which the notice applies; the name of at least one of the authors; and, if available, the original copyright registration number (sub-subsections (b)(1)(i)–(iii)).

Sub-subsections (b)(1)(iv) and (v) contain two potentially problematic requirements. Sub-subsection (iv) requires that the claimant provide "[a] brief statement reasonably identifying the grant to which the notice of termination

90. *Extension of Copyright Terms,* U.S. Copyright Off. Circular 15T (rev. Jan. 2010), http://copyright.gov/circs/circ15t.pdf.

applies." In some cases this is easy to comply with—such as when the grant applies to a single song or a single piece of artwork. In other cases, this requirement can require a very complex analysis and submission. In cases where the grant involved a series of works, including rights to stories and separately copyright-protected characters, such as was the case in the Superman and Marvel universe (Jack Kirby's creations) or for a motion picture, which is a work of bundled copyrights for a story, a sound recording, a visual (the film itself), and other elements (i.e., original art, costumes, etc.), complying with this requirement can be very difficult. It is necessary, in such cases, to separate out the elements your client owns, remembering further that if the ownership interest is in less than half of the total of the work, it may not be possible to terminate and recapture the grant.

Sub-subsection (b)(1)(v), asking for the effective date of the termination, requires knowledge of the relevant five-year period in which the termination can be made and an affirmative statement that the effective date of termination complies with that period and the service period referenced previously. Again, failure to get these dates right can lead to a rejection of the filing by the Copyright Office and can doom an otherwise valid claim.

The remainder of subsection (b) requires claimants to confirm that termination of renewal rights under section 304(d), which can only be done once, has not been done previously and then in a detailed series of sub-subsections, 201.10(b)(1)(vii) to (2)(i)–(vii), explains the various requirements for identification of all of the claimants and their relationship with the author if the author is deceased and the claimants are heirs, such as widows, children, surviving children of deceased children, etc. Practitioners submitting claims on behalf of heirs will need to review these subsections with care in order to make sure the signatories to the claim are authorized to make the claim and that within the claim their entitlement is described in detail.

Sub-subsections (c)(1)–(5) detail the requirement for signing the claim, noting that for each proportional share of a work referred to in the notice, the owner of each such proportion, or his or her duly authorized agent, must provide a handwritten signature. While updated versions of this section don't expressly provide for electronic signatures, the E-Sign law, found in 15 U.S.C. section 7001, likely now applies to the signature of a termination claim, allowing an electronic signature to be used as well.

The requirements for service of process of the claim, which must be done in addition to the filing of the claim in the Copyright Office, are addressed in sub-subsections (d)(1)–(4). The claimant is required to effect service by personal service or by first-class mail sent to an address that, after reasonable investigation, is found to be the last known address of the grantee or successor in title. "Reasonable investigation" can include, but is not limited to, a search of the records in the Copyright Office or the offices of performing rights societies (in the case of a music publishing grant—in the United States these societies are ASCAP, BMI, and SEASAC).

The technical requirements for filing the claim outlined in section 201.10 conclude with the terms of sub-subsection (f), under the heading *Recordation*. An exact copy of the notice served on the grantee must be filed with the Copyright Office, together with payment of the then-applicable fee.[91]

Sub-subsection (f)(4) reserves to the Copyright Office the right to refuse recordation of a notice of termination if, in the judgment of the office, the notice is untimely under the requirements of the statute. In such cases, the office will offer to record the document as a "document pertaining to copyright," but it will not index the document as a notice of termination. Presumably this offer will facilitate restoration of the document as a valid notice of termination if the claimant either is able to persuade the office to revise its conclusion or seeks judicial relief and gets a court order validating the notice.

Finally, sub-subsection (f)(6) makes it clear that a claimant may not rely on the timely and proper recordation of the notice of termination as being evidence of the legal sufficiency of that notice. Any party is free to claim that the legal and/or the formal requirements for valid notice have not been complied with, despite the filing of the notice by the Copyright Office.

Returning to section 304(c), a claimant, having completed these procedural steps in preparing and serving a claim of termination, is by no means out of the woods with his or her claim. Subsection 304(c)(5) pertains to the right to terminate a grant even if a grantor has previously agreed to waive that termination right. This subsection provides: "(5) Termination of the grant may be effected notwithstanding any agreement to the contrary, including an agreement to make a will or to make any future grant."

The purpose of this subsection could not be clearer. It was Congress's way to send the message that section 304 overrules the outcome in the *Fisher v. Witmark* case. A claimant cannot waive the right of termination this law provides, and no agreement the claimant signed, whether done voluntarily or as a result of being induced to sign an agreement by offers of additional benefits, can operate to waive the right to terminate the grant. In sum, the termination right under section 304 is inalienable.

Having gone through the discouraging experience of seeing its intent to give authors a second bite at the apple undermined by the decision in *Witmark* and knowing full well that if it didn't make its intentions clear in this statute, grantee's counsel would argue that "if Congress intended to prevent contrary

91. As of early 2021, the basic fee for recording a notice of termination is $125 if only one title and one legal transaction are involved. The fee goes up in increments based on the number of additional transactions and titles involved. For further information, the Copyright Office provides detailed listings for how to determine the relevant fee at https://www.copyright.gov/about/fees.html.

agreements being executed, it would have said so," Congress, in this subsection, said so. Case closed, right?

Not so fast. Despite what would seem to be an unconditional, clear statement that grantees shouldn't even bother to try to entice grantors with waiver agreements, the allure of the freedom-of-contract argument remained strong, and two key appellate districts have issued several decisions that have sent the interpretation of section 304 right back into the realm of *Fisher.* These decisions in the highly influential Second and Ninth Circuit Courts of Appeal threaten to undermine congressional intent to protect authors' interests. Considered in conjunction with the broad interpretation of the work-for-hire doctrine in pre-1976 independent-contractor cases, this is where we see that the good intentions of Congress to protect the interests of authors have gone awry.

CHAPTER 5

The Question for Parody and Satire: Is It Transformative?

Fan-created works often take a popular television show or other work and, in the course of using it as a basis, poke fun at social conventions or other aspects of the original work. Most of these works poke gentle fun at the original work because the fan creator wants his or her new work to be either an homage or at least a positive nod to the underlying work, as opposed to offering what might be viewed as damaging criticism.

Literary works that adopt this style are referred to as parodies. Google's dictionary defines "parody" as "an imitation of the style of a particular writer, artist, or genre with deliberate exaggeration for comic effect."[1] A key element of this definition is that for a work to be a parody, it has to be about the style of a particular writer, artist, or genre—and that as a result, it is necessary for the parodist to use enough of the underlying work for the reader to recognize it and appreciate the humorous twist given to it. You can't appreciate the parody of a work if you don't recognize that underlying work.

For that reason, parody presents a high degree of risk for the creator. Unless the creator/owner of the original work consents to the parody, the parody writer runs the risk of a copyright infringement lawsuit, and an easy one at that for the original work's owner, since by its nature a parody is clearly an unauthorized copying. So how is it that parodies exist and are often seen in pop culture?

The answer is found in the protections afforded creators under the First Amendment and under the fair-use doctrine in U.S. copyright law. While it remains risky to create an unauthorized work based on someone else's original

1. *Parody Defined*, GOOGLE, https://www.google.com/search?client+firefox-b-1-d&q=Parody+defined (last visited Jan. 20, 2021).

work, for decades U.S. courts have found that such works are an exception to the prohibition against unauthorized derivative works. And while there are no cases that specifically hold that gentle parodies are authorized and mean-spirited or harsh parodies don't also get protection, those edgier works are more likely to draw a lawsuit by an offended original creator.

Two examples of hardcopy printed works that specialized in largely gentle parody treatments of many elements of pop culture are the *National Lampoon Magazine*, published from 1970 through the end of 1998, which was inspired by the *Harvard Lampoon*, a classic college humor magazine; and *Mad Magazine*, which ended an historic 68-year run in 2019, opting to end publication of its monthly edition in favor of collections of past issues in the collectibles market. *Mad Magazine* proudly asserts that it has never lost an infringement lawsuit, relying on its First-Amendment and fair-use defenses.

For many years, a key distinction in cases where a parody defense was raised was the question of whether the work at issue was truly a parody or a satire. The focus and purpose of a satire is to offer a comment on society, religion, and/or politics and the news of the day by holding things or people up to ridicule via exaggeration and irony. Thus the difference has been summarized as being that parody makes fun of a person or thing, whereas satire uses the person or thing as an example of a larger point about society and culture.

The importance of this distinction was that parody was generally protected by the First Amendment and the fair-use doctrine, whereas satire was not afforded those protections. The consequence was that if an accused infringing work could establish its parody credentials, it would escape infringement liability, whereas satire could result in a costly finding of infringement.

Prior to the development and application of the transformative doctrine, understanding these distinctions was a critical necessity for fan creators in particular, since their works, by definition, were based on underlying works they didn't create and typically didn't have permission to use. The transformative doctrine has changed this equation and has made it less important to be aware of the satire/parody distinction. A review of the key cases that defined that shift is worth understanding and is the subject of this chapter of the book.

A. *Dr. Seuss Enterprises v. Penguin Books USA Inc.: The Cat Not in the Hat* Case

Here is the cover illustration of the original book at issue in this case—note that the face of the cat is replaced by a drawing of O.J. Simpson in the Dr. Juice book.[2]

2. Dr. Seuss Enters., The Cat in the Hat (Random House 1957, renewed 1985). No claim of copyright ownership of these images is made by the author herein; the use of these images is done under the auspices of the fair-use doctrine of U.S. copyright law.

In 1957, Theodor Geisel, writing under the pseudonym "Dr. Seuss," published the iconic children's book *The Cat in the Hat*. The story begins on a cold and rainy afternoon, where Sally and her brother sit bored in their suburban home. Their parents are gone—Dad is at work and Mom is out running errands. As they sit wondering what to do to entertain themselves, the siblings hear a knock on the door. Answering it, they welcome into their home the Cat in the Hat, a creature with a vaguely human body and a face unlike that of any real cat (cats don't have eyebrows and round ears on the side of their face). The Cat also wears a banged-up red-and-white-striped top hat, a broad red bow tie, and, as was common among cartoon characters of this era, a pair of white gloves on his hands (no paws either).

The Cat commences entertaining the children with an array of tricks and juggling work, bringing in his two companions, named Thing One and Thing Two, to add to the somewhat destructive chaos. After making a huge mess of the house, and with their mother approaching from afar, the Cat exits, leaving the children with the prospect of explaining to their mother how the house got trashed. Then the Cat reappears with a huge machine, which he deploys to the task of clearing the house. The house is returned to its original condition just in the nick of time, and the Cat disappears just as mother enters the house and is curious to find that her children have no answer to her question asking them what they did while she was gone.[3]

Thirty-eight years later, in 1995, author Alan Katz and illustrator Chris Wrinn, Penguin Books USA, Inc., and Dove Audio, Inc., published *The Cat Not in the Hat!*, which they subtitle "A Parody." It's a mashup, taking the basic story of a catlike creature who enters a home and causes a great deal of disruption, then escapes at the last minute after putting the house in order, and weaving into that basic story the idea that the catlike creature, whose face is that of O.J. Simpson, enters the house of his ex-wife, Nicole Brown Simpson, and murders her in cold blood, later escaping the house and cleaning up all evidence of his involvement in the crime.

Katz and Wrinn borrow liberally from Dr. Seuss's other books as well. Thus the iconic line "One fish/two fish/red fish/blue fish./Black fish/blue fish/old fish/new fish" becomes "One Knife?/Two Knife/Red Knife/Dead Wife." Needless to say, the estate of Theodor Geisel was not amused and brought suit against Penguin Books, the publisher of the forthcoming book, and Dove Audio, which plans to distribute an audiobook version of the work. The complaint alleged copyright and trademark infringement (Geisel owned trademarks in "Dr. Seuss" and "Cat in the Hat"). The appeals court summarized the gist of the complaint and how the trial court handled it as follows:

> Seuss filed suit under the enforcement provisions of the Copyright Code, 17 U.S.C. §§ 501-02; the Lanham Act, 15 U.S.C. § 1125(a); the Federal Trademark Dilution Act of 1995, 15 U.S.C. § 1125(c)(1); and the California Unfair Competition Statute, § 17200 et seq. and § 14330. The district court denied the request for the temporary restraining order, but it set a hearing date for the preliminary injunction. Penguin and Dove went forward with the production schedule. Seuss incorporated additional infringement claims from other Dr. Seuss texts-Horton Hatches the Egg and One Fish Two Fish Red Fish Blue Fish-in its request for injunctive relief. On March 21, 1996, the district court granted Seuss' request for a preliminary injunction. About 12,000 books, at an expense of approximately $35,500, had been printed to date but now were enjoined from distribution. Penguin and Dove brought a motion for reconsideration and Katz filed a second declaration admitting to drawing from the other two Dr. Seuss works. Seuss then withdrew its claim regarding an illustration from Horton for purposes of its motion for injunctive relief.

3. This summary is derived from the one found on the SuperSummary website, www.supersummary.com/the-cat-in-the-hat/summary/ (last visited Jan. 20, 2021).

> While the district court modified its order in reconsidering these new claims, it did not dissolve the preliminary injunction. The court found that Seuss had demonstrated: (1) a strong likelihood that Katz and Wrinn had taken substantial protected expression from The Cat in the Hat but not from Horton or One Fish Two Fish; (2) a strong likelihood of success on the copyright claim raising a presumption of irreparable harm; (3) a strong likelihood of success on the parody as fair use issue; (4) serious questions for litigation and a balance of hardships favoring Seuss on the trademark violations; and (5) a minimal likelihood of success on the federal dilution claim. Penguin and Dove timely appealed.[4]

Katz and Wrinn, in their marketing and packaging for *The Cat Not in the Hat!*, repeatedly characterized the book as a parody. The outcome of this case reflects that taking this approach, while it likely won't hurt, doesn't have any actual impact on how the case will be decided. Calling a work a parody doesn't make it so.

Circuit Judge O'Scannlain, writing for the three-judge panel that also included Judges T.G. Nelson and Hawkins, notes that the case was before the Ninth Circuit on an "interlocutory" appeal, meaning an appeal taken during the proceedings in a case before it reached the trial stage. In this instance, the District Court, acting as the first-level trial court, had granted the preliminary injunction, effectively stopping the publication of *The Cat Not in the Hat!* before a single copy of the book had been distributed. At issue, he notes, is whether the plaintiffs had presented enough of a showing of copyright and trademark infringement that the injunction was properly issued and should remain in place throughout the rest of the handling of the case—since this was an appeal of a preliminary injunction, the Ninth Circuit was not ruling on whether the injunction should become permanent; that decision would be made only after the final trial of the case.

This is a good opportunity to step away from the analysis of this case in particular to note the legal tactic of using injunctions in copyright infringement cases. This is a very effective strategic move plaintiffs often opt for in these cases. The application to a court to issue an injunction against the defendant's act of publishing and/or distributing the alleged infringing work, if granted, can bring the case to a conclusion shortly after the case has begun and months, if not years, before it comes to trial. It is an enormously powerful stratagem, because once granted, it can end the defendant's distribution of the work, effectively achieving the main goal of the plaintiff's case right from its outset. For the defendant who is on the losing side of an injunction-motion fight, that loss

---

4. Dr. Seuss Enters., LP v. Penguin Books USA, Inc., 109 F.3d 1394, 1395 (9th Cir. 1997) (citation omitted).

often takes the fight out of the case, and many cases settle at this early stage of the litigation.

On the other hand, defendants who successfully hold off an injunction motion are emboldened to dig their feet in and fight on in the principal case. This is because in order to win an injunction, the plaintiff must show that there is a substantial likelihood of prevailing on the merits in the principal case—so if the plaintiff loses the motion, it sends a strong message to the plaintiff that they are not likely to win their case.

Counsel handling infringement cases should be looking for the viability of injunctive relief at the initiation of the case, and if they can't make a case for the granting of that relief, it is a signal that the underlying case may be weak and the decision to go forward with that case should be reevaluated. No one's interest is served by prosecuting a weak infringement case.

Copyright infringement cases primarily come in two flavors—direct or literal copying cases, which require plaintiffs to simply prove that they are the owners of the work and that defendant copied it without authorization; and indirect copying cases—where elements of the original work have been copied or otherwise used in creating a new work derived from the original.

Returning to the analysis of the *Seuss* case, Judge O'Scannlain next focused on the elements needed to prove copyright infringement in a case where the defendant didn't engage in literal copying but instead created an unauthorized derivative work. In such cases, plaintiffs must first prove that they hold a valid copyright registration in the work, which in this case was not in question.

The second element required is evidence that the alleged infringing work is substantially similar to the original work. There is a two-part test that is generally used to find substantial similarity, a test the Court applies here. The test comes from the case of *Sid & Marty Krofft Television Productions, Inc. v. McDonald's Corp.*[5]

The first part of this two-part test, referred to as the extrinsic part, asks if there is a similarity of ideas, and a concept known as analytic dissection is used to make this determination. The second part of the test, known as the intrinsic test, asks if an "ordinary reasonable person" would perceive a substantial taking of protected expression. The Court notes that these test elements have been criticized and modified in a number of cases, concluding that "the two tests are more sensibly described as objective and subjective analyses of expression."[6] Reviewing the efforts made by the trial court in conducting this analysis, Judge

---

5. Sid & Marty Krofft Television Prods., Inc. v. McDonald's Corp., 562 F.2d 1157, 1164 (9th Cir. 1977).

6. Dr. Seuss Enters., LP v. Penguin Books USA, Inc., 109 F.3d 1394, 1397 (9th Cir. 1997).

O'Scannlain finds no error in the conclusion the court reached that infringement of the copyright occurred.[7]

Addressing the defendants' argument that their story is a fair-use parody of the original work, the Court analyzes and applies each of the four factors of the fair-use test to the content of *The Cat Not in the Hat!* It's always important in this context to remember that all factors must be considered by the court in evaluating a fair-use claim—it is reversible error for a court to reach a conclusion on fair use based on an analysis that does not consider all four factors.

The first factor, the purpose and character of the use, requires the Court to evaluate whether *The Cat Not in the Hat!* is a transformative use of the material in the original book. Judge O'Scannlain notes that in a series of cases, courts have found that parodies are transformative works—leading him to conclude, under the *Acuff-Rose* test,[8] that the threshold question when fair use is raised in defense of a parody is whether a parodic character in the work may be reasonably perceived.[9] Citing that decision, the Court notes that

> [t]he difference between parody (in which the copyrighted work is the target) and satire (in which the copyrighted work is merely a vehicle to poke fun at another target): "Parody needs to mimic an original to make its point, and so has some claim to use the creation of its victim's (or collective victims') imagination, whereas satire can stand on its own two feet and so requires justification for the very act of borrowing."[10]

Applying this criterion to *The Cat Not in the Hat!*, the Court finds that the stanzas in that work don't mimic the style of the original—they have "no critical bearing on the substance or style" of *The Cat in the Hat.* Based on that analysis, the Court concludes that there is "[n]o effort to create a transformative work with 'new expression, meaning or message,' and therefore the infringing work's commercial use further cuts against the fair use defense."[11]

The Court cites the rule in the circuit for the distinction between protectable parody and unprotected satire, noting that its approach is consistent with dictionary definitions of "parody." The Court makes it clear that while the parody may address more than the work itself, for example offering criticism of aspects of modern society, at least in part it must also make fun of the underlying work. The audience must be aware of the existence of that underlying work for the parody to work.[12]

---

7. *Id.* at 1398.
8. Campbell v. Acuff-Rose, 510 U.S. 569 (1994).
9. *Id.*
10. *Dr. Seuss Enters., LP,* 109 F.3d at 1398.
11. *Id.* at 1398–99.
12. *Id.* at 1399.

The Court makes short work of the analysis of the second factor, "the nature of the copyrighted work," noting only that the distinction here is that creative works of expression are "closer to the core of intended copyright protection" than informational and functional works and therefore more likely to be entitled to protection.[13]

Turning its attention to the third factor, "the amount and substantiality of the portion used in relation to the copyrighted work as a whole," the Court notes that the image of the Cat and his Hat, which appears on the front and back cover of defendants' book, as well as appearing 13 times within the book, is the "highly expressive core of Dr. Seuss' work."[14] Which in turn leads the Court to consider if it was necessary to the purpose of defendants' book to make that extensive a use of this iconic character.

Rather than summarizing the argument defendants make that they have created a protectable parody, the Court includes in its decision a verbatim quote from the defendants' opening brief, which encapsulates their position. Defendants argue that their parody is a commentary about the events surrounding the murders of Ms. Brown and Mr. Goldman and the subsequent trial of O.J. Simpson for those crimes. They assert that they are exploring the contradictions between the childish style and moral content of Dr. Seuss's works and the moral gravity of the cultural reaction to the Simpson murder case. Their Cat is a real "trickster" cat, they argue, who creates real mayhem and then magically cleans it up at the end, "leaving a moral dilemma in his wake."

The Court fully rejects the argument in the kind of language a lawyer never wants to see in a court of appeals opinion against a client's position: "We completely agree with the district court that Penguin and Dove's fair use defense is 'pure shtick' and that their post-hoc characterization of the work is 'completely unconvincing.'"[15]

Ouch. So while it is generally true that fair-use doctrine is often applied with a high degree of leniency by courts, that didn't happen here.

Finally, the Court completes its fair-use analysis with the fourth factor—"the effect of the use upon the potential market for or value of the copyrighted work." Citing the Second Circuit decision in *MCA Inc. v. Wilson*,[16] the Court characterizes this analysis as one balancing

> the benefit the public will derive if the use is permitted and the personal gain the copyright owner will receive if the use is denied. The less adverse effect that an alleged infringing use has on the copyright

---

13. *Id.* at 1400 (citing *Acuff-Rose*, 510 U.S. at 586).
14. *Id.* at 1401.
15. *Id.*
16. MCA v. Wilson, 677 F.2d 180, 183 (2d Cir. 1981).

owner's expectation of gain, the less public benefit need be shown to justify the use.[17]

Applying that standard, the Court notes that having shown that the use was nontransformative and admittedly commercial, it is at least more certain than not that some degree of market substitution is likely and that harm to the market for the original work may be "more readily inferred." This last point seems a bit of a stretch, to the extent it suggests that people who might be disposed to buy *The Cat in the Hat*, a book marketed toward children, would choose instead to buy *The Cat Not in the Hat!*, a parodic work not likely sold through the same marketing channels or displayed in the children's section of brick-and-mortar or online stores.

Finally, finding that there are serious questions and some evidence supporting Dr. Seuss's claims of trademark infringement, and based also on the absence of a fair-use defense, the Court affirms the District Court's grant of an injunction barring the sale of *The Cat Not in the Hat!*[18] And so in this case, decided 23 years before I wrote these words, it seemed that the fair-use test and transformative doctrine could not be relied on by fan creators who wanted to use a work in pop culture to offer a satirical comment about contemporary events. But would that principle hold over the next two decades? A subsequent case, about an equally if not more iconic work of American fiction, would give us an indication that the winds of change were upon us.

B. *Suntrust Bank v. Houghton Mifflin Co.*: *The Wind Done Gone* Case

As the Court in this Eleventh Circuit decision notes, Margaret Mitchell's book, *Gone with the Wind* (GWTW), published in 1936, is one of the best-selling books in the world, second in sales only to the Bible. The Mitchell Trust, which holds and manages the copyright in the work, has granted numerous licenses for different products relating to and versions of the original work. Suntrust Bank brought the suit in its capacity as trustee for The Mitchell Trust.

At the time of this decision, in 2001, Alice Randall had written and, through publisher Houghton Mifflin, had published her book entitled *The Wind Done Gone* (TWDG), a fictional work unmistakably based on GWTW. Randall's book is written from the perspective of black slaves on Tara, the plantation ultimately owned by Scarlett O'Hara, a key character in GWTW, whose pursuit of Rhett Butler is the central love story in GWTW. Randall, the Court notes,

17. Dr. Seuss Enters., LP v. Penguin Books USA, Inc., 109 F.3d 1394, 1402 (9th Cir. 1997).
18. *Id.* at 1403.

"persuasively claims that her novel is a critique of GWTW's depiction of slavery and the Civil-War era American South."[19]

Suntrust sued Houghton, seeking an injunction against TWDG, arguing it should not be published due to alleged copyright violations. Specifically, Suntrust argued that Randall appropriated the characters, major scenes, and plot from GWTW and copied in addition character traits and relationships, including in some instances verbatim copying of character dialogues and descriptions from GWTW.[20]

Houghton did not contest these allegations, arguing instead that there was no substantial similarity between the two works or, in the alternative, that the uses made were fair use because TWDG is primarily a parody of GWTW. In a step common to copyright infringement cases where the publication of the alleged infringing work is ongoing, Suntrust first sought an injunction to bar further publication and distribution of the book.

As I discussed previously, this kind of motion is a bet-the-farm step—if the injunction is issued, it often ends the litigation and leads to a quick settlement. If denied, it signals a significant weakness in the underlying case, which often also leads to a settlement, albeit not one that is very beneficial to the plaintiff.

What happened in the *Suntrust* case was a bit out of the ordinary—after a hearing at the District Court level, the motion was granted and the injunction was issued, barring sale of TWDG. And while that usually is the end of these kinds of cases, Houghton took the unusual step of seeking review of the decision by the U.S. Court of Appeals for the Eleventh Circuit.

The Eleventh Circuit Federal Court of Appeals handles appeals from U.S. District Courts in Florida, Alabama, and Georgia from its headquarters in Atlanta, Georgia. Although it isn't as big a hub for entertainment business activity as the Second Circuit, based in New York City, or the Ninth Circuit, based in San Francisco, the Eleventh Circuit has often been the locale for entertainment cases arising out of the Miami and Atlanta entertainment business areas.

In this case, Circuit Judge Stanley F. Birch felt it necessary to "review the history of the Constitution's Copyright Clause and understand its relationship to the First Amendment."[21] He begins that analysis with the history and development of the Copyright Clause, first in England and then in the United States from its initial incarnation in 1783 through to the Copyright Act of 1976. He summarizes the importance of copyright law to public education and access to

19. Suntrust Bank v. Houghton Mifflin Co., 268 F.3d 1257, 1259 (2001).
20. *Id.*
21. *Id.* at 1260.

knowledge, then moves to the entitlement of the public to have works enter the public domain after the protection of copyright law expires.[22]

Discussing the exclusive rights of the author under U.S. copyright law, Judge Birch makes a point often forgotten—the author of a work owns the copyright in the work but not the work itself. He illustrates that point by noting that once a work goes into the public domain, the author loses all rights to it—both ownership and the copyright. The work continues to exist, but ownership of all rights to it has passed to the public in general.

This fact reinforces the argument that copyright in a work does not include all rights in the work and that the U.S. system is organized around the concept that the creator of the work retains control over it for only a limited time. And while critics decry the term of current copyright (life of the author plus 70 years) as being too long, arguing that the constitutional grant of exclusive rights for a limited term[23] should not support such a long period of time, when viewed from the perspective that the work's existence continues indefinitely, the grant of life plus 70 years is indeed a grant for a limited time.

Judge Birch then addresses the classic conflict between the protections authors have in copyright law and how those rights conflict with the broad grant of freedom of expression afforded by the First Amendment. The balance between these two is, he notes, "[p]reserved, in part, by the idea/expression dichotomy and the doctrine of fair use."[24] The fact that protection is not granted to uncopyrightable facts and ideas and that works of scholarship and commentary are protected by the fair-use doctrine is how First Amendment protections share the expressive space with copyright protections. And so, he concludes, in order to determine if TWDG is protected by the First Amendment and the fair-use doctrine, it must be reviewed using the substantial-similarity test for infringement and the four-part test for the fair-use defense.

Judge Birch concurs with the District Court's determination that Randall incorporates many of the key elements in GWTW in TWDG. While some names are changed, many are the same, and the place and time are also identical. His careful review concludes that TWDG encapsulates and exploits GWTW characters, story lines, and settings as "the palette for the new story."[25]

Houghton Mifflin doesn't dispute these similarities but argues that the works are not substantially similar because TWDG is "an inversion" of GWTW—the same characters, places, and events are viewed in a different light, and strong characters in the original book are now seen as weak and vice versa. The Court acknowledges this but does not find it changes the

---

22. *Id.* at 1261–63.
23. *Id.* at 1263 (citing U.S. Const. art. I, § 8).
24. *Id.*
25. *Id.* at 1267.

substantial-similarity analysis, holding: "While we agree with Houghton Mifflin that the characters, settings, and plot taken from GWTW are vested with a new significance when viewed through the character of Cynara in TWDG, it does not change the fact that they are the very same copyrighted characters, settings, and plot."[26]

Moving into the fair-use analysis, the Court notes that parody, as defined in the *Acuff-Rose* case, can be interpreted either narrowly as being directed toward comic effect or ridicule or more broadly as simply offering a "commentary" on the original. For the purpose of this decision, the Court adopts the broader standard. This means that the Court will find that TWDG should be deemed a parody if its aim is to comment upon or criticize a prior work by appropriating elements of the original in creating a new artistic, as opposed to scholarly or journalistic, work. And that is exactly what the Court finds TWDG has done, so it finds:

> TWDG is not a general commentary upon the Civil-War-era American South, but a specific criticism of and rejoinder to the depiction of slavery and the relationships between blacks and whites in GWTW. The fact that Randall chose to convey her criticisms of GWTW through a work of fiction, which she contends is a more powerful vehicle for her message than a scholarly article, does not, in and of itself, deprive TWDG of fair-use protection.[27]

And with this framework established, Judge Birch begins his careful analysis of the four fair-use factors. Addressing the first factor, the purpose and character of the allegedly infringing work, the Court notes that in the past, the principal inquiry was whether the work was done for profit or for an educational or other nonprofit use. Works done for profit have a harder time qualifying as a fair use, since the infringer is profiting from the unauthorized use. And here, notwithstanding the fact that TWDG is offering timely social criticism, the Court has to acknowledge that the for-profit nature of TWDG, as a commercially for-sale book, would ordinarily mean this factor would favor the Mitchell Trust and Suntrust Bank.

But times have changed, and the Court must now, in considering this first factor, also consider to what extent TWDG is a transformative work. And as much as I am a critic of what sometimes seems to be the overbreadth of the scope of what is considered transformative, it's hard to argue with Judge Birch's analysis of how the doctrine applies to TWDG. That said, it can also be argued that it wasn't necessary to go through a transformative analysis here, relying instead on the already existing body of cases finding that parodies, as opposed to satires, are protectable fair uses. The parodic nature of TWDG having been

26. *Id.* (citation omitted).
27. *Id.* at 1268–69.

established, was it really necessary to apply the transformative doctrine? It seems a fair question, at least.

That said, this is the direction the Court took, and its finding is that TWDG uses many of the plot, character, and scenic elements of GWTW to attack its "romantic, idealized portrait of the antebellum South during and after the Civil War." The Court goes on to note that the first half of TWDG attacks the premises behind GWTW, and the second half offers a new story about the new characters added to the story. The Court notes that Cynara, the lead character in TWDG, uses language that is a departure from Margaret Mitchell's original prose. Cynara is the voice of Randall's inversion of GWTW. The traditional race roles depicted in GWTW are flipped in Randall's story line—the effect is to demystify GWTW and to strip the romanticism from that iconic work. The Court finds TWDG is a "completely new story" that features a new story with new and original plot points, despite being based on GWTW characters.[28]

Given the Court's view that TWDG offers a valuable and timely different view of the society depicted in GWTW, it is no surprise that the Court finds that this different view isn't simply a lazy substitute for the original work but instead offers a new, creative take on GWTW. The Court points out that parody requires the parodist to appropriate elements of the original work in order to offer commentary about that work. Acknowledging that a work can be a fair use without being transformative, the Court notes that the more transformative a work is, the less important the other fair-use factors will become. Applying that principle to this case, the Court finds that the transformative nature of the work means that the showing needed regarding the other factors is less important here.[29]

It seems accurate to say, charting the history of the transformative doctrine, that this case suggests that a parody that, while making fun of an underlying work, also offers a valid social commentary, to the extent that in doing so it crosses the line into satire as well, the inclusion of parodic content likely allows that work to survive an infringement challenge. Fan creators should take note that an effectively done parody may allow them to incorporate satirical elements as well, without negative consequences.

Consideration of the second factor, the nature of the copyrighted work, tracked the analysis of the Court in the *Seuss* case, finding that the creative nature of GWTW supports a finding that copying its elements is an infringing act. However, the Court here adds that an exception exists for cases involving parody: "This factor is given little weight in parody cases, however, 'since parodies almost invariably copy publicly known, expressive works.'"[30]

---

28. *Id.* at 1270.
29. *Id.* at 1271.
30. *Id.* (citing Campbell v. Acuff-Rose, 510 U.S. 569, 586 (1994)).

The third factor, the amount and substantiality of the portion used in relation to the copyrighted work as a whole, required a more extensive analysis by the Court. The reason this factor is complicated in this case is important for fan creators to be aware of—parody by its nature requires the parodist to take enough of the original work to be able to "'conjure up' at least enough of the original to make the object of its critical wit recognizable."[31] Yet, after doing that, the parodist must be careful that any further taking specifically serves the new work's parodic aims.[32]

So if in reading this, you are thinking this is a difficult path to tread, you are right. How can you know, if you are a fan creator writing a parody of a popular work, how much you can take to meet the need of conjuring up enough of the original to make the object of your parody recognizable, and then to add some more references to the original work that specifically serve your parodic aims, without crossing a line that some court, years later, will view as going too far, exposing you to infringement liability? Unfortunately, this is not a question that can be answered with any precision. So the only suggestion I can offer to fan creators of parodies is to have someone with an understanding of this area of the law review your work before you publish it—based on the benefit of having trained eyes review the work to see if it is likely to spark a claim. Such a review will probably allow you to catch material that is clearly over the line, but more subtle cases will test your—and, if you use an outside publisher, their—risk tolerance. Should you do this in all cases, for all parodies? Probably not. If you are writing expressly nonprofit fan fiction, with no aspirations for the work other than to self-publish it on a fan-fiction site, you probably have no need to be concerned, as the work is not likely to draw attention that might result in an infringement claim—whereas posting an hour-long fan-film parody of a currently popular work, like *The Handmaid's Tale*, might be a work that you should be cautious about.

Finally, the Court, looking at the fourth factor—the effect that the publication of TWDG will have on the market for or value of Suntrust's copyright in GWTW—assessed the likelihood that market substitution would occur; would people not buy GWTW and instead purchase TWDG? And here, as is likely to be the case with most, if not all, fan-created parodies, the Court concludes "that Suntrust's evidence falls far short of establishing that TWDG or others like it will act as market substitutes for GWTW or will significantly harm its derivatives. Accordingly, the fourth fair use factor weighs in favor of TWDG."[33]

And with that final factor considered, the Court concludes overall that the district court's finding that Suntrust had established its likelihood of success

---

31. *Id.*
32. *Id.*
33. *Id.* at 1273.

on the merits is valid, so it is their conclusion that TWDG was entitled to a fair-use defense.

So what lessons do these two cases teach? For fan creators, it is important to understand that for a parody to be a protected fair use, it must stick pretty closely to the original work as the focus of the new piece, and you need to be careful not to veer into commentary unrelated to the original piece. That said, there is a lot of room within the context of direct parody to offer social commentary, as Randall did in TWDG.

With this lesson in mind, another question that often comes up in the fan-creator context is whether, and to what extent, you can create a mashup of more than one pop-culture work, more as an homage than a direct parody, and still prevail in an infringement lawsuit. At least one case in the Ninth Circuit as of the writing of this book has answered the question with a finding that this kind of work is also a transformative, allowed fair use.

C. *Dr. Seuss Enterprises, L.P. v. ComicMix, LLC: Oh the Places You'll Boldly Go!*

Dr. Seuss Enterprises, L.P. (DSE), owner by assignment of the copyrights in the works of Theodor S. Geisel, writing as Dr. Seuss, brought suit in November 2016 seeking damages for copyright infringement, trademark infringement, and unfair competition against publisher ComicMix LLC, its co-owner Glenn Hauman, writer David Gerrold, and artist Ty Templeton. At issue was a graphic novel the defendants had created and published, entitled *Oh the Places You'll Boldly Go!*—a mashup project whose title took Dr. Seuss's beloved book *Oh the Places You'll Go!* and mixed it with a portion of the opening lines of the *Star Trek* television show, read by lead actor William Shatner: "These are the voyages of the starship *Enterprise*. Its five-year mission: to explore strange new worlds; to seek out new life and new civilisations; to boldly go where no man has gone before."[34]

Having previously been successful in *The Cat Not in the Hat!* case, DSE likely believed that it would be able to obtain a similar result in this case and that the courts would reject the fair-use defense and find infringement. Oh what a difference 20 years makes. The trial court, ruling on cross-motions for summary judgment, rejected DSE's infringement claim, accepting the defendants' fair-use defense on the grounds that their work was transformative.

34. https://www.clivebanks.co.uk/Star%20Trek%20Intro.htm (spelling of "civilizations" in the original form).

Similar to the creation process for *The Cat Not in the Hat!*, the creators of *Oh the Places You'll Boldly Go!* made a careful study of the artwork style of Dr. Seuss and the costumes, facial features, and some of the landscapes found on the *Star Trek* series and creatively mashed up the two to produce their work. They encountered difficulties in finding a publisher for their book, in part likely because they had not sought a license from DSE, preferring to rely on their belief that their work was a transformative parody and therefore a fair use.[35]

Defendants knew they were treading a thin line between defensible fair use and infringement. They included two different disclaimers on their completed draft of *Boldly*, writing "This is a work of fair use, and is not associated with or endorsed by CBS Studio or Dr. Seuss Enterprises, L.P." and then "Copyright Disclaimer under Section 107 of the Copyright Act of 1976, allowance is made for 'fair use' for purposes such as criticism, comment, news reporting, teaching, scholarship, education, research, and parody."[36]

They further acknowledged the danger they knew they faced in going forward with the project in a statement they made in the "Risks and Challenges" section of their Kickstarter campaign to raise funds for the project, writing:

> While we firmly believe that our parody, created with love and affection, fully falls within the boundary of fair use, there may be some people who believe that this might be in violation of their intellectual property rights. And we may have to spend time and money proving it to people in black robes. And we may even lose that.[37]

These efforts did not stop DSE from seeking to halt the publication of *Boldly*. They sent DMCA takedown notices to Kickstarter and sent three cease-and-desist letters to defendants. When these demands were refused, DSE filed suit in November 2016, seeking damages for copyright infringement, trademark infringement, and other claims.[38] The trademark claim is an interesting one, as the holders of copyrights on pop-culture material occasionally create a character or logo that becomes so popular that its use transcends its origins to become a brand name or graphic for the company that owns or otherwise licenses the right to use it as a brand. Examples include the Spiderman mask, which has become a trademark of Marvel Comics, or the use of the stylized lettering for the name "Superman" and the distinctive "S" design on the character's chest.

---

35. Dr. Seuss Enter., L.P. v. ComicMix LLC, et al., Case No. 16-CV-2779JLS (BGS), Order granting (1) defendants' motion for summary judgement, (2) denying plaintiff's motion for summary judgement, and (3) denying as moot plaintiff's motions to strike and to exclude, at 4–6 (S.D. Cal. filed Mar. 12, 2019).

36. *Id.* at 6.

37. *Id.* at 7.

38. *Id.* at 8.

In this case, DSE licenses the use of its characters and designs for a wide array of commercial goods, including clothing, games, toy designs, etc. Based on those uses, it claimed that *Boldly* violated its rights in those distinctive marks.

Defendants responded by filing a motion to dismiss the copyright claims on the grounds of fair use and the trademark claims on the grounds that DSE held no cognizable trademark rights to the title, artistic style or fonts used in *Boldly*. They also argued that even if DSE did have trademark rights, defendants were protected by the First Amendment and by "nominative" fair use—the version of fair use that applies to trademark cases.

In reaching a decision on a motion to dismiss, the court is limited to the allegations made in the complaint and is required to assume the statements made are true and can be proven in the course of the case. If the court finds that the complaint is sufficiently pled, it will deny the motion. Courts are reluctant to grant these motions, since a dismissal of the case brings it to an end, without plaintiffs ever getting their day in court to present their claims. It is, therefore, a questionable strategy to bring this kind of motion, since the court's ability to analyze the claims is so limited and the preference is to allow the case to move forward.

Strategically, the better approach often is to bring a motion for summary judgment to resolve the case without the necessity and cost of going forward to trial. A summary-judgment motion is usually brought after all discovery in a case has been completed. If by the time the motion is filed, the evidence doesn't support plaintiff's claim and there is no issue of fact left for a jury to decide, a successful summary-judgment motion can bring a case to a speedy conclusion—although you do have to incur the cost and time for that discovery to conclude and to prepare, file, and argue the motion.

One benefit a motion to dismiss can offer is that it gives the court a means to communicate to counsel and the parties whether the court sees the case as either very weak or very strong. A court can do this by denying the motion, while at the same time pointing out serious weaknesses in the plaintiff's case—in essence sending a message to the plaintiff that it has a weak case, which it should probably settle.

And that is precisely what the Court in the Central District of California (Los Angeles) did with this first motion to dismiss. As to the copyright infringement claim, the Court found that *Boldly* "[i]s no doubt transformative" and further found that it "[d]oes not supplant the market for *Go!* or the other relevant Dr Seuss works."[39]

The Court did note, however, that since on a motion to dismiss it had to accept plaintiff's allegations as true, it had to

---

39. *Id.* at 10.

> "[p]resume some degree of harm to Plaintiff's licensing opportunities, although this presumed harm is neutralized somewhat by the fact that *Boldly* does not substitute for the original and serves a different market function than *Go!* because *Boldly*'s market relies on consumers who have already read and greatly appreciated *Go!* and Dr. Seuss' other works, and who simultaneously have a strong working knowledge of the Star Trek series," rendering it "unlikely that *Boldly* would severely impact the market for Dr. Seuss's works."[40]

And yet, despite this critique that appeared to support defendants' position, the Court concluded that "given the procedural posture of this motion and near-perfect balancing of the factors, the Court denied Defendants first motion as to fair use."[41]

The Court's reaction to the defendants' effort to obtain a dismissal of the trademark claims illustrates another risk in bringing a motion to dismiss at the initial stages of a lawsuit. The Court granted defendants' motion to dismiss because it found that *Boldly* "does not explicitly mislead as to its source or contents"[42] and because the DSE marks were not used by defendants as a trademark, which lent credence to defendants' nominative fair-use defense. And yet the Court, even while granting the motion to dismiss as to the trademark and unfair competition claims, nonetheless granted DSE leave to file an amended complaint on those claims.

This is the risk taken in a motion to dismiss—it is common practice for a court, in granting this motion, to allow plaintiff an opportunity, at least once in the process, to amend its complaint in an effort to cure the defect in the pleadings that led the court to grant that dismissal. Experienced litigators often decline to file these motions, because they know that in many cases, all they will accomplish is to educate the other side as to the weaknesses in their complaint. Doing so gives the defendant an opportunity, via the court's grant of leave to amend the complaint, to strengthen their complaint. Often, the better practice is to hold off from filing this motion, allow the plaintiff to proceed into the litigation with a weak or poorly drafted complaint, and win the case via a strong summary-judgment motion.

Defendants took a different approach—they doubled down and after DSE filed its first amended complaint again filed a motion to dismiss, and although they managed this time to get the trademark infringement claims dismissed, the copyright claims survived again, with the court concluding that there was

40. *Id.*
41. *Id.*
42. *Id.*

evidence relevant to the fourth fair-use factor, that the publication of *Boldly* did present the prospect of harm in the market for plaintiff's derivative works.

After some additional motions clarified disputed points about the fonts, title graphics, and illustration styles, the parties moved forward with their litigation battle, and after discovery was completed, defendants filed a motion for summary judgment on the copyright issues. Now, with discovery completed, they were able to argue that with all the evidence disclosed, there was no material issue of fact left for a jury to decide and that all of the facts and related evidence supported their claim that fair use and the First Amendment protected *Boldly* from DSE's infringement claim.[43]

The Court responded to the motion by conducting a fair-use analysis. Looking at the first factor, the purpose and character of the use, the Court notes that defendants did not engage in literal copying of Dr. Seuss's works—instead, although they borrowed liberally from the designs and themes of those works, in all instances,

> [t]he copied elements are always interspersed with original writing and illustrations that transform *Go!*'s pages into repurposed, *Star Trek*-centric ones. Defendants did not copy verbatim text from *Go!* in writing *Boldly*, nor did they replicate entire illustrations from *Go!* Although Defendants certainly borrowed from *Go!*—at times liberally—the elements borrowed were always adapted or transformed. The Court therefore concludes, as it did previously, that Defendants' work, while commercial, is highly transformative.[44]

Turning to the second factor, the nature of the copyrighted use, the Court and the parties agreed to leave unchanged the previous ruling on the motion to dismiss that this factor slightly favors DSE. The Court notes that the Dr. Seuss books are highly creative works, which would normally be a significant factor in DSE's favor, but in this case the Court finds the impact of this is slight, because the works have been published for a long time and *Boldly* does not supplant them.[45]

The Court then moves to consideration of the third factor, the amount and substantiality of the portion used compared to the work as a whole. Here, the Court focuses on the fact that in *Boldly*, although the creators used a number of Seuss-like graphics, in virtually all instances, they mashed up those elements with ones from *Star Trek*, which diminishes the extent of their taking of Seussian elements. Because of that usage that combines the two works, the Court concludes:

---

43. *Id.* at 14.
44. *Id.* at 17.
45. *Id.* at 18.

> Yes, these are elements significant to the Copyrighted Works, but Defendants ultimately did not use Dr. Seuss' words, his character, or his universe. The Court therefore stands by its prior conclusion that Defendants took no more from the Copyrighted Works than was necessary for Defendants' purposes, *i.e.* a "mash-up" of *Go!* and *Star Trek*, and that consequently, this factor does not weigh against Defendants.[46]

Finally, the Court looks at the fourth fair-use factor, the market effect of the use. The Court begins that analysis by noting that its determination that *Boldly* is transformative requires DSE, in turn, to meet the burden of proof that there is a likelihood of future market harm. The Court further notes that this showing must be by a preponderance of the evidence—a tough standard to meet.[47]

The Court concludes that DSE failed to meet its burden of proof. Citing a number of prior cases as precedent, the Court begins the explanation for its conclusion by noting that the market for *Boldly* is generally a different one than for *Go!* The Court notes that the market for *Boldly* is more of an adult demographic, because *Star Trek* is skewed to an adult audience. The Court notes, for example, a sequence in *Boldly* where the character with *Star Trek*'s Captain Kirk's face is shown pulling on his boots. They explain that in the *Star Trek* series, scenes of the captain pulling on his boots are always preceded by scenes of the captain with various women from Earth and other planets, and the implication is always clear—Captain Kirk is getting dressed after having sex with these women. This, the Court suggests, is not the kind of fare that Dr. Seuss's stories trade in—and is targeted to the audience of *Star Trek* fans, not to fans of Dr. Seuss's children's books.[48]

The Court acknowledges that the issue of whether *Boldly* could affect *Go!*'s considerable market for derivative works and graduation gifts is a closer question. The Court acknowledges that *Boldly*'s publisher hopes the book will sell well in those markets but also notes that DSE failed to offer any evidence—only speculation—that sales of *Boldly* would have a market impact on sales of *Go!* or its derivatives.

Having now concluded that all four factors support defendants, the Court grants their motion for summary judgment as to fair use.[49] DSE did not accept this outcome and filed an appeal to the Ninth Circuit Court of Appeals. Literally on the day I completed my final draft of this book, on December 18, 2020, the Ninth Circuit three-judge panel that heard the appeal shocked the

---

46. *Id.* at 22.
47. *Id.* at 23.
48. *Id.* at 27–28.
49. *Id.* at 38.

copyright legal community by unanimously reversing the District Court on the copyright holdings in the case, while affirming the trademark decision.[50, 51]

The Ninth Circuit flatly rejected the District Court's fair-use analysis, principally on the grounds that *Boldly,* in the Court's view, was not a transformative work. In coming to that conclusion, the Ninth Circuit relied on its prior decision in the *Cat Not in the Hat!* case, discussed previously. The Court, drawing from that case and the *Campbell* case, reiterated that for a work to be transformative, it had to "add something new, with a further purpose or different character, altering the first with new expression, meaning or message."[52]

The Court went on to reject the argument that *Boldly* was a parody, finding that similar to the *Cat Not in the Hat!, Boldly* does not use Seuss elements for the purpose of making fun of them or to make another point about *Go!*—so "lacking critical bearing on the substance or style of Go, Boldly cannot be characterized as a parody."[53]

As has been seen in other cases dealing with fair use and the transformative doctrine, once a court finds a work is not transformative, the remaining three factors of the fair-use test are viewed in a different light. The Ninth Circuit has no problem, having found against the transformative and parody claims and that the nature of the work, as a commercial venture, also works against a fair-use finding. They find that *Boldly* uses a substantial amount of the original Seuss work in *Go!* and that there is at least a likelihood that some market displacement may occur, which supports a finding that the fourth factor also weighs in favor of DSE.[54]

As this decision has come down as this book goes to the publisher, it is unknown whether the copyright bar, and the many scholars who supported the fair-use finding of the District Court, will appeal the case to the U.S. Supreme Court. What can be said is that this decision renders the ground underpinning the transformative doctrine continually shaky and unpredictable.

---

50. Dr. Seuss Enters. v. ComicMix LLC, No. 19-55348, op. (9th Cir. filed Dec. 18, 2020).

51. For a comprehensive analysis of the merits of the arguments on appeal, see Brief of *Amici Curiae* Professors Mark A. Lemley et al. in Support of Defendants-Appellees and Affirmance, Dr. Seuss Enters. v. ComicMix LLC, No. 19-55348 (9th Cir. Dec. 18, 2020).

52. *Dr. Seuss Enters.,* No. 19-55348, at 12.

53. *Id.* at 13–14.

54. *Id.* at 19–30.

D. Conclusions: The Impact of the Transformative Doctrine on Fair-Use Defenses for Fan-Created Works

Before the introduction and adoption of the transformative doctrine to copyright law, fair-use analysis was dominated almost entirely by evidence regarding the fourth factor—the effect on the market. A use that interfered with the current or future market for the goods was likely to be found not to be a fair use. The application of the transformative doctrine has changed that focus—now it is the first factor that is the key element in the analysis. If a work is found to be a transformative use of the underlying work, plaintiffs must produce evidence of substantial harm to their market position in order to overcome the support a transformative use gives to a fair-use defense. The likely outcome of this shift is to broaden the range of fan-created works that can now be created, particularly in the area of mashups—a media format long popular in fan works.

While the focus of this section of the book has been on legislation from 1909 and 1976, there are at least two other pieces of legislation that have significant impact on the works of fan creators: the PROTECT Act and the CASE Act. We examine those in the next chapter.

CHAPTER 6

Related Legislation: The PROTECT Act and the CASE Act

A. *United States v. Handley*: The PROTECT Act Protects Whom from What?

Of the various traps for the unwary fan and creator of pop culture–based works, many of which have already been discussed in this book (i.e., the transformative doctrine, works for hire, etc.), none looms as large or poses as much of a risk as the prospect of running afoul of state and/or federal law prohibiting the creation, distribution, possession, or even mere reading of explicit sexually oriented materials, referred to in the law variously as "obscenity" or "pornography."

Notwithstanding the oft-repeated statement of Supreme Court Justice Potter Stewart, who, in his concurring opinion in *Jacobellis v. Ohio*,[1] famously wrote,

> I have reached the conclusion, which I think is confirmed at least by negative implication in the Court's decisions since *Roth* and *Alberts*, that under the First and Fourteenth Amendments criminal laws in this area are constitutionally limited to hard-core pornography. I shall not attempt further to define the kinds of material I understand to be embraced within that shorthand description, and perhaps I could never succeed in

1. Jacobellis v. Ohio, 378 U.S. 184 (1964). Justice Stewart's quote is often incorrectly recast as "I can't define it, but I know it when I see it." As you can see, his actual words are a bit more nuanced than this recast version; however, the essential message—being the vagueness and ambiguity that plague the definition of obscene and/or pornographic material—remains valid.

> intelligibly doing so. But I know it when I see it, and the motion picture involved in this case is not that[,][2]

whether a work is obscene or pornographic is rarely something that all viewers or readers of it can unanimously agree on. And it is that chilling uncertainty that can lead to terrible results when a creator, distributor, or even simply a reader finds him- or herself ensnared in a legal battle, with years in prison at stake, over whether a given work is obscene.

The comic-book genre has not been immune from claims that a given book or series of books is obscene. Fortunately for comics writers, artists, publishers, distributors, and readers, there is an organization dedicated to offering protection to them when they are charged with the criminal offense of involvement with obscenity. Enter the Comic Book Legal Defense Fund.

1. The Origins of the Comic Book Legal Defense Fund[3]

By the fall of 1986, Denis Kitchen had been involved in the comic art and business fields for over 20 years. He was part of the group of artists who were active in the underground comix movement, which also included the now-famous artists Robert Crumb and Art Speigelman. Kitchen got involved in publishing during that time and founded the eponymous Kitchen Sink Press, a company he ran until 1999. Currently he is a co-owner and founder of a number of comics-related businesses, including Kitchen, Lind, and Associates, a company that packages books and represents cartoonists to the mainstream literary marketplace.[4] In December 1986, Kitchen received a telephone call from Frank Magiaracina, owner of a chain of comics stores in Indiana and Illinois called Friendly Franks. Frank told him that his store in Lansing, Illinois, had been the subject of a police raid. Six police officers had come into the shop and seized seven comic titles, including *Omaha the Cat Dancer, Weirdo,* and *Heavy Metal.* They arrested the store manager, Michael Correa, on charges of having obscene books on display and closed the Friendly Franks store for a five-day period.[5]

The arresting officer, Sgt. Jack Hoestra, told the *Gary Post-Tribune* newspaper that in addition to the legal charges of obscenity, he noticed a "satanic

2. *Id.* at 197.

3. This subsection dealing with the Comic Book Legal Defense Fund and the Charles Handley case is adapted from Chapters 9 and 10 of my book COMIC ART, CREATIVITY AND THE LAW (Edward Elgar Publ'g, Ltd. 2014).

4. Charles Brownstein, *Who Is Denis Kitchen? Snapshots from an Oddly Compelling Life, in* THE ODDLY COMPELLING ART OF DENIS KITCHEN 48 (Dark Horse Books 2010).

5. Press Release, Denis Kitchen, Origins of the Comic Book Legal Defense Fund 1 (2005) (on file with author). A few weeks after the original raid, the police added *Elektra: Assassin, Love & Rockets, Ms. Tree, Bodessey,* and *Elfquest* to the list of allegedly obscene material. *Id.*

influence" in many of the shops' comics. "Oh yes, there was absolutely a lot of satanic influence in the comics there," he told the paper. "If you know what you're looking for, you can see the satanic influence all over. Three-quarters of the rock groups today show satanic influence, and it's all over the television."[6]

Kitchen was appalled at the total lack of merit of the police action. He felt a personal sense of responsibility to try to help Magiaracina and Correa, because one of the titles seized, *Omaha the Cat Dancer,* was distributed by Kitchen Sink Press.[7] A short time after the raid, while he was attending a comics convention in St. Paul, Minnesota, he discussed with a few colleagues, who were equally outraged by the police action, what they could do to lend support to the legal defense effort. Kitchen came up with the idea of creating and selling limited-edition prints by an impressive array of artists under the rubric of a First Amendment portfolio. Adding his own contribution, he put together a group of 14 artists to create the portfolio and found a printer to print the work at cost. The resulting effort yielded a net profit of $20,000, which he put into a bank account that he named the Comic Book Legal Defense Fund.[8]

Before the funds raised could be put to use, the charges against the defendants went to trial, and the trial judge found Correa guilty of corruption charges. Using the money raised, Kitchen hired Burton Joseph, a well-known attorney who specialized in First Amendment cases and who had represented the Playboy Foundation, to appeal the conviction. The appeal was successful, and the conviction was overturned.[9]

Following the successful conclusion of the *Correa* case, Kitchen found that several thousand dollars remained in the bank fund. After discussing options with his colleagues in the venture, he decided that the Friendly Franks raid wasn't likely to be an isolated incident, so he took steps to create a 501(c)(3) nonprofit organization, using the same name he'd applied to the bank account—The

6. *Id.*

7. *Id.* Kitchen notes that although *Omaha the Cat Dancer* contains adult content (primarily nudity by the lead character, an anthropomorphic feline creature who works as a dancer in a strip club), the book had received critical praise all over the world and was one of the few comics in 1986 with a high female readership. *Id.*

8. *Id.* at 2. The artists contributing to the portfolio, and the work they were known for, were Sergio Aragones (*Mad Magazine*), Hilary Barta (*Plastic Man*), Reed Waller (*Omaha the Cat Dancer*), Steve Bissette (*Swamp Thing*), Bob Burden (*Flaming Carrot*), Richard Corben (*Bodessey*), Robert Crumb (*Weirdo* and *Zap*), Howard Cruse (*Wendel*), Will Eisner (*The Spirit*), Frank Miller (*Batman: The Dark Knight* and *Electra*), Mitch O'Connell & Don Simpson (*Megaton Man*), and Eric Vincent (*Alien Fire*).

9. *Id.* at 3. *See also CBLDF Case Files—Illinois v. Correa,* CBLDF, http://cbldf.org/about-us/case-files/correa (last visited Jan. 21, 2021); James A. Morrisard, *Comics Relief: CBLDF Comes to Legal Aid of Comic-Book Artist, Publishers, and Sellers,* Balt. City Paper (March 4, 1998). Kitchen points out the somewhat ironic circumstance that the judge in the case, Cook County Circuit Court Judge Paul Foxgrover, later pled guilty to charges of theft, forgery, and official misconduct that stem from his endorsement of $27,534 in restitution checks paid by defendants who appeared before him. *See, e.g., Ex-Judge Foxgrover Enters Guilty Plea,* Chi. Tribune (June 6, 1992), http://articles.chicagotribune.com/1992-06-06/news/9202200388_1_foxgrover-charges-guilty.

Comic Book Legal Defense Fund. The nonprofit status was obtained in 1990, and through additional fundraising, enough money was raised to hire a full-time executive director and a small staff and to fund an office. Originally located in Massachusetts, near Kitchen's home, the organization subsequently moved to New York City, where it presently occupies offices at 255 West 36th Street, Suite 501, in the heart of the city.

In the years that have followed the *Correa* case, the CBLDF has provided aid and assistance to comics creators, retailers, and even readers. The cases they have handled have included trademark law issues and copyright issues. The most frequent requests for their assistance continue to come on cases that go to the heart of the creative process of many comics writers and graphic artists—works of a sexually explicit nature that trigger obscenity prosecutions.

On occasion, the CBLDF is asked to provide expert witnesses for the defense in comics-related cases in which it is not initially involved or requested to provide counsel. The case of *United States v. Handley* is one such instance. The statutory basis for Handley's prosecution is so alarming and the outcome of the case is so unfortunate that they merit discussion in this chapter.

Christopher Handley fits a classic definition of what is known as a fanboy in the comics world. At the time of his arrest in May 2006, he was a single white male, sexually a virgin, living in a small town in Iowa at home with his mother.[10] Handley had done a term of service in the U.S. Navy and now worked as a computer programmer following a medical discharge from the service. His chief social outlets were his work and a Bible fellowship. He spent most of his spare time at his house, taking care of his mother and playing online fantasy games and reading comic books in the basement of the house.[11] He was an avid manga collector, owning several thousand manga comic books. A small subset of his collection included hentai manga, which is defined as sexually explicit manga featuring drawings of characters that appear as young girls, known as lolicon.[12]

The case began in May 2006, when Handley went to the post office to pick up a shipment of manga books he had received from Japan. The postal inspector had obtained a search warrant to search the package, based on the belief that it might contain cartoon images of objectionable content.[13] The inspector's

10. *CBLDF Case Files—U.S. v. Handley*, CBLDF, at 1–2, http://cbldf.org/about-us/case-files/handley (last visited Jan. 21, 2021).

11. *Id.*

12. *Id.* Of the over 1,200 manga comics in his collection, only a handful were hentai manga, and of those, only seven books were the focus of the government case. *Christopher Handley's Attorney Comments on His Case*, GoCollect (Mar. 2, 2010), https://blog.gocollect.com/christopher-handley-s-attorney-comments-on-his-case/.

13. Press Release, CBLDF to Serve as Special Consultant in PROTECT Act Manga Case 1 (Oct. 9, 2008), https://www.animenewsnetwork.com/press-release/2008-10-09/cbldf-to-serve-as-special-consultant-in-protect-act-manga-case (on file with author).

review of the package contents confirmed this suspicion, and law enforcement officials then waited for Handley to pick up the package. As he drove away from the post office, Handley was followed by a small flotilla of law enforcement officers, with representatives from the Postal Inspector's Office, the Immigration and Customs Enforcement Agency, special agents from the Iowa Division of Criminal Investigation, and officers from the local Glenwood Police Department all in the vehicles following him.[14] He was pulled over and ordered to proceed to his home, which the officers then searched, and they seized over 1,200 manga comic books, hundreds of DVDs, VHS tapes, laser disks, seven computers, and other documents.[15]

Handley hired well-known local defense attorney Eric Chase to represent him. Chase enlisted the CBLDF to provide expert testimony in the case. CBLDF's veteran legal counsel, Burton Joseph, explained why the fund was willing to help in the case:

> In the lengthy time in which I have represented CBLDF and its clients, I have never encountered a situation where criminal prosecution was brought against a private consumer for possession of material for his personal use in his own home. This prosecution has profound implications in limiting the First Amendment for art and artists, and comics in particular, that are on the cutting edge of creativity. It misunderstands the nature of avant-garde art in its historical perspective and is a perversion of anti-obscenity laws.[16]

The relevant language of the statute at issue in the *Handley* case, known as the PROTECT Act, provides as follows:

18 U.S.C. § 1466A: Obscene visual representations of the sexual abuse of children

A.

(a) In General.—Any person who, in a circumstance described in subsection (d), knowingly produces, distributes, receives, or possesses with intent to distribute, a visual depiction of any kind, including a drawing, cartoon, sculpture, or painting, that—

(1)(A) depicts a minor engaging in sexually explicit conduct; and

(B) is obscene; or

(2)(A) depicts an image that is, or appears to be, of a minor engaging in graphic bestiality, sadistic or masochistic abuse, or sexual intercourse,

14. *Id.*
15. *Id.*
16. *Id.*

including genital-genital, oral-genital, anal-genital, or oral-anal, whether between persons of the same or opposite sex; and

(B) lacks serious literary, artistic, political, or scientific value; or attempts or conspires to do so, shall be subject to the penalties provided in section 2252A(b)(1), including the penalties provided for cases involving a prior conviction.

(b) Additional Offenses.—Any person who, in a circumstance described in subsection (d), knowingly possesses a visual depiction of any kind, including a drawing, cartoon, sculpture, or painting, that—

(1)(A) depicts a minor engaging in sexually explicit conduct; and (B) is obscene; or

(2)(A) depicts an image that is, or appears to be, of a minor engaging in graphic bestiality, sadistic or masochistic abuse, or sexual intercourse, including genital-genital, oral-genital, anal-genital, or oral-anal, whether between persons of the same or opposite sex; and (B) lacks serious literary, artistic, political, or scientific value; or attempts or conspires to do so, shall be subject to the penalties provided in section 2252A(b)(2), including the penalties provided for cases involving a prior conviction.

(c) Nonrequired Element of Offense.—It is not a required element of any offense under this section that the minor depicted actually exist.

(d) Circumstances.—The circumstance referred to in subsections (a) and (b) is that—

(1) any communication involved in or made in furtherance of the offense is communicated or transported by the mail, or in interstate or foreign commerce by any means, including by computer, or any means or instrumentality of interstate or foreign commerce is otherwise used in committing or in furtherance of the commission of the offense; (2) any communication involved in or made in furtherance of the offense contemplates the transmission or transportation of a visual depiction by the mail, or in interstate or foreign commerce by any means, including by computer; (3) any person travels or is transported in interstate or foreign commerce in the course of the commission or in furtherance of the commission of the offense; (4) any visual depiction involved in the offense has been mailed, or has been shipped or transported in interstate or foreign commerce by any means, including by computer, or was produced using materials that have been mailed, or that have been shipped or transported in interstate or foreign commerce by any means, including by computer; or (5) the offense is committed in the special maritime and territorial jurisdiction of the United States or in any territory or possession of the United States.

(e) Affirmative Defense.—It shall be an affirmative defense to a charge of violating subsection (b) that the defendant—(1) possessed less than 3 such visual depictions; and (2) promptly and in good faith, and without retaining or allowing any person, other than a law enforcement agency, to access any such visual depiction—(A) took reasonable steps to destroy each such visual depiction; or (B) reported the matter to a law enforcement agency and afforded that agency access to each such visual depiction.

(f) Definitions.—For purposes of this section—(1) the term "visual depiction" includes undeveloped film and videotape, and data stored on a computer disk or by electronic means which is capable of conversion into a visual image, and also includes any photograph, film, video, picture, digital image or picture, computer image or picture, or computer generated image or picture, whether made or produced by electronic, mechanical, or other means; (2) the term "sexually explicit conduct" has the meaning given the term in section 2256(2)(A) or 2256(2)(B); and (3) the term "graphic," when used with respect to a depiction of sexually explicit conduct, means that a viewer can observe any part of the genitals or pubic area of any depicted person or animal during any part of the time that the sexually explicit conduct is being depicted.[17]

There are two important issues of concern in the enforceability of this section of the PROTECT Act. The first issue is that the section targets visual "representations" of the sexual abuse of children and is therefore not limited to photographs, film, or even drawings of actual children engaged in actual conduct—as subpart (c) notes, the minor depicted need not actually exist.[18] Thus a drawing of a fictional person, who appears to be a child, can form the basis of a violation of this law. This strikes at the heart of the creative process. A creator who creates a drawing of a person engaged in sexual activity of the nature proscribed by the statute may face prison for the creation of this artwork.

The second issue is that although subpart (a) limits offenses to those involving distribution, creation, receipt, or possession with intent to

17. 18 U.S.C. § 1466A (Obscene visual representations of the sexual abuse of children). The PROTECT Act appears to be Congress's response to the Supreme Court's decision in *Ashcroft v. Free Speech Coalition*, 534 U.S. 234 (2002), a case in which the Court found the Child Pornography Prevention Act of 1996 (CPPA), 18 U.S.C. § 2251 *et seq.*, abridges the freedom of speech. The CPPA attempted to extend the federal prohibition against child pornography to sexually explicit images that appeared to depict minors but were produced without using any real children—primarily through the use of digital techniques like morphing and using software (Photoshop) to create the impression that a photograph was one of a child, when in fact the body was of an adult and the head or face that of a child. The Supreme Court found that by prohibiting child pornography that did not depict an actual child, the statute went beyond the decision in *New York v. Ferber*, 458 U.S. 747 (1982), which had allowed a ban on child pornography even if the work was not obscene, per *Miller*, because of the state's interest in protecting the children exploited by the production process. *Ashcroft*, 534 U.S. at 239–41.

18. 18 U.S.C. § 1446A(c).

distribute, subpart (b) allows a finding of a violation of the law for mere possession, regardless of the presence of an intent to distribute.[19] Each of these issues presents serious constitutional concerns.

Turning to the first issue, that this law doesn't require an actual minor to be involved, this raises a real problem in determining that a violation has occurred, based on the age of the child involved. The definition of a minor, for purposes of this statute, is "any person under the age of eighteen years."[20] The problem this presents in an illustration of a fictional character is that a drawing isn't a person—it's a drawing. As the famous Magritte painting of a pipe notes, *Ceci n'est pas une pipe* ("this is not a pipe")—it is a drawing of a pipe.[21] The picture is not the thing it represents.

This begs the real question: how are we to determine the age of the minor if the picture depicts a representation of a person—who can say that the depiction is of a child below the age of 18, unless the text expressly states it is? It is difficult, if not impossible, to tell whether a person is under the age of 18 based solely on their physical appearance or clothing, except in the case of an infant or a very small child—once you depict a person in his or her teens, with obvious signs of having reached puberty, the actual age is very difficult to determine with any certainty. As a matter of law, this creates a terrible vagueness problem. And for creators, it creates a chilling effect and directly affects their work . . . draw a childish-appearing character, and you may face liability if any act depicted in connection with that character violates the rights of a living child under the relevant law.

The second issue, that the law makes mere possession of the prohibited materials an offense, seems to be in direct contradiction of the time-honored precedent established by the Supreme Court in its decision in *Stanley v. Georgia*,[22] in which the Court held that the possession of obscene materials in the privacy of one's own home was not unlawful.[23]

Both of these arguments were submitted by Eric Chase in support of a motion to dismiss the charges against Christopher Handley.[24] The District Court, engaging in some tortured logic, rejected both arguments.

19. 18 U.S.C. § 1446A(a).

20. 18 U.S.C. § 2256(1).

21. *See, e.g.*, www.artscenecal.com/ArticlesFile/Archive/.../RMagritteA.html, describing the 1929 painting by surrealist artist Rene Magritte of a tobacco pipe, with the words "Ceci n'est pas une pipe" written underneath it. Magritte's point is that the painting is not the thing—only a representation of the thing.

22. Stanley v. Georgia, 394 U.S. 557 (1969).

23. *Id.* at 559. Justice Marshall, writing for the majority: "For reasons set forth below, we agree that the mere possession of obscene matter cannot constitutionally be made a crime." *Id.*

24. CBLDF Case File, United States v. Christopher S. Handley, Case No. 1:07-cr-00030-JEG, U.S. Dist. Ct. Judge James E. Gritzner, Order on Motion to Dismiss, at 4–10 (S.D. Iowa July 2, 2008) (on file with author).

With respect to the argument that the definition of what "appears to be" a "minor" is void language due to vagueness, the Court, citing the Supreme Court's decision in *United States v. Williams*,[25] disagreed with Chase's argument, holding:

> The determination of what is, or appears to be, a minor does not require a wholly subjective judgment. The term "minor" has a statutory definition contained within the PROTECT Act and has a commonly understood meaning of being an individual under the age of eighteen. The phrase "appears to be" is not subject to differing interpretations, and the plain meaning of the phrase is clear.[26]

Clear as mud. This portion of the Court's order simply ducks the difficult question posed by Chase—how was Handley supposed to know that the fictional characters depicted in the manga books he purchased were under the age of 18? How can anyone tell if a character is 17 years, 11 months, and 29 days old, and thereby a minor, or two days older, and therefore no longer a minor and a lawful subject of illustration? As ridiculous as this distinction seems, when we acknowledge that making this distinction is the determining factor in whether you spend five years in jail, the absurdity of it takes on a much more sinister cast.

Judge Gritzner's order also makes short work of the *Stanley v. Georgia* argument on similarly shaky analysis. The Court finds that Handley was not being charged with mere private possession of obscene materials—he was charged with receipt of obscene materials that were transported in interstate commerce.[27] Judge Gritzner, citing the decisions in several prior federal and Supreme Court cases,[28] concludes:

> Thus, while an individual has a limited right to possess obscene materials in the privacy of his own home, there exists no right to receive or possess obscene materials that have been moved in interstate commerce, and that is the illegal conduct with which Defendant is charged.[29]

There are at least two problems with this analysis. If you are entitled to possess obscene material in the privacy of your own home, but you may not

---

25. United States v. Williams, 553 U.S. 285 (2008).
26. CBLDF Case File, *supra* note 24, at 10.
27. *Id.* at 5.
28. Judge Gritzner cites *United States v. 12 200-Foot Reels of Super 8mm. Film*, 412 U.S. 123, 126 (1973) (holding that *Stanley* was decided on privacy, and not First Amendment, grounds); *United States v. Orito*, 413 U.S. 139, 141 (1973) (rejecting the argument that *Stanley* created a correlative right to receive, transport, or distribute obscene materials in interstate commerce); and *United States v. Whorley*, 386 F. Supp. 2d 693 (Dist. Ct., E.D. Va. 2005) (holding that the zone of privacy in *Stanley* was limited and didn't extend to the receipt of legally offensive materials from the Internet). *Id.*
29. *Id.*

receive it via interstate commerce, how is it supposed to get into your home? Does this mean only locally, in-state-created obscene material may make its way lawfully into your home? How would law enforcement authorities be able to make such a distinction?

A second problem with this holding is that the language of *Stanley* does not appear to be as restrictive as the Court suggests it is. In fact, the Supreme Court in the *Stanley* decision speaks repeatedly about the freedom of individuals to "receive" information and ideas; as Justice Marshall wrote:

> It is now well established that the Constitution protects the right to receive information and ideas. "This freedom [of speech and press] . . . necessarily protects the right to receive . . . ." *Martin* v. *City of Struthers,* 319 U. S. 141, 143 (1943); see *Connecticut,* 381 U. S. 479, 482 (1965); *Lamont* v. *Postmaster General,* 381 U. S. 301, 307-308 (1965) (BRENNAN, J., concurring); cf. *Pierce* v. *Society of Sisters,* 268 U. S. 510 (1925). This right to receive information and ideas, regardless of their social worth, see *Winters* v. *New York,* 333 U. S. 507, 510 (1948), is fundamental to our free society. Moreover, in the context of this case—a prosecution for mere possession of printed or filmed matter in the privacy of a person's own home—that right takes on an added dimension. For also fundamental is the right to be free, except in very limited circumstances, from unwanted governmental intrusions into one's privacy.[30]

Justice William A. Douglas made it clear, in his concurrence with Justice Black's dissent in *United States v. Thirty-Seven (37) Photographs (Luros, Claimant),*[31] that unless the Court was reversing *Stanley,* it had to allow people to receive obscene materials for private use:

> Since the plurality opinion offers no plausible reason to distinguish private possession of "obscenity" from importation for private use, I can only conclude that at least four members of the Court would overrule Stanley. Or perhaps in the future that case will be recognized as good law only when a man writes salacious books in his attic, prints them in his basement, and reads them in his living room.[32]

---

30. Stanley v. Georgia, 394 U.S. 557, 564 (1969).

31. *United States v. Thirty-Seven (37) Photographs (Luros, Claimant),* 402 U.S. 363 (1971) (upholding a conviction for violation of the Tariff Act of 1930, 19 U.S.C. § 1305(a), against Milton Luros for bringing in his luggage on a return trip into the United States from Europe 37 allegedly obscene photos). Luros argued that under *Stanley v. Georgia* he was entitled to bring the photos into the country for his personal use. The U.S. District Court for the Central District of California agreed with this argument, and the government appealed. The majority held that *Stanley* did not extend to bringing materials into the country. *Id.* at 376–77.

32. *Id.* at 382.

Justice Douglas joined Justice Black in an expression of concern that the Court was abandoning "cherished freedoms," perhaps in response to political pressures of the times (this was the era of the Nixon presidency and the rejection of the findings of the President's Commission on Obscenity and Pornography[33]). Douglas wrote:

> I do not understand why the plurality feels so free to abandon previous precedents protecting the cherished freedoms of press and speech. I cannot, of course, believe it is bowing to popular passions and what it perceives to be the temper of the times. As I have said before, "Our Constitution was not written in the sands to be washed away by each wave of new judges blown in by each successive political wind that brings new political administrations into temporary power." *Turner* v. *United States,* 396 U. S. 398, 426 (1970) (BLACK, J., dissenting). In any society there come times when the public is seized with fear and the importance of basic freedoms is easily forgotten. I hope, however, "that in calmer times, when present pressures, passions and fears subside, this or some later Court will restore the First Amendment liberties to the high preferred place where they belong in a free society." *Dennis* v. *United States,* 341 U. S. 494, 581 (1951) (BLACK, J., dissenting).[34]

Judge Gritzner was not the judge who was going to restore Justice Douglas's cherished freedoms. While he did find one section of the PROTECT Act to be unconstitutional for failing to require a finding of obscenity as to certain materials prohibited by the Act, he also found that the remaining two sections of the Act, which do require a finding of obscenity under the standards set forth in *Miller v. California,* 413 U.S. 15 (1973), were constitutional.[35] Based on those findings, he found that there remained sufficient evidence of a possible violation of the Act to allow the case to go forward to trial.[36]

This left Handley facing a criminal trial with the possibility of a felony conviction and a five-year prison sentence. Handley accepted a plea bargain and pled guilty to "possessing obscene visual representations of the sexual abuse of children and mailing obscene material." On February 10, 2010, he was sentenced to six months in prison, plus a three-year supervised release

---

33. *See, e.g.,* Richard Nixon, *Statement about the Report of the Commission on Obscenity and Pornography,* AM. PRESIDENCY PROJECT (Oct. 24, 1970), https://www.presidency.ucsb.edu/node/240090.

34. *Thirty-Seven (37) Photographs,* 402 U.S. at 388.

35. CBLDF Case File, United States v. Christopher S. Handley, Case No. 1:07-cr-00030-JEG, U.S. Dist. Ct. Judge James E. Gritzner, Order on Motion to Dismiss, at 14 (S.D. Iowa July 2, 2008) (on file with author). Judge Gritzner found sections 1466(a)(2) and (b)(2), which banned pornography without making a determination that the materials either were obscene or involved the use of actual minors, were overbroad and unconstitutional. *Id.*

36. *Id.* at 18.

(psychological treatment) running concurrent with five years of probation, and he forfeited his entire manga collection and his other property that was seized.[37]

Commenting on the impact of this sorry result, CBLDF Executive Director Charles Brownstein noted:

> From start to finish, the case against Christopher Handley was an appalling abuse of the justice system. Chris Handley is going to jail not because of anything he did, but because of what he reads and thinks . . . . Putting Chris Handley in jail protects no one—he and his family are the only victims. . . . Chris Handley could be any of us. He was prosecuted not because he had engaged in any actions that were a danger to members of his community, but because of his tastes in entertainment. . . . When the government begins locking people up for the content of their intellect we are entering dangerous waters. Chris' case is appalling. One hopes that it is not a harbinger of things to come.[38]

So what is the fandom community to make of the *Handley* case? A few important take-away points emerge.

Obscenity laws exist in both state law and federal law contexts, so whether you are charged with a violation of federal or state law may depend on the context in which the charges are brought. If, for example, you are involved in the transmittal of sexually explicit materials via the U.S. mail system, or online where your communication crosses state lines, you are engaged in the kind of interstate commerce that may trigger federal law, and any works involved will be subject to federal laws like the PROTECT Act.

On the other hand, if you are simply in possession of explicit sexual materials or have limited your distribution of them to within your state, or if you are a retailer of items charged as being pornographic, you may be subject to state obscenity laws, many of which are closely modeled after federal laws but some of which can have significant differences. So bottom line, if you are

37. *CBLDF Case Files—U.S. v. Handley*, CBLDF, at 1, http://cbldf.org/about-us/case-files/handley (last visited Jan. 21, 2021); *Christopher Handley's Attorney Comments on His Case*, GoCollect 1 (Mar. 2, 2010), https://blog.gocollect.com/christopher-handley-s-attorney-comments-on-his-case/. Chase notes that the sentencing recommendation was that Handley spend the six-month sentence in a halfway house, as opposed to jail. *Id.*

38. *CBLDF Case Files—U.S. v. Handley*, CBLDF, at 2, http://cbldf.org/about-us/case-files/handley (last visited Jan. 21, 2021). It is important to note that the five cases summarized here are not all of the cases handled by CBLDF since the fund began its work. Other cases have dealt with issues relating to parody and fair use, which are beyond the scope of this chapter. It is also appropriate to acknowledge that in many instances, CBLDF is able, by retaining counsel and sending a letter to a district attorney or prosecutor who is threatening to bring criminal obscenity charges against a comic store owner, distributor, creator, or collector, to head off the threatened prosecution by pointing out the available First Amendment defense arguments.

engaged in fan-created sexually explicit materials, you would be wise to familiarize yourself with the applicable laws relating to that kind of material in your jurisdiction.

The other point to consider is that whose standards apply in the determination of whether a given work is deemed obscene is a legal minefield of uncertainty. When the Supreme Court, in the *Miller v. California* case, established that obscenity had to be determined based on "local community standards," they failed to define what the relevant community was. The decision refers generally to the standards of the citizens of the state of California, which of course is a meaningless term. In my hometown of San Francisco, standards of what people consider obscene vary from street to street, neighborhood to neighborhood—with no clear standard at all. Multiply this level of uncertainty to the point of asking what is the community standard definition of obscenity on the entire Internet, and the absurdity of the question becomes manifest.

But this is not just a theoretical discussion—people go to jail for violating the local community standard, so the only practical approach to take, if you are going to be creating fan works, is to spend some time canvassing your community, talking to district attorneys and arts groups in the community, and making a diligent effort to determine what local law enforcement is going to view as a violation of those community standards. And also, if you think there is at least a possibility that your creation may land you in trouble, have the phone number and email address for CBLDF on speed dial—you might need them.

B. The CASE Act: Addressing the Problem of Orphan Works and Related Issues

"Orphan works" have posed problems for creators and copyright lawyers for decades. The basic problem is this—despite the fact that copyright-protected works pre-1909 had to bear a copyright notice identifying the name of the creator and the year of creation, and post–1976 Act works are still encouraged to display the same identifying information, many works are published without that information, or even if they do have the information, the whereabouts of the current owner of the work may be unknown, for various reasons. The work, and accompanying copyright, may have been transferred to a third party; the original owner may have died and the work is now in the hands of heirs. And many such works, particularly photographs, were published without proper, traceable information identifying who the owner is and how to find him or her. Because the parent of the work is not findable, the work is deemed an orphan work.

So why is this a problem? It is a problem because using a work that does not belong to you, when you know that the original owner, who now can't be found, at one time claimed copyright in the work—a copyright that might still be in force—subjects you to liability for willful copyright infringement, which carries a statutory penalty of up to $150,000! And even if your unauthorized use is found only to be unintentional, rather than willful, the statutory penalty could reach $30,000.

Faced with such a risk, many creators hesitate to use or incorporate orphan works into their own work—often depriving them of great material that could be of value in their new work. A fan writing a book in the style of Jack London who finds a great photo of London he wants to use in his book may be unable to do so if he can't find the owner of the copyright in the photo. And sometimes, taking the risk that the orphan work's true owner will never find out what you have done with the work leads to negative, and expensive, outcomes, as the following anecdote from my own practice illustrates.

Some years ago, I met with two clients who recounted the following situation: they had decided, together with a group of friends, that they wanted to create a musical adaptation for the stage of a well-known romantic comedy film from the 1940s. This was a mainstream film that had experienced great box-office results when it was released and was still remembered fondly by many fans.

The clients explained that they had exercised due diligence in trying to track down the owners of the rights to the underlying story the film was based on. They started with the name of the author of the story but ran into a dead end. The author had died years ago, and there was no record of a widow or any children. A relative of the author was contacted but had no helpful information on the location of any heirs. The owners of the long-defunct film production company could offer no help—they confirmed that the only rights they owned were for the film adaptation of the work. So far as they knew, the author still held the rights to theatrical adaptations.

Convinced that there simply were no heirs who retained any rights to the literary work and that it was a truly orphaned work, my clients had developed a script, hired a few cast members, and sponsored a series of well-publicized backer's auditions in New York City, as they went about the expensive process of raising the funding for a Broadway play. What happened next brought them into my law office in San Francisco, which was their home base as well.

They had received a letter from a firm of British solicitors[39] in London, advising them that the firm represented the son and daughter of the author of the work. The author had engaged in a short-lived marriage to a British woman, which had ended in divorce, but only after the birth of the two children, who

39. Lawyers who do not do trial work in the United Kingdom are known as solicitors; lawyers who go to trial are called barristers.

had spent their entire life using their mother's maiden name and living in Britain, which is why my clients weren't able to find them.

The solicitor advised that his clients were opposed to the proposed production, were not willing to license use of the work to my clients, and threatened that unless my clients ceased all efforts to go forward with this adaptation project, they would engage barristers in London, and litigators in New York, and sue for intentional copyright infringement. All efforts at negotiation or settlement of the matter were rejected.

And so ultimately my clients, in order to avoid what was likely going to be a substantial undertaking to litigate their claim to be entitled to produce the show, recognizing that the likelihood was that they would lose in the litigation, gave up. They settled with the heirs by agreeing to relinquish any claim to the rights, to destroy all production-related materials, and to cease all efforts on the project in exchange for a release that allowed them to avoid being sued. This is only one example of many for how misunderstanding the law related to orphan works could lead to disastrous consequences for fans who want to create a work based on a popular work from the past.

As stories of problems like this one reached Congress, members began to think something needed to be done. And so for a number of years in the early 2000s, a series of bills were proposed in Congress under the general heading of the Orphan Works bill. Most of the versions of this bill shared similar properties—they provided for the creation of a registry of copyright-protected works, in which all works granted statutory copyright were to be listed. This way, if a creator wanted to use any or all of the previously created work, the creator could check the registry, and if they found the work, they could contact the owner of the original work and negotiate an appropriate license and fee.

The key part of the Act was that if the true owner could not be found, after a diligent search of the registry and other efforts, the creator could not be sued for statutory damages under the Copyright Act, and damages instead would be limited to the fair market value of a license for the work—which, the theory went, was all the original owner was really entitled to.

Support for the various iterations of the Orphan Works bills was far from unanimous. In particular, photographers were strongly opposed. They argued that eliminating their ability to seek statutory damages would make it impossible for them to recover damages in infringement cases, because the cost of litigation would far exceed the fair market value of the license fee they would be seeking to recover. Public archives similarly objected to terms in the bills requiring them to pay a nominal fee for use of orphan works, arguing that there should be no fee imposed at all. In sum, an array of stakeholders objected to each iteration of the Orphan Works bill and succeeded in ending its prospects in Congress.

One concern from the Orphan Works debate survived—the idea of addressing the concerns of photographers that the cost of pursuing infringement actions was too high, so they needed to retain the right to pursue statutory damages to offset those high costs. Congress's solution to that concern is the Copyright Alternative in Small Claims Enforcement Act of 2019, also known as the CASE Act.

Opinions regarding the merits of the CASE Act vary widely. While I don't always quote verbatim from sources other than case decisions, in this instance I am including full and direct quotes of the opinions voiced by the various stakeholders in the CASE Act debate so readers can get the full flavor of the debate, which will help you understand why it remains an unresolved matter.

In a statement submitted to the Subcommittee on Intellectual Property of the U.S. Senate Judiciary Committee, Register of Copyrights (the register is the director of the U.S. Copyright Office) Karyn A. Temple outlined the need for, and parameters of, the proposed Copyright Small Claims Court that is the heart of the CASE Act:

> I would also like to take the opportunity to discuss one policy issue for which the Copyright Office has provided legislative support over the past few years: the possibility of a small claims tribunal within the Copyright Office. The Copyright Office identified the creation of such a small claims tribunal as a topic worthy of further study as far back as 2006, during its participation in Congress' review of the orphan works problem.
>
> As we discussed in our 2013 report, Copyright Small Claims, the costs and burdens of federal copyright litigation effectively prevent many who do not have extensive resources from bringing suit to enforce their rights or to obtain a declaratory judgment of non-infringement. In 2017, the median cost to litigate a copyright infringement suit with less than $1 million at stake was estimated at $200,000.
>
> Given the complexity of complying with the Federal Rules of Civil Procedure and Federal Rules of Evidence, as well as the vigorous motion practice typical of infringement cases in district court, few parties would be capable of proceeding without an attorney. However, according to a survey conducted by the American Bar Association's section on intellectual property law, only thirty-two percent of the lawyers surveyed indicated that they would be willing to accept a case with less than $30,000 at stake, which would exclude many individual artists and creators from representation.
>
> Federal litigation is also a very time-consuming business, with the median time to trial in the Southern District of New York at 720 days. As we found in our study, these hurdles have an appreciable negative

impact on small creators of all kinds. The Songwriter's Guild of America, while noting that individual online infringements of their works "may seem unimportant," pointed out that, "taken in the aggregate, they have an effect on the livelihoods of individual creators akin to the infamous torture 'death by a thousand cuts.'"

As the Copyright Office heard during the course of its study regarding a small claims tribunal, a songwriter, musician, artist, app developer, or author often lacks the ability to enforce their copyright interests against unauthorized uses of their work, even in markedly commercial contexts. Similarly, individual creators on YouTube can find their viewership and incomes negatively impacted when their videos are improperly taken down and they are unable to obtain a timely declaration of non-infringement.

The experiences of individual photographers and other visual artists are particularly compelling. These artists work under a "high volume, low value" business model, and typically earn $50,000 or less per year from licensing their work at rates of just a few hundred dollars (or less) per use. As a result, they are often unable to invest the resources necessary to enforce their copyrights in federal district court.

For this reason, many photographers and visual artists strongly support the idea of a copyright small claims tribunal. Jenna Close, a commercial photographer, spoke at a September 2018 hearing of the Committee on the Judiciary of the U.S. House of Representatives about her support for a small claims bill. As part of her testimony, Ms. Close relayed her personal experience of "witness[ing] [her] photos enlarged as the backdrop to a competitor's tradeshow booth, while [her] paying client was rightfully using the same art work at the same trade show in their own booth."

Despite this, she did not pursue a claim due to the fact that "[f]ederal court litigation is too burdensome and too expensive." Overall, this means that low-dollar but still valuable copyrighted works are frequently infringed with impunity, and individual creators and small businesses often lacking [sic] an effective remedy. The cost of federal court litigation can likewise be prohibitive for an independent filmmaker that wants to obtain a declaration of non-infringement for their use of copyrighted footage in a documentary, but cannot afford to spend $200,000 or more on litigation to obtain a declaratory judgement. Such hurdles may be insurmountable, even if the filmmaker has a strong fair use defense or is otherwise using a copyrighted work pursuant to an exception or limitation that allows such use.

For this reason, the Copyright Office strongly supports a small claims tribunal structured along the lines of the proposal detailed in the Copyright Office's 2013 report. Specifically, such a tribunal should

> be situated in the Copyright Office, with officers recommended by the Register and appointed by the Librarian of Congress, who should, between them, have a background of representing both copyright owners and users. Unlike federal district court, this would ensure that the individuals hearing a claim have specialized expertise in copyright law, and would promote a balanced tribunal. Likewise, to address constitutional and due process concerns, the Copyright Office strongly believes that participation in such tribunal should be voluntary. After studying the matter, the Copyright Office concluded that either an opt-out or an opt-in system would adequately address these concerns. The CASE Act's experience requirements for the CCB officers would further ensure that all claims are resolved by individuals with a significant understanding of and grounding in federal copyright law. These provisions, combined with the extensive notice requirements and due process safeguards for respondents, would provide important safeguards against the use of the CCB by bad faith claimants to ensure that the CCB remains focused on resolving the larger body of cases involving situations of clear infringements for which the copyright holder is unable to realistically access federal district courts due to the high cost of litigation, or clear instances where a declaration of non-infringement is appropriate.[40]

As described, this small-claims process certainly seemed like a solution to the problem of the high cost and complexity of copyright infringement litigation that was precluding worthy, but small-dollar-value, cases from being prosecuted. The CASE Act was passed with bipartisan support by the House of Representatives and sent to the Senate Judiciary Committee. It was subsequently reported out to the full Senate—and after much delay was finally passed by the Senate, and was thereafter signed by the president. Perhaps one reason it was stalled for so long is that in the months that followed Temple's statement, significant stakeholders in the copyright arena voiced strong objection to a number of its provisions.

Katharine Trendacosta, writing on the webpage of the Electronic Frontier Foundation (EFF),[41] in an article entitled "Congress Continues to Ignore the Dangerous Flaws of the CASE Act,"[42] summarized the leading criticisms of the Act as follows:

---

40. Statement of Karyn A. Temple, U.S. Register of Copyrights, before the Subcomm. on Intellectual Prop. Comm. on the Judiciary, U.S. Senate (July 30, 2019), https://www.copyright.gov/laws/hearings/testimony-of-karyn-temple-for-july-30-oversight-hearing.pdf.

41. The EFF characterizes itself as "[t]he leading nonprofit defending digital privacy, free speech and innovation" (https://www.eff.org, last visited Jan. 22, 2021).

42. Katharine Trendacosta, *Congress Continues to Ignore the Dangerous Flaws of the CASE Act*, Elec. Frontier Found. (Sept. 11, 2019), https://www.eff.org/deeplinks/2019/09/congress-continues-ignore-dangerous-flaws-case-act.

The Copyright Alternative in Small-Claims Enforcement Act (CASE Act) is one of those (mostly) bad ideas that just won't go away. It feels like a simple and easy solution to a thorny problem in copyright law: streamlining the dispute process. But as often happens, this solution is neither simple nor easy.

The U.S. House of Representatives' Committee on the Judiciary followed its counterpart in the Senate by passing the CASE Act out of committee. This means that the whole House could vote to pass it, without bothering to fix any of its many flaws.

That would be a profound mistake.

The CASE Act's goal is to make it simple and fast for copyright holders to get paid for infringement claims. The method it employs is to create a quasi-judicial body in the Copyright Office called the "Copyright Claims Board," which would be able to award damages as high as $30,000 per proceeding, while also strictly limiting the ability of parties to appeal the decisions. $30,000 judgments issued by people who are not judges but rather officers of the Copyright Office, who see copyright *holders*—not the general public—as their customers, are not "small claims." These are judgments that could ruin the lives of regular people; people who are engaging in the things we all do when we're online: sharing memes, sharing videos, and downloading images.

During the mark up hearing, we once again heard the CASE Act described as a "voluntary" small claims system.

The CASE Act is not as "voluntary" as its boosters say it is. It cannot be emphasized enough how inadequate an "opt-out" system is. The way the CASE Act is currently structured, the Copyright Office sends a notice about the complaint to someone along with information about how to opt out. If they don't opt out within 60 days of the notice—in whatever way the Copyright Office decides is the proper way to opt out—then the person is bound to whatever decision is made by the Claims Board, even if they don't respond at all or don't show up.

This is hardly a clear and easy process, particularly since it will come from a board most regular people have never heard of. Companies and people who have lawyers will know if they should to [sic] opt out. But the average Internet user will not, which means they will risk facing a huge judgment, potentially without ever having presented their side of the story.

Instead of a friendly and "voluntary" dispute system, CASE will create a new procedure for copyright trolls. Copyright trolls don't make money through creating art, but through litigation and legal threats that target infringers and non-infringers alike. Courts have been reining in this activity, but the Copyright Claims Board will have none of

> the protections that those courts have established. Thus, CASE creates a quick and cheap way to collect on a large number of claims, without the review they might receive in a real court. And, given the amounts the CASE Act empowers the Claims Board toward, it will also make it easy for trolls to file a claim and then simply tell their targets to settle for what is still a significant amount, but less ruinous than the worst-case scenario of going through the full CASE Act process.
>
> All of these problems don't even include another huge flaw in the CASE Act: its new dispute system has to pass Constitutional muster. First, it's not clear that Congress can just assign some copyright disputes to an administrative tribunal—particularly given that they may implicate fundamental speech concerns. Second, the proposed "opt-out" process is not just unfair—it's potentially a violation of your constitutional right to due process.
>
> There are just too many problems with the CASE Act for it to be a viable solution to the problem it's supposed to solve. Tell your representatives to vote "no" on the CASE Act.[43]

Similar concerns were voiced by New York IP attorney and writer Mitchell Stein, writing on the IP Watchdog site, who offered this commentary:

The Case Act: Good Intentions but Bad Policy

> On October 22, the U.S. House of Representatives passed, by a vote of 410-6, the Copyright Alternative in Small-Claims Enforcement Act (the "CASE Act"). The Act proposes to set up what is in essence a voluntary administrative procedure conducted in the U.S. Copyright Office whereby artists and other copyright holders can protect their copyrights without the cost, expense and difficulty associated with filing a full-blown copyright infringement litigation in federal court.
>
> Based on the vote in the House, the CASE Act appears to enjoy widespread, bipartisan support in Congress—a rarity these days, to be sure. The appeal is simple: give individual artists and small companies an affordable mechanism to enforce their rights in their creative works. But although the political appeal of the CASE Act is obvious, the practical reality of the CASE Act is something entirely different. Indeed, there are three gaping holes in the CASE Act which may cause the small claims process it sets forth to have only very narrow appeal and to be an effective dispute resolution mechanism in only a narrow subset of cases.

43. *Id.*

Big Companies and Trolls Still Win

The first of these holes is that the process is voluntary for both plaintiff and defendant. If an individual artist wishes to take on a big company under the CASE Act, the better-funded big company may decide to opt out of the proceeding, putting the plaintiff in the exact same bind the CASE Act was designed to cure. Alternately, if the big company is clearly or probably liable, it may decide to keep the proceeding in the Copyright Office, to benefit from the $30,000 cap on liability under the Act. In either event, the big company gets its preferred choice of forum.

The second hole derives from unusual features of the Copyright Act itself. Unlike most U.S. statutory claims, and all common law claims in the United States, a plaintiff who prevails on a copyright infringement case in federal court may recover their reasonable attorney's fees. This fee-shifting provision of the Copyright Act was enacted to provide poorly funded plaintiffs and their counsel with a financial incentive to protect their copyrights; such plaintiffs would be made whole financially by recovering both attorney's fees and damages. Indeed, the threat of having to pay a plaintiff both damages and their attorney's fees is perhaps one of the leading factors contributing to early copyright settlements. Even if damages are low, a prolonged copyright case that a defendant loses could end up costing a lot of money to compensate a prevailing plaintiff for attorney's fees. Additionally, the Copyright Act provides for recovery of "statutory damages" of up to $30,000 per copyright infringed, or, in the case of willful infringement, up to $150,000 per copyright infringed, even if the plaintiff's actual damages were nominal.

The fact that the Copyright Act permits fee-shifting and statutory damages has contributed to the rise in recent years of "copyright troll" law firms, whose business model involves representing as many photographers and artists as they can find, then threatening to file infringement lawsuits and trying to obtain quick settlements under the threat that a prolonged suit will end up costing the defendant the plaintiff's attorney's fees and/or statutory damages. Clients of copyright trolls often do not pay the firm's hourly rates, but instead agree that the firm may keep a portion of the recovery. By way of example, one of these firms has been reported to have filed over 500 cases between 2016 and 2018. The number of demand letters the firm has sent and received a settlement payment prior to filing in addition to filing suits is unknown.

For copyright trolls and the artists they represent, proceeding in the Copyright Office under the CASE Act has little to no appeal. The financial leverage on which they rely—threats of recovering attorney fees and statutory damages for willful infringement—are not available under the

> CASE Act. Also, there is no cost savings to the clients of copyright trolls, as they are enjoying the benefit of representation without having to pay attorney hourly rates.
>
> *The Benefits Aren't Broad Enough*
>
> The third major hole in the CASE Act is that, under the current legislation, a decision by the Copyright Office in a CASE Act proceeding regarding who owns a contested copyright is not a binding decision and cannot be enforced in court. For this subset of copyright disputes, CASE Act proceedings will not provide a satisfactory outcome.
>
> So, who will find CASE Act proceedings an attractive alternative? Certainly, individual and small business copyright owners who want to prevent other individuals and small businesses from using their copyrighted works. Individuals and companies named as a defendant in a CASE Act proceeding that can afford the costs of federal litigation, however, will opt to stay in a CASE Act proceeding only in rare circumstance where the benefits of the Act's $30,000 liability cap outweigh the tactical and strategic advantages that can be gained by "lawyering up" and being better funded than one's opponent in a federal litigation. Finally, copyright trolls and their clients should have no interest in starting CASE Act proceedings, as doing so leaves their best weapons—the threat of attorney's fees and recovery of statutory damages for willful infringement—on the sidelines.[44]

And finally, Judy Perry Martinez, the American Bar Association's then-president, weighed in with the ABA's official position on the CASE Act, which was as follows:

> Congress has an opportunity to join together and pass legislation that will provide authors, artists and other creators with a meaningful way to protect their work. Both houses of Congress will soon be voting on the Copyright Alternative in Small-Claims Enforcement Act of 2019 (the "CASE Act"), which creates an alternative forum to pursue low value claims of copyright infringement.
>
> Under the current system, authors whose work has been copied or infringed upon have no cost-effective way to get compensated. The high cost of legal action they need to take (sometimes tens of thousands of dollars) could significantly outweigh the damages they might be awarded. They also can't bring a claim in a state court because the law requires copyright cases to be heard in federal court.

---

44. Mitchell Stein, *The Case Act: Good Intentions but Bad Policy*, IP Watchdog (Nov. 4, 2019), https://www.ipwatchdog.com/2019/11/04/case-act-good-intentions-bad-policy/id=115539/.

> Copyright owners with small infringement claims essentially have a right without a remedy. When the cost of bringing a federal lawsuit significantly outstrips the value of their claims, this hinders copyright law from fulfilling its central function of incentivizing the creation of new expressive works.
>
> If enacted, the CASE Act will avoid costly copyright lawsuits by establishing a Copyright Claims Board within the United States Copyright Office to resolve claims up to $15,000 for a single work and up to $30,000 in one proceeding in which two or more claims are asserted.
>
> While the CASE Act will provide more cost-effective protection for plaintiffs, copyright defendants will also benefit from the proposed legislation. Currently, defendants can be burdened with significant legal costs and drawn out suits, even where their use is a fair use or otherwise lawful. Participation in a small claims proceeding would cap their damages and likely provide a faster resolution of the dispute.
>
> Participation in the program would be entirely voluntary, and parties could proceed with or without attorneys. Proceedings could be held through phone or videoconferences. Lawyers well-versed in copyright and alternative dispute resolution would decide the claims. The CASE Act would bring positive change to the copyright system by providing copyright holders with a realistic means to protect their works.
>
> Critics have expressed concern that the proposed legislation could deny defendants the right to appeal decisions. Opponents are also opposed to making defendants opt-out of the proceedings if they do not want to participate rather than opting-in if they do. The ABA believes the legislation provides ample opportunity for challenge and review of decisions consistent with constitutional norms. We also consider the "opt-out" path the right one since it provides the parties a better ability to pursue claims against uncooperative respondents.
>
> Both the Senate and House Judiciary committees have already passed the CASE Act this summer. The legislation is now ready to be brought to the floor of both chambers for a full vote. The ABA urges all senators and representatives to support this important legislation.[45]

For fan creators of works based on pop-culture materials, the ability to use orphan works without fear of punishingly expensive copyright infringement claims is an important benefit. Whether the CASE Act is the best vehicle to achieve that goal isn't clear. With the bill finally moving from Congress to the president's desk for signature, we'll see if it lives up to its promises. After 14

45. Judy Perry Martinez, *The Case for the CASE Act*, The Hill (Oct. 21, 2019), https://thehill.com/blogs/congress-blog/judicial/466742-the-case-for-the-case-act.

years of attempting to resolve the orphan-works problem, the solution remains elusive—stay tuned.

C. Two Short Notes on Fandom and Trademark Law and Right-of-Publicity Law

These last two areas of the law that, to the extent they apply to any aspect of fan-created works, apply to all of them, are also areas that for good reason have little overall applicability to fandom. So while it would be an error of omission to not mention them, they warrant only these few brief words.

Trademark law is the law that helps the general public avoid being confused about the source of the goods and services they purchase or acquire and that secondarily allows the owners of the brands by which those items are identified the right to exclusive use of those brands and the right under the law to prosecute infringements. Those rights of prosecution are limited, however, in ways that render the appearance of brands in fan-created works not likely to draw an infringement action.

The principal limitation relevant here is what is called the defense of nominative fair use. This defense allows the use of a trademark so long as it doesn't cause confusion as to the source of the goods and doesn't dilute or tarnish the good reputation of well-known trademarks/brands. So a fan-fiction story in which Tony Stark and Pepper Potts go out to a McDonalds on Sunset after a long night of crime fighting isn't going to draw a complaint from McDonalds. Their trademark is used in a nominative manner—one that doesn't attempt to make use of the mark in a way that will confuse anyone or suggest that the brand is owned by the author of the story.

For that reason, we have seen virtually no lawsuits for trademark infringement related to fandom or fan-created works that made it into the courts, particularly up to the courts of appeal where we would see a published court opinion on the case. The one slightly odd exception to this pattern arose as a result of a late-2015 application by a company that sought to obtain a federal trademark on the word "FANDOM," which they claimed they used, according to their application to the Trademark Office, in connection with entertainment services, specifically an ongoing series of documentary films and a related website.[46]

This petition was filed by the Organization for Transformative Works, a nonprofit organization supportive of fandom and fan culture (discussed in detail in Chapter 7). The petition argues with great strength and clarity that

46. Petition for Cancellation of the Mark: FANDOM, Reg. No. 4,863,676, https://www.transformativeworks.org/wp-content/uploads/2016/08/Petition-to-cancel-FANDOM-mark.pdf (last visited Jan. 22, 2021).

the term "fandom" is a generic term in wide use by the general public and is therefore not an appropriate subject for a grant of exclusive trademark rights. Apparently the company that filed the application recognized its overreach, and the application was withdrawn. Other than this one instance, there simply doesn't appear, as of this writing, to have been any suits filed for trademark infringement in the fandom space.

That said, I would be remiss in leaving this subject without sounding a warning bell for creators on this subject. Trademark holders take a very dim view of creators whose works unduly disparage or falsely accuse the brand of any wrongdoing, or faulty quality in the goods or services, and will be quick to file trade disparagement claims in the form of defamation claims or trademark infringement by tarnishment or dilution claims.

An example of this is the 1996 lawsuit filed by the famous Ringling Bros. circus,[47] holder of the trademarked phrase "The Greatest Show on Earth," against the state of Utah, which was using the clever play on words "The Greatest Snow on Earth" to promote winter sports tourism. While Ringling lost the suit, because the Court found no evidence that anyone was confused by the two slogans and the circus's reputation was not tarnished by the reference, it has only been in these kinds of cases that we have seen any kind of claims filed.

The right of publicity (ROP) presents a different profile in the law. This right, which began its life as one of the four rights of privacy, gives an individual the right to control the manner in which his or her name, image, and/or likeness may be used in commercial contexts. In sum, it prevents a third party from using the right of publicity of the individual without consent in commercial contexts (such as using a person's picture to help sell a product or service). The most common context in which these cases arise is when a well-known person, and/or a celebrity, claims his or her right of publicity has been misappropriated. Over the years, a series of court decisions expanded the "elements of identifiability," which comprise the right of publicity, to include slogans about people (like "Here's Johnny"), the sound of their voice, and their characteristic clothing.[48] Some judges argue that these extensions go too far and unduly limit First Amendment rights.[49]

For a fairly obvious reason, we again rarely see cases of alleged violation of the right of publicity in the context of fan-created works. That reason is that virtually all fan-created works are, by definition, versions of fictional stories, featuring fictional, rather than real living, people. Since the right of publicity requires that the claim be filed by an actual real person, a fictional character can't qualify, and since authors don't own the right of publicity of their characters, it follows that ROP cases typically don't arise in the fandom space.

---

47. Ringling Bros. v. Utah Div. of Travel, 955 F. Supp. 598 (E.D. Va. 1997).
48. *See, e.g.*, Vanna White v. Samsung Elecs., 971 F.2d 1395 (1992).
49. *Id.* at 1402 (dissenting and concurring opinion of Alarcon, J.).

Moreover, fan-created works don't tend to generate either the money or the reputational damage that typifies ROP cases.

In recent years, we have seen a few exceptions to this general principle, which, while interesting cases that involve other legal doctrines discussed in this section, do not involve fan-created works. The first of these cases dealt with a close friend of one of two actresses involved in a legendary feud. At issue was how she, as a real person, was portrayed by another actress in a docudrama.

So legendary was their battle that the name of the television movie that sparked the case was *Feud*, produced by FX Networks. The docudrama focused on the battle between iconic actresses Bette Davis and Joan Crawford. Another famous actress of the same era, Olivia de Havilland, brought suit against FX, alleging that the manner in which she was portrayed in the movie, among claims of defamation and related arguments, also violated her right of publicity. Relying on the oft-used defense in such cases, that the First Amendment protected FX from suit, the California Court of Appeals for the Second Circuit reversed the trial court's order denying dismissal of the case at the pleadings stage, and that ended that.[50]

In the second instance, a series of cases involved college football players whose real names and images were used to create characters in computer video games, without their consent. In *Hart v. Electronic Arts*,[51] a college football player argued that a videogame manufacturer violated his right of publicity by creating an avatar with his features, name, and characteristics for use in the game. The Ninth Circuit Court of Appeals in California, which has handled many ROP cases, rejected the player's claims, once again on First Amendment grounds.

So while creative lawyers may someday in the future come up with allegations of violations of these laws that will apply to works created by fans, we aren't at that point yet—with one possible exception, arising in cases where a fictional character becomes identified with a particular actor and that actor's image is depicted in a work of fan art—more about that in Chapter 8.

50. De Havilland v. FX Networks, LLC, 21 Cal. App. 5th 845 (2018).
51. Hart v. Elec. Arts, 717 F.3d 141 (2013).

SECTION 3

The Narrow Brush: Legal Doctrines and Fan Fiction, Art, Film, and Cosplay

CHAPTER 7

Fan Fiction

Adding to the definitions of "fan fiction" I offered in the introduction is this one, written by a law student in 1997—a student who would become one of the leading scholars in, and an acafan of, fan fiction: professor (and then student) Rebecca Tushnet. Her definition was: "'Fan fiction,' broadly speaking, is any kind of written creativity that is based on an identifiable segment of popular culture, such as a television show, and is not produced as 'professional' writing."[1] Based on that definition, she begins her article by repeating the generally accepted view that fan fiction had its origins in stories based on the *Star Trek* television series and its iconic characters. Many of those stories focused on romantic relationships between the characters, prominently including homosexual relationships between Captain Kirk and Chief Officer Spock, which in turn sparked the creation of the phrase "slash" fiction, referring to fan fiction about same-sex romantic relationships.[2]

In the pre-Internet era, fan-fiction writers had few outlets for submission of their works and few readers as well. The digital revolution irrevocably changed fan fiction into a huge, global activity. An unverified 2018 report claimed that FanFiction.Net (FFN), the largest repository of fan fiction, had over 12 million registered users and was hosting submissions from over 40 countries.

A 2011 research report on fan-fiction demographics conducted by researchers at FFN, at a point when they had a little over 6 million registered users, found that the majority of the users were in the United States and that 78 percent of the

1. Rebecca Tushnet, *Legal Fictions: Copyright, Fan Fiction, and a New Copyright Law*, 17 Loy. L.A. Ent. L. Rev. 651 (1997).

2. *Id.* at 655.

members/users were female and 22 percent were male. At the time of this study, the average age of FFN users was 15.8 years and the median age was 15.[3]

These age and gender statistics, coupled with the amateur status of most fan-fiction creators, has led not surprisingly to criticism of fan fiction as being in some way less legitimate than other forms of fiction. The dependence in fan fiction on the original characters and their universe, created by the primary author, also gives rise to claims that fan-fiction writers lack originality and overall writing talent.

In a brilliant and mordant article entitled *When Men Write Fanfiction, It Isn't Fanfiction Because It's Academic*, writer Kaila Hale-Stern, writing on The Mary Sue webpage,[4] is critical of a male fan-fiction writer who had reworked author Stephen King's iconic horror tale *The Shining*. She noted that he made a strenuous effort to avoid having his work called "fan fiction," insisting instead that it was a form of scholarly critique on the underlying work. Hale-Stern explains this reluctance to accept the label of fan fiction, noting:

> Fic is primarily created by women, trans, genderqueer and just plain queer people—for free, for each other—and as such it's often derided and dismissed. Made mostly by girls? For no profit or acclaim? Must be amateurish and trashy, goes much of the knee-jerk response you get when you mention fic to people in the mainstream.[5]

Hale-Stern emphasizes the inaccuracy of this viewpoint, noting that half of the fanfiction authors she knows are academics (remember that if the median age of users is 15, that still leaves a lot of users who are adults) and that the unpolished nature of some fan fiction is because it is a space where "young writers go to learn and cut their teeth."[6]

The primary legal tension in fan fiction is between the desire and intent of the authors of the original works the fan fiction is based on to protect their copyright, and both their economic and moral rights of control over their work, and the First Amendment freedom afforded to fan creators to express themselves through the creation and dissemination of their work. Protecting both of these interests is a tricky project, and efforts to do so have met with mixed results.

Prof. Tushnet's early article notes one way that fan creators seek to achieve this balance is through the liberal use of disclaimers on their work. Among

---

3. *Fan Fiction Demographics in 2010: Age, Sex, Country*, FFN Rsch. (Mar. 18, 2011), http://ffnresearch.blogspot.com/2011/03/fan-fiction-demographics-in-2010-age.html.

4. Kaila Hale-Stern, *When Men Write Fanfiction, It Isn't Fanfiction Because It's Academic*, The Mary Sue (Mar. 1, 2018), https://www.themarysue.com/when-men-write-fanfiction-it-isnt-fanfiction-because-its-academic. The Mary Sue is a website that self-describes as "the geek girl's guide to the universe" (https://www.themarysue.com/about/, last visited Jan. 25, 2021).

5. Hale-Stern, *supra* note 4, at 4.

6. *Id.* at 5.

other examples, she cites a disclaimer of a *Star Trek*–based fan fiction that read: "Star Trek is the property of Paramount Studios, the following is a non-profit work of fan fiction. Distribution is free, but tampering with the story or removal of this disclaimer is actionable by law."[7]

Note the two key elements of this disclaimer—a statement that this is a nonprofit work of fan fiction and the acknowledgment that the original work is the property of Paramount Pictures. Giving attribution to the creator and/or owner of the underlying work both acknowledges that ownership right and makes it clear that the author is not trying to pass off those elements from the underlying work as elements that the author created on his or her own. Making it clear that you are not attempting to misappropriate the work will likely help you mitigate any damages that may be awarded if an infringement action is successful and is also likely to be viewed as evidence of your good-faith belief that you were legally allowed to make the use you did make in creating your story based on the underlying work of the original creator.

The nonprofit reference is an interesting one. The Copyright Act does not contain any provision that allows the copying of otherwise protected work if the copier doesn't plan to, or actually, make a profit from the copying. The simple act of copying a protected work, even without subsequent distribution of it, is an infringement of the copyright. So why include any reference to the nonprofit status of the use?

The answer lies in the first element of the four-part fair-use test, discussed extensively in Section Two. That first element, which focuses on the nature and purpose of the use of the work by the alleged infringer, is focused at this point in time on whether the use is transformative. However, before that doctrine was adopted, the first element of the fair-use test was whether the use made was a for-profit use or a nonprofit use. If the latter, the case for a fair-use defense to infringement was strengthened. So in aid of the potential fair-use defense to an infringement claim against a fan-fiction work, the nonprofit nature of the work is referenced in the disclaimer.

The nonprofit nature of fan fiction is also an element that supports the fourth element of the fair-use test—the effect of the fan-fiction work on the market for the original work. Fan fiction is posted on sites like FanFiction.Net and others for free—readers pay no charge to read the works. And since they generally offer a positive view of the underlying original work, they are not likely to draw a complaint that they tarnish or otherwise disparage that original work. So while it may be possible to offer an argument that the fan-fiction work has an adverse effect on an original work, the recent cases like *Suntrust Bank v. Houghton Mifflin Co.*, previously discussed, suggest that this is not likely to be a successful argument.

---

7. Tushnet, *supra* note 1, at 664 n.66.

The poor treatment of comic-book creators, dealers, and readers led to the creation of the Comic Book Legal Defense Fund, profiled in Chapter 6. I see a parallel in the creation of an organization that operates today as a highly successful archive of fan fiction as well as an advocate, both in legal matters as well as in raising awareness of the benefits and value of fan fiction. That organization is the Organization for Transformative Works (OTW) and its related fan-fiction archive, the Archive of Our Own, also referred to by the acronym AO3.

The OTW, founded in May 2007, and AO3, which was created by the OTW in 2008, primarily exist as an extremely robust online site and archive. The organization's purpose, mission, and values incorporate most of the principles that drive fandom, as discussed in Chapter 1. Rather than try to paraphrase their words, I think it best to let them speak for themselves. Here is their self-description:

What We Believe

Our Mission

> The Organization for Transformative Works (OTW) is a nonprofit organization established by fans to serve the interests of fans by providing access to and preserving the history of fanworks and fan culture in its myriad forms. We believe that fanworks are transformative and that transformative works are legitimate.
>
> The OTW represents a practice of transformative fanwork historically rooted in a primarily female culture. The OTW will preserve the record of that history as we pursue our mission while encouraging new and non-mainstream expressions of cultural identity within fandom.

Our Vision

> We envision a future in which all fannish works are recognized as legal and transformative and are accepted as a legitimate creative activity. We are proactive and innovative in protecting and defending our work from commercial exploitation and legal challenge. We preserve our fannish economy, values, and creative expression by protecting and nurturing our fellow fans, our work, our commentary, our history, and our identity while providing the broadest possible access to fannish activity for all fans.

Our Values

> 1. We value transformative fanworks and the innovative communities from which they have arisen, including media, real person fiction, anime, comics, music, and vidding.
> 2. We value our identity as a predominantly female community with a rich history of creativity and commentary.

3. We value our volunteer-based infrastructure and the fannish gift economy that recognizes and celebrates worth in myriad and diverse activities.
4. We value making fannish activities as accessible as possible to all those who wish to participate.
5. We value infinite diversity in infinite combinations. We value all fans engaged in transformative work: fans of any race, gender, culture, sexual identity, or ability. We value the unhindered cross-pollination and exchange of fannish ideas and cultures while seeking to avoid the homogenization or centralization of fandom.

Our Goals

During our first seven years, the OTW has laid the groundwork for a vibrant and creative organization by:

- Establishing the OTW as an IRS-recognized nonprofit organization.
- Creating infrastructure for OTW by establishing a board and creating committees, soliciting membership and donations, forming alliances, and holding elections.
- Encouraging community interaction and input via the OTW's Web site and across the online and offline spaces where fans congregate.
- Designing, programming, and launching the Archive of Our Own, a Web archive to host transformative fanworks.
- Exploring ways to make fanworks as accessible as possible.
- Establishing a legal advocacy project and forming alliances to defend fanworks from legal challenge.
- Creating a fan wiki to preserve the history of transformative fanworks and the fandoms from which they have arisen.
- Establishing a refereed academic journal to promote scholarship on fanworks and fan practices.
- Developing a long-term plan for the organization.
- Undertaking additional projects relevant to transformative fandom, such as the preservation of fan history and fanworks, building and maintaining infrastructure for use by fans, and sponsoring academic scholarship on fandom.[8]

The OTW has put its goals and values into effect over the past 13 years of operation. Guided initially by founding board member Professor Rebecca Tushnet, the OTW has made its presence known as a legal advocate for fandom

8. *What We Believe*, Org. for Transformative Works, https://www.transformativeworks.org/what_we_believe/ (last visited Jan. 22, 2021).

and the rights of fan creators, principally through the filing of amicus briefs in support of various cases.

The study and preservation of the history of fan culture is also the subject of OTW activity—it publishes the Fan Fiction Studies Reader and has partnered with the University of Iowa's libraries on a project to preserve fanzines and other nondigital forms of fan culture.

Perhaps the jewel in the crown of the OTW is AO3. With over 4 million uploaded fan works as of 2018 and over 1.5 million registered users, with fan works in over 30,000 fandoms, it is one of the larger fan-fiction sites in the world and one of the most popular ones as well.[9] Its ability to advocate for its users through its Legal Advocacy program is one of the elements that distinguishes OTW from other fan-fiction sites.[10]

A review of the legal advocacy undertaken by the OTW over the past 13 years reveals that the organization has filed amicus briefs in a number of the copyright infringement cases discussed in the previous section of this book. But overall, it is just a handful of cases, and none of them involved the kind of fan fiction that dominates sites like FanFiction.Net and AO3—the kind of alternate universe or slash fiction that is hugely popular. Which leads to another observation and question—with many millions of fan-fiction works posted on websites all over the world, why is it that only a handful of lawsuits for copyright infringement have been filed? It would seem, given that virtually all fan fiction is made up of derivative works based on earlier works by other creators, that we would be awash in copyright infringement claims. Why aren't we?

There are a few reasons for the paucity of lawsuits. A prominent one has to do with the lack of damage caused by fan fiction. Most fan-fiction creators write their works about shows or other pop-culture elements out of the great joy and pleasure those programs give them and out of a desire to share that joy, and a dialogue about the programs, with other fans. Far from having a damaging effect, these fan creators spread the word about their favorite programs and in some cases lead efforts to prevent the shows from being cancelled. They are some of the programs' most loyal fans, and on occasion, the ideas they put

---

9. Organization for Transformative Works, https://www.transformativeworks.org (last visited Feb. 22, 2021).

10. The OTW is not without its detractors. Shortly after it commenced operation, in 2008, one commentator posted a legal commentary on the FindLaw website challenging the OTW's advocacy of equal rights for fan fiction with other literary forms, arguing that fan fiction was a lesser form of literature because of its essentially derivative nature and the lack of professionalism of the work of some contributors. *See* Julie Hilden, *The Organization for Transformative Works and Its Bid to Protect Fan Fiction: Are Its Proposed Changes to Copyright Law, Creating Immunity for Suits against FanFic, a Good Idea?*, FindLaw (Jan. 21, 2008), https://supreme.findlaw.com/legal-commentary/the-organization-for-transformative-works-and-its-bid-to-protect-fan-fiction-are-its-proposed-changes-to-copyright-law-creating-immunity-for-suits-against-fanfic-a-good-idea. In subsequent years, these views, although still extant, seem to not have gained significant traction.

into their works are picked up by the show runners for television shows and incorporated into upcoming episodes.

And since fan fiction is a nonprofit activity, with many fan-fiction sites run primarily by unpaid volunteers, there simply is no money to be made suing these writers, many of whom, as minors, are hardly likely to be able to respond to a damages claim. Moreover, there simply are no damages arising from these fan works. It is only in the rare case, like *The Wind Done Gone*, or possibly in *Oh the Places You'll Boldly Go!*, where we can see the glimmer of a possibility that the alleged infringing work will have some impact on the market for the underlying work. But a story about forbidden love between Worf and Data (characters in the *Star Trek* universe)—read only by fans of a television show that ceased production of new episodes in 1994—is just not going to cause damage to anyone.

This is not to say, however, that the litigation landscape is completely devoid of cases arising out of fan fiction. This is particularly so when fan-fiction creators become so popular that they move out of the fan-fiction space into the "professional writer" space—marked primarily by their beginning to receive income for their work.

A fascinating and somewhat disconcerting example of this is found in the litigation case pending as of the writing of this book that pits two authors of fan fiction in what is known as the Omegaverse at odds with each other to such a degree that they are in court battling each other.

A. Trouble in the Omegaverse

The combatants in this battle are Addison Cain, author of the *Alpha's Claim* series of books, and Zoey Ellis, author of the *Myths of Omega* series of books, all of which take place in the fantasy realm of the Omegaverse. What is the Omegaverse?

The answer to that question, and one of the best discussions of the Cain/Ellis dispute, is found in Alexandra Alter's article *In a FanFic Feud, Deep (and Kinky) Questions Emerge*—a deep dive into the Omegaverse whose placement as the cover story in the Sunday business section of the *New York Times* is reflective of the prominence fan fiction has come to have in American culture.[11]

Alter describes the Omegaverse as a genre of fan fiction that arose about a decade ago, when devotees of the CW television series *Supernatural* began writing love stories involving the two male leads. As she describes these stories, "One would be the dominant alpha male. The other man would be a feminized

11. Alexandra Alter, *In a FanFic Feud, Deep (and Kinky) Questions Emerge*, N.Y. Times, May 24, 2020, Bus. sec. at 1, 4–5.

omega, often with the ability to become impregnated—a trope known as MPreg. Canine, and then lupine, sex stuff got mixed in."[12]

The genre, Alter notes, grew rapidly in popularity:

> The premise was wildly popular, and tropes were rapidly adopted by writers in other fandoms, including NBC's *Hannibal* and MTV's *Teen Wolf*. The sprawling body of work that followed came to be known as the Omegaverse, with its own rules, plot elements and terminology.
>
> Some Omegaverse stories involve lycanthropes (werewolves), vampires, shape shifters, dragons, space pirates; others feature regular humans. But virtually all Omegaverse couples engage in wolf-like behavior. Alphas "rut" and Omegas go through heat cycles, releasing pheromones that drive Alphas into a lusty frenzy. One particular physiological quirk that is ubiquitous in Omegaverse stories, called knotting, comes from a real feature of wolf penises, which swell during intercourse, causing the mating pair to remain physically bound to increase the chance of insemination.
>
> The appetite for such tales is large and growing. In the past decade, more than 70,000 stories set in the Omegaverse have been published on the fan fiction site Archive of Our Own. As it became more popular, the Omegaverse transcended individual fandom and became an established genre on its own.
>
> Writers began publishing Omegaverse stories with original characters and settings, and authors started to publish them for profit. On Amazon, there are hundreds of novels for sale, including titles like "Pregnant Rock Star Omega," "Wolf Spirit: A Reverse Harem Omegaverse Romance" and "Some Bunny to Love: An M/M MPreg Shifter Romance," an improbable tale involving an Alpha male who can transform into a rabbit.[13]

It was into this developing genre that Addison Cain, an American raised in Orange County, California, who had been writing fanfic featuring Batman's nemesis Bane, ventured when she published *Born to Be Bound*, an adaptation of her prior fan fic. Set in an Earth of the future, the book describes a postplague planet whose few survivors live under a dome. The society has devolved to a hierarchical one, akin to a wolf pack, populated by dominant Alphas, submissive Omegas, and neutral Betas. Scenes of aggressive wolfish sex between the Alpha, Shepherd, and his captive Omega, Claire, are an important element of the book.

---

12. *Id.* at 4.
13. *Id.* at 4.

Cain followed this book with several other titles, *Born to be Broken, Reborn, Stolen,* and *Corrupted,* all featuring cover graphics of the shirtless, muscular Alpha male character, Shephard. According to her publisher, the series grossed in excess of $370,000—meaning Cain had successfully transitioned from amateur fan fic into the realm of a professional genre writer.

She followed this success with other works over the next few years, churning out a new book every few months and building a brand in what she called "the erotica pool," noting, "There's nothing to do here but make money."[14]

She wasn't the only one to think that way. In 2018, she heard about a new series of books, the *Myth of Omega,* whose inaugural title, *Crave to Conquer,* and succeeding volumes, *Crave to Capture* and *Crave to Claim,* had generated a great deal of buzz and book sales. Cain, reading these works, became progressively outraged at the similarities these books, written by Zoey Ellis, had to her *Bound* series. Among other things that likely angered Cain was the use of similar shirtless muscular men as book cover models, as exemplified by this graphic:

---

14. *Id.*

At Cain's urging, Blushing Books, publisher of her *Bound* series, sent copyright violation notices to a number of online retailers of the *Myth of Omega* series. The goal of those notices was to get those retailers, including Barnes and Noble, iTunes, Apple Store, Google Play, and others, to remove the *Myth of Omega* series from their sites. The tactic worked, and Ellis saw an immediate drop in revenue.

So how could Cain accomplish this result with just a few letters from her lawyers? The answer is found in a yet-undiscussed section of the Copyright Act of 1976.

Section 512 of the Act is popularly known as the "Notice and Take-Down" section. The intent of the section was to address the problem of holding Internet service providers (an ISP is defined as a business that provides access to the Internet and its sites—so Google, Yahoo, AOL, and many other sites qualify as ISPs) liable for content posted through their systems that infringes copyright. The ISPs have argued, with some merit, that the huge volume of content posted every hour of the day makes it unfair and unreasonable to hold them liable for posted content that infringes on the copyright of another party. The ISPs argued that unless they had notice of the claimed infringement, and an opportunity to respond by taking down the alleged infringing work, their due process rights would be violated.

So section 512, and specifically subsection (c) of that section, provides a way to allow companies to avoid that liability by taking down the alleged offending work. Subsection 512(c) provides:

> (c) Information Residing on Systems or Networks At Direction of Users.—
>
> (1) In general.—A service provider shall not be liable for monetary relief, or, except as provided in subsection (j), for injunctive or other equitable relief, for infringement of copyright by reason of the storage at the direction of a user of material that resides on a system or network controlled or operated by or for the service provider, if the service provider—
>
> . . .
>
> (C) upon notification of claimed infringement as described in paragraph (3), responds expeditiously to remove, or disable access to, the material that is claimed to be infringing or to be the subject of infringing activity.[15]

The ISP is required to designate an agent to receive these notices and to thereafter take down the alleged infringing material. The subsection has very detailed requirements for what the notice to the ISP must include:

> (3) Elements of notification.—
>
> (A) To be effective under this subsection, a notification of claimed infringement must be a written communication provided to the designated agent of a service provider that includes substantially the following:
>
> (i)
>
> A physical or electronic signature of a person authorized to act on behalf of the owner of an exclusive right that is allegedly infringed.
>
> (ii)
>
> Identification of the copyrighted work claimed to have been infringed, or, if multiple copyrighted works at a single online site are covered by a single notification, a representative list of such works at that site.
>
> (iii)
>
> Identification of the material that is claimed to be infringing or to be the subject of infringing activity and that is to be removed or access to which is to be disabled, and information reasonably sufficient to permit the service provider to locate the material.
>
> (iv)
>
> Information reasonably sufficient to permit the service provider to contact the complaining party, such as an address, telephone number,

15. 17 U.S.C. § 512(c).

> and, if available, an electronic mail address at which the complaining party may be contacted.
>
> (v)
>
> A statement that the complaining party has a good faith belief that use of the material in the manner complained of is not authorized by the copyright owner, its agent, or the law.
>
> (vi)
>
> A statement that the information in the notification is accurate, and under penalty of perjury, that the complaining party is authorized to act on behalf of the owner of an exclusive right that is allegedly infringed.[16]

So once a service provider receives a properly constructed notice, it must immediately take down the alleged infringing content. So long as it does so, the ISP avoids liability to the copyright holder for contributing to the infringement (the liability of the ISP here is what is referred to as either contributory or secondary liability—the ISP isn't doing the direct infringement but is facilitating the distribution of the offending content).

Sounds like a pretty good system for shielding an ISP, right? But like many things in the law, it is not so easily done. What happens, for example, if the party who posted the material believes that he or she is legally entitled to do so and that the notice is not valid, for any number of reasons?

Section 512 has an answer for that problem. Subsection (g) of section 512 provides for a right of a posting party to submit a counternotification, which asserts that the material was posted legally, for any number of reasons, including that the posting party had a license or other right to post the content, that the claim of copyright by the alleged owner is invalid, that the posting party has a First Amendment right to post the material, etc. The subsection also provides a list of elements that the counternotification must include, as follows:

> (g) Replacement of Removed or Disabled Material and Limitation on Other Liability.—
>
> (1) No liability for taking down generally.—
>
> Subject to paragraph (2), a service provider shall not be liable to any person for any claim based on the service provider's good faith disabling of access to, or removal of, material or activity claimed to be infringing or based on facts or circumstances from which infringing activity is apparent, regardless of whether the material or activity is ultimately determined to be infringing.
>
> (2) Exception.—Paragraph (1) shall not apply with respect to material residing at the direction of a subscriber of the service provider on a

---

16. *Id.* § 512(c)(3).

system or network controlled or operated by or for the service provider that is removed, or to which access is disabled by the service provider, pursuant to a notice provided under subsection (c)(1)(C), unless the service provider—

(A)

takes reasonable steps promptly to notify the subscriber that it has removed or disabled access to the material;

(B)

upon receipt of a counter notification described in paragraph (3), promptly provides the person who provided the notification under subsection (c)(1)(C) with a copy of the counter notification, and informs that person that it will replace the removed material or cease disabling access to it in 10 business days; and

(C)

replaces the removed material and ceases disabling access to it not less than 10, nor more than 14, business days following receipt of the counter notice, unless its designated agent first receives notice from the person who submitted the notification under subsection (c)(1)(C) that such person has filed an action seeking a court order to restrain the subscriber from engaging in infringing activity relating to the material on the service provider's system or network.

(3) Contents of counter notification.—To be effective under this subsection, a counter notification must be a written communication provided to the service provider's designated agent that includes substantially the following:

(A)

A physical or electronic signature of the subscriber.

(B)

Identification of the material that has been removed or to which access has been disabled and the location at which the material appeared before it was removed or access to it was disabled.

(C)

A statement under penalty of perjury that the subscriber has a good faith belief that the material was removed or disabled as a result of mistake or misidentification of the material to be removed or disabled.

(D)

The subscriber's name, address, and telephone number, and a statement that the subscriber consents to the jurisdiction of Federal District Court for the judicial district in which the address is located, or if the subscriber's address is outside of the United States, for any judicial district in which the service provider may be found, and that the subscriber will accept service of process from the person who provided notification under subsection (c)(1)(C) or an agent of such person.

(4) Limitation on other liability.—

A service provider's compliance with paragraph (2) shall not subject the service provider to liability for copyright infringement with respect to the material identified in the notice provided under subsection (c)(1)(C).

Finding that her books were disappearing from ISP sites, Ellis had her counsel send out counternotifications, which, over the course of several months, led to the relisting of her books. But damage was done in the meantime: both the loss of sales for that unlisted period and damage to her reputation in the fan-fic universe—with questions about her integrity and the quality of her work now circulating.

So in response to these actions, Ellis brought suit in Federal District Court in Oklahoma, where her digital distributor is based. Her lawsuit seeks damages of $1.25 million, based on claims of defamation and interference with her career and for the filing of the copyright notices and take-down requests, which she claims were false when filed. As of this writing, the suit remains active and has not yet been resolved, either through settlement or trial.

Ellis, interviewed for the *New York Times* article, explained that she first heard about the dispute when a reader of her books e-mailed her and told her that her books were no longer available for purchase at the Barnes and Noble site. Ellis discovered that other sites had pulled her works as well, because of the copyright infringement notices they had received.

Ellis was baffled, noting,

> I couldn't see how a story I had written using recognized tropes from a shared universe to tell a story that was quite different than anything else out there commercially could be targeted in that way . . . . There are moments and scenarios that seem almost identical, but it's a trope that can be found in hundreds of stories.[17]

Ellis's lawyers filed the requisite counternotices, and after a period of several weeks, and in some cases, months, the works were restored to those sites. But the lost revenue during those times could not be recovered, which is now part of her lawsuit. So her lawsuit contains claims for $1.25 million in damages based on theories of defamation, interference with economic advantage, and filing allegedly false copyright notices. She has enlisted an expert witness, Kristina Busse, author of *Framing Fan Fiction,* who has written essays dealing with the Omegaverse. Busse asserts about both Cain's and Ellis's books, "They

---

17. Alter, *supra* note 11.

are not very original, either one of them . . . . They both stole from fandom or existing tropes in the wild."[18]

At the core of this dispute are two copyright doctrines: the transformative doctrine, which I have already examined, and the doctrine of *scene a faire*, defined as a plot element that is standard for a particular genre.[19] In copyright law, *scene a faire* elements are not protectable. So in a classic Western story, a shootout at high noon on a dusty main street between the hero and the villain is not protectable. In a murder mystery, the gathering of suspects for an announcement by the detective of the identity of the killer similarly is not protectable.

For fan fiction, the doctrine of *scene a faire* operates as a double-edged sword.[20] If you want to use a trope or *scene a faire* expression, you are free to do so without fear of infringement claims. But if you do, as Cain did in creating her version of an Omegaverse story, you also run the risk that a successor writer will do with your work what you did with those who came before you.

As I read the account of the Cain/Ellis dispute and discovered, what I thought was for the first time, the world of Omegaverse, I had a nagging suspicion that I had seen something of this genre before. After a bit of recollection, I placed it. Seminal fantasy and horror author Anne Rice had explored this turf years before in her two werewolf romance fantasies, *The Wolf Gift* and *The Wolves of Midwinter*, which made up her series *The Wolf Gift Chronicles*.

I was a fan of this series and had the pleasure of meeting Anne Rice in July 2013 at the San Diego Comic-Con, where she signed a copy of *The Wolf Gift* and graciously and patiently allowed an assistant to take this picture of us with my camera:

Marc H. Greenberg and Anne Rice at the San Diego Comic-Con, July 2013. Photo by Anne Rice's assistant, using Marc Greenberg's camera.

---

18. *Id.*

19. *Scene a Faire*, MERRIAM-WEBSTER, https://www.merriam-webster.com/dictionary/scene%20a%20faire (last visited Jan. 25, 2021).

20. And yes, this expression is a trope or a *scene a faire* expression as well.

So why, I wondered as I read about the Cain/Ellis dispute, is it that in the materials I read about the Omegaverse, there was no reference to any fan fic based on the iconic characters found in Anne Rice's many books? It didn't take too much research to find the answer. Anne Rice doesn't allow fan fiction to be written about her characters and storylines.

In an April 2018 post on the Fanlore Wiki, the question was posed thusly: "Where has Anne Rice fanfiction gone?" In the body of the post, the question is posed and answered.

> **Where Can I Read Fanfiction Based on Anne Rice's Books?**
>
> Nowhere. You can't. On April 7, 2000 Anne Rice had the following message to say on her webpage:
>
> "I do not allow fan fiction.
>
> The characters are copyrighted. It upsets me terribly to even think about fan fiction with my characters. I advise my readers to write your own original stories with your own characters.
>
> It is absolutely essential that you respect my wishes."[21]

The post notes that Rice's attorneys and others have attacked Anne Rice fan-fiction writers, threatening copyright infringement claims and attacks on businesses that the fan-fic authors owned, as well as personal attacks sent to authors' e-mail addresses and related conduct the post describes as harassment. The post notes: "Suffice to say, Anne Rice made her displeasure clear."[22]

In her blog *Business of Writing*, *New York Times* best-selling author Ilona Andrews commented on the Cain/Ellis dispute in a post entitled "Plagiarism and Other Fun Things." Andrews talks about the different views authors, including her, hold about fanfic:

> A lot of writers are comfortable with fan fiction use of their work; others are not. Anne Rice is not. Neil Gaiman is. We don't mind, but we don't want to read it in any way, shape or form. Not even a paragraph. It is a stance shared by a good portion of fiction writers.[23]

So where does that leave fan-fic authors who want to write fan fic based on an individual author's iconic characters and/or storyline? Are there any guidelines or benchmarks that can inform you if you will encounter resistance from the author?

---

21. *Where Has Anne Rice Fanfiction Gone?*, Fanlore, https://fanlore.org/wiki/Where_has_Anne_Rice_fanfiction_gone%3F (last visited Jan. 25, 2021).

22. *Id.*

23. Ilona Andrews, *Plagiarism and Other Fun Things*, Business of Writing (May 26, 2020), https://ilona-andrews.com/2020/plagiarism-and-other-fun-things.

While the short and simple answer is no—there aren't any guidelines, and the best advice is for the fan-fic author to reach out to the author whose work inspired him or her to ask for permission, one possible earmark is worth considering. If the work you are inspired by, and the characters you want to write about, are characters only one author has ever written about, such as Anne Rice's iconic vampire, Lestat, there is a greater likelihood that the author will feel pretty possessive about that character and be resistant to fan-fic authors adding their take on the character to the world. On the other hand, if the author is one of many who have written stories about the character, for example the legion of writers who have done stories about Superman or Spiderman, then chances are those writers will feel less of an attachment to the characters and be more objective about fan fic based on them.

Bottom line—fan-fic authors are well advised to do their due diligence before writing fanfic about well-known characters. If the result of that investigation tells you that the author may be resistant to your efforts, particularly if he or she isn't given any notice about the work coming out, you have a decision to consider.

On one hand, you can take the position that between the transformative doctrine and the difficulty the author will have proving any damage as a result of your fan-fiction work, it is so unlikely that you will get sued that you can simply go ahead and publish the story, regardless of how the author will feel about it. On the other hand, if you are a fan of this author and don't want to incur his or her ire, there is another approach you can consider. Write directly to the author or company that owns the rights to the characters and ask for permission. Even if you get a "no" response and decide that your version will be sufficiently transformative to avoid a successful infringement prosecution, you will know going in that such a claim from the owner is a possibility. And of equal importance, you can, and should, share that knowledge with any publisher who is publishing your work—giving a publisher a heads up so it can assess the risks and decide if it wants to go forward is not only the fair and decent thing to do but also allows a greater chance that you and the publisher can present a united front in the event a claim is filed. One consideration in taking this approach is that you will be letting the author know about your work, and if he or she would otherwise never become aware of it, staying anonymous may allow you to avoid any claims.

Of additional importance is the change in the legal landscape wrought by the ascendancy of the transformative doctrine. Production companies and publishers alike who have watched and learned from the experiences of the Margaret Mitchell Trust, Dr. Seuss Enterprises, and others are wary of facing and prevailing in a case where the alleged infringer raises the transformative doctrine as a defense. Litigation of all stripes is an expensive endeavor. Copyright litigation, which must be conducted in federal court, is more expensive than other cases because of the need to engage expert witnesses and the fact that most such cases are tried before juries, requiring more weeks to complete (and are more expensive) than court trials.

A final reason fan fiction doesn't typically draw infringement litigation has to do with the concern of prospective plaintiffs that they are essentially, in bringing such a suit, suing their own fans, the people who buy their original works. In recent years, we have seen a trend, both in fan fiction and in the other areas we will look at in the next few chapters in this section, of production companies attempting to engage with those fans rather than sue them and to assist them in their creative endeavors, while at the same time attempting to exercise some extrajudicial controls over the content created.

Marvel Comics has taken this approach with the launch, in 2017, of Marvel's Create Your Own platform, which allows fans to create original comic strips using characters from the Marvel universe, accompanied by stock background graphics.

The use of those Marvel graphics and characters, now owned by Disney, is subject to a pretty extensive set of conditions. Here are some of the relevant terms governing that use, which Disney characterizes as a license, as of July 2020:

> **2. License Grant and Restrictions**
>
> The Disney Products, including, but not limited to, movies, television shows, entertainment or informational programming, trailers, bonus material, scripts, code, images and artwork, are our copyrighted, patented or trademarked property or the copyrighted, patented or trademarked property of our licensors and all copyrights, trademarks, service marks, trade names, trade dress, patents and other intellectual property rights in the Disney Products are owned by us or our licensors (who may be third-party beneficiaries of this contract) and protected by the copyright, trademark, patent and other laws of the United States and international treaties.
>
> A. Consumer License. If a Disney Product, or third party providing Disney Products subject to this Agreement, is configured to enable the use of software, content, virtual items or other materials owned or licensed by us, we grant you a limited, non-exclusive, non-sublicensable, non-transferable license to access and use in the United States such software, content, virtual item or other material for your personal, noncommercial use only, only for as long as that Disney Product is made available to you by us, or an authorized third party, and only in accordance with this Agreement and/or the specific terms

that apply to that Disney Product, with no right to reproduce, distribute, communicate to the public, make available to the public, or transform any Disney Product, in any media format or channel now known or hereafter devised (except as may be expressly described or contemplated within the Disney Product). This is a license agreement and not an agreement for sale or assignment of any rights in the Disney Products. Except as we specifically agree in writing, no element of the Disney Products may be used or exploited in any way other than as part of the authorized Product made available to you. You may own the physical media on which elements of the Disney Products are made available to you, but we retain full and complete ownership of the Disney intellectual property. We do not transfer title to any portion of the Disney websites, software, applications, content, virtual items or other materials and/or services to you. Likewise, the purchase of a license to use any Disney Product does not create an ownership interest in the Disney websites, software, applications, content, virtual items or other materials and/or services.

B. Restrictions on Your Use of Disney's Products. You agree that as a condition of your license, you will not:

i. circumvent or disable any content protection system or digital rights management technology used in connection with the Disney Product;

ii. copy the Disney Product (except as expressly permitted by us);

iii. rebroadcast, transmit or perform the Disney Product;

iv. create derivative works of the Disney Product or any part thereof, except as and only to the extent that any foregoing restriction is prohibited by applicable law;

v. move, decompile, reverse-engineer, disassemble, or otherwise reduce to human-readable form the Disney Products and/or the video player(s), underlying technology, any digital rights management mechanism, device, or other content protection or access control measure incorporated into the video player(s);

vi. modify the Disney Products, including, but not limited to, by removing identification, copyright or other proprietary notices from the Disney Products, or by framing, mirroring, or utilizing similar techniques;

vii. access or use the Disney Products in a manner that suggests an association with our products, services or brands;

viii. use the Disney Products for any commercial or business related use or build a business utilizing the Products, whether or not for profit;

ix. bypass, modify, defeat, tamper with or circumvent any of the functions or protections of the Disney Products;

x. access, monitor or copy, or permit another person or entity to access, monitor or copy, any element of the Disney Products using a robot, spider, scraper or other automated means or manual process without our express written permission;

xi. damage, disable, overburden or impair the Disney Products;

xii. use the Disney Products in any unlawful manner, for any unlawful purpose, or in any manner inconsistent with this Agreement; and

xiii. allow third parties to violate the above restrictions.

C. Violation. Any attempt to perform any of the restricted actions listed above is a violation of the rights of Disney and/or the intellectual property rights holder.

. . . .

7. Submissions, User Generated Content, DMCA Takedown Notices

A. Submissions and Unsolicited Ideas Policies. Our long-standing company policy does not allow us to accept or consider unsolicited creative ideas, suggestions or materials. In connection with anything you submit to us—whether or not solicited by us—you agree that creative ideas, suggestions or other materials you submit are not being made in confidence or trust and that no confidential or fiduciary relationship is intended or created between you and us in any way, and that you have no expectation of review, compensation or consideration of any type.

B. User Generated Content. The Disney Products may ask for or allow you to communicate, submit, upload or otherwise make available text, chats, images, audio, video, contest entries or other content ("**User Generated Content**"), which may be accessible and viewable by the public. Access to these features may be subject to age restrictions. Whether a Disney Product made available by us or in connection with Disney Products appears on a Disney website, service and/or platform or is integrated with a third-party website, service, application, and/or platform, you may not submit or upload User Generated Content that is defamatory, harassing, threatening, bigoted, hateful, violent, vulgar, obscene, pornographic, or otherwise offensive or that harms or can reasonably be expected to harm any person or entity, whether or not such material is protected by law.

In most instances, we do not claim ownership of your User Generated Content; however, you grant us a non-exclusive, sub-licensable, irrevocable and royalty-free worldwide license under all copyrights, trademarks, patents, trade secrets, privacy and publicity rights and other intellectual property rights for the full duration of those rights to use, reproduce, transmit, print, publish, publicly display, exhibit, distribute, redistribute, copy, index, comment on, modify, transform, adapt, translate, create derivative works based upon, publicly perform, publicly communicate, make available, and otherwise exploit such User Generated Content, in whole or in part, in all media formats and channels now known or hereafter devised (including in connection with the Disney Products and on third-party websites, services, applications, and/or platforms), in any number of copies and without limit as to time, manner and frequency of use, without further notice to you, without attribution (to the extent this is not contrary to mandatory provisions of applicable law), and without the requirement of permission from or payment to you or any other person or entity. You agree that submission of User Generated Content does not establish any relationship of trust and confidence between you and us, and that you have no expectation of compensation whatsoever (except as may be specifically stated in the provisions of the Disney Products in connection with the submission, or arising from it).

You represent and warrant that your User Generated Content conforms to this Agreement and that you own or have the necessary rights and permissions including, without limitation, all copyrights, music rights and likeness rights (with respect to any person) contained in the User Generated Content, without the need for payment to any other person or entity, to use and exploit, and to authorize us to use and exploit, your User Generated Content in all manners contemplated by this Agreement; and you agree to indemnify and hold us harmless from any claims or expenses (including attorneys' fees) by any third party arising out of or in connection with our use and exploitation of your User Generated Content resulting from your breach of this Agreement. You also agree to waive and not to enforce any moral rights, ancillary rights or similar rights in or to the User Generated Content against us or our licensees, distributors, agents, representatives and other authorized users, and agree to procure the same agreement to waive and not to enforce from others who may possess such rights.

To the extent that we authorize you to create, post, upload, distribute, publicly display or publicly perform User Generated Content that requires the use of our copyrighted works, we grant you a non-exclusive license to create a derivative work using the specifically referenced copyrighted works as required for the sole purpose of creating such a work, provided that such license shall be conditioned upon your assignment to us of all rights worldwide in the work you create for the duration of copyright in the User Generated Content, in all formats and media known or unknown to date, including for use on Disney Products and on third party sites and platforms. If such rights are not assigned to us, your license to create derivative works using our copyrighted works shall be null and void.

We may monitor, screen, post, remove, modify, store and review User Generated Content or communications sent through a Disney Product, at any time and for any reason, including to ensure that the User Generated Content or communication conforms to this Agreement, without prior notice to you. We may terminate your account and access to the Disney Products if your User Generated Content violates this Agreement, including unlawful postings or content, without prior notice to you. We are not responsible for, and do not endorse or guarantee, the opinions, views, advice or recommendations posted or sent by users.

C. Claims of Copyright Infringement. Notifications of claimed copyright infringement and counter notices must be sent to our designated agent:

Attn: Lance R. Griffin
The Walt Disney Company
500 South Buena Vista Street
Burbank, California 91521, USA
Phone: +1 818-560-1000
Fax: +1 818-560-4299
Email: designated.agent@dig.twdc.com

We are only able to accept notices in the languages in which this Agreement is made available by us.

We will respond expeditiously to claims of copyright infringement committed using the Disney Products that are reported to our designated copyright agent, in accordance with the U.S. Digital Millennium Copyright Act of 1998 ("**DMCA**") or, as applicable, other laws. With respect to Disney Products hosted in the United States, these notices must include the required information set forth in the DMCA and described in detail here.[24]

The most notable language in this license is this excerpt from Section 8:

You may not submit or upload User Generated Content that is defamatory, harassing, threatening, bigoted, hateful, violent, ***vulgar, obscene, pornographic, or otherwise offensive or that harms or can reasonably be expected to harm any person or entity, whether or not such material is protected by law.***

24. *Disney Terms of Use,* https://disneytermsofuse.com/english/#License-Grant-and-Restrictions (last visited Jan. 26, 2021).

> In ***most*** instances, we do not claim ownership of your User Generated Content; ***however, you grant us a non-exclusive, sublicensable, irrevocable and royalty-free worldwide license*** under all copyrights, trademarks, patents, trade secrets, privacy and publicity rights and other intellectual property rights for the full duration of those rights to use, reproduce, transmit, print, publish, publicly display, exhibit, distribute, redistribute, copy, index, comment on, modify, transform, adapt, translate, create derivative works based upon, publicly perform, publicly communicate, make available, and otherwise exploit such User Generated Content, in whole or in part, in all media formats and channels now known or hereafter devised (including in connection with the Disney Products and on third-party websites, services, applications, and/or platforms), in any number of copies and without limit as to time, manner and frequency of use, without further notice to you, without attribution (to the extent this is not contrary to mandatory provisions of applicable law), and without the requirement of permission from or payment to you or any other person or entity. You agree that submission of User Generated Content does not establish any relationship of trust and confidence between you and us, and that you have no expectation of compensation whatsoever (except as may be specifically stated in the provisions of the Disney Products in connection with the submission, or arising from it, you may not submit or upload User Generated Content that is defamatory, harassing, threatening, bigoted, hateful, violent, vulgar, obscene, pornographic, or otherwise offensive or that harms or can reasonably be expected to harm any person or entity, whether or not such material is protected by law.[25]

These two sections are problematic for creators who want to work with Marvel characters under the terms of this license. First is the problem of warranting that your work using these characters is not "vulgar, obscene or otherwise pornographic." Given that the standard for making obscenity/pornography determinations is impossibly vague and subject to the muddled rule of the Supreme Court in *Miller v. California*[26] and that what is "vulgar" to one person is not to another, granting an absolute warranty that your work doesn't violate these "standards" is well-nigh impossible and opens the door to a liability finding that may carry criminal or serious financial penalties.

The second part of this section is equally problematic in that it grants a broad license to Disney to make whatever use they choose to make of your

25. *Id.* sec. 8 (emphasis added).
26. Miller v. California, 413 U.S. 15 (1973).

creation, including an unlimited right to modify that creation or even to create derivative works based on it.

One remaining problem worthy of discussion closes out this chapter on fan fiction—the problem arising from the duration and term of copyright and the kind of issue that arises with popular-culture works of significant vintage. While it is fair to say that much of fan-created content is focused on current elements of fandom, there is also quite a lot of fan-created work based on content that is so old that in some cases the original work has passed out of copyright protection. To date, due to the length of that protection under copyright law (life of the author plus 70 years), few works of interest in pop culture qualify—but some very significant works are fast approaching that benchmark and will soon go into the public domain; the character of Mickey Mouse is one such example.

A recent case shows us the lengths to which both sides of this equation are willing to go to protect their respective interests. In *Klinger v. Conan Doyle Estate,*[27] the issue arose regarding one of popular culture's oldest and most revered icons—the famous detective Sherlock Holmes, originally created by Sir Arthur Conan Doyle.

At issue in this case was the fact that some 46 of Doyle's stories, plus four novels, including those that introduced readers to the detective, his trusted friend Dr. Watson, and his home at 221b Baker Street, were published before 1923. Those elements and characters were therefore, under U.S. copyright law, now in the public domain and available for use by fan creators without infringement liability—much to the distress of the Doyle estate. However, the last ten stories written by Doyle, featuring these characters and introducing a few new characters and stories, had been published between 1923 and Doyle's death in 1927 and were still under the protection of the copyright law, with copyright registrations that were set to expire at various dates between 2018 and 2022.

Author Leslie Klinger, a fan of the Sherlock Holmes stories, coedited a collection of stories inspired by, and featuring, Sherlock Holmes and other characters from Doyle's books, entitled *A Study in Sherlock: Stories Inspired by the Sherlock Holmes Canon.*[28] Klinger felt that he didn't need permission from the estate of Arthur Conan Doyle to publish this anthology, because the copyright to the Holmes character and the books had expired. The estate disagreed and demanded Random House pay a $5,000 licensing fee. Random House paid the fee, and the anthology was published and sold well enough that Klinger decided to put together a second anthology, entitled *In the Company of Sherlock Holmes,* this time to be published by Pegasus Books. The estate again demanded

27. *Klinger v. Conan Doyle Estate,* 755 F.3d 496 (7th Cir. 2014).

28. Leslie Klinger, A Study in Sherlock: Stories Inspired by the Sherlock Holmes Canon (Random House 2011).

a licensing fee, which Pegasus insisted would have to be paid directly from Klinger to the estate. Klinger declined to pay, opting instead to sue for what the law refers to as declaratory relief, a claim filed when the party filing believes that there is a question about the legal status of a matter and seeks guidance from the courts as to what his or her legal rights and responsibilities are.

Klinger alleged that the anthology's stories were all based on the first 50 Sherlock Holmes works, which were out of copyright protection, and that the remaining ten stories still protected under the law would not be featured in the anthology. Based on those facts, Klinger argued that the anthology did not need to pay any license fee to the estate. In reply, the estate argued that the characters of Holmes, Watson, et al., were complicated characters, that they were continuing to evolve in the last ten stories, and that as a consequence, all 60 of the stories were still under protection and would remain so until the last story had passed its copyright term—which would occur in 2022, some eight years after the litigation was initiated.

The case worked its way through the trial court and ultimately ended up before the Seventh Circuit U.S. Court of Appeals, located in Chicago. Noted judge Richard Posner wrote the decision.[29]

Pointing out that the estate was seeking to extend the copyright term of Doyle's works to a period of 135 years (1887–2022), Judge Posner rejected the estate's claims:

> We cannot find any basis in statute or case law for extending a copyright beyond its expiration. When a story falls into the public domain, story elements—including characters covered by the expired copyright—become fair game for follow-on authors, as held in Silverman v. CBS Inc., 870 F.2d 40, 49–51 (2d Cir. 1989), a case much like this one. At issue was the right to copy fictional characters (Amos and Andy) who had appeared in copyrighted radio scripts. The copyrights covered the characters because they were original. As in this case the characters also appeared in subsequent radio scripts that remained under copyright, though the copyrights on the original scripts in which the characters had appeared had expired. The court ruled that "a copyright affords protection only for original works of authorship and, consequently, copyrights in derivative works secure protection only for the incremental additions of originality contributed by the authors of the derivative works." Id. at 49; see Leslie A. Kurtz, "The Methuselah Factor: When Characters Outlive Their Copyrights," 11 U. Miami Entertainment & Sports L. Rev. 437, 447–48 (1994). The copyrights on the derivative works, corresponding to the copyrights on the ten last Sherlock Holmes stories, were not extended

29. *Klinger*, 755 F.3d 496.

> by virtue of the incremental additions of originality in the derivative works.
>
> And so it is in our case. The ten Holmes-Watson stories in which copyright persists are derivative from the earlier stories, so only original elements added in the later stories remain protected. Id. at 49–50. The "freedom to make new works based on public domain materials ends where the resulting derivative work comes into conflict with a valid copyright," Warner Bros. Entertainment, Inc. v. X One X Productions, 644 F.3d 584, 596 (8th Cir. 2011)—as Klinger acknowledges. But there is no such conflict in this case.[30]

Judge Posner makes an important point here, one fan creators need to pay attention to. If you are dealing with a series of stories and characters whose stories include works no longer under copyright protection and later stories dealing with the same characters that remain protected, only the new and original elements added to those later stories may still be subject to an infringement claim—the original story lines, and characters, will now be in the public domain and fair game for your version.

Judge Posner summarizes the policy concerns this case posed—what he colorfully terms the "spectre of perpetual copyright":

> With the net effect on creativity of extending the copyright protection of literary characters to the extraordinary lengths urged by the estate so uncertain, and no legal grounds suggested for extending copyright protection beyond the limits fixed by Congress, the estate's appeal borders on the quixotic. The spectre of perpetual, or at least nearly perpetual, copyright (perpetual copyright would violate the copyright clause of the Constitution, Art. I, § 8, cl. 8, which authorizes copyright protection only for "limited Times") looms, once one realizes that the Doyle estate is seeking 135 years (1887–2022) of copyright protection for the character of Sherlock Holmes as depicted in the first Sherlock Holmes story.[31]

This case again illustrates the careful balance courts dealing with fan-fiction works strike between the First Amendment rights of fan-fiction authors and the rights of original authors and their heirs to protect the legacy and work of those original authors. But does that balance shift in any way when the fan-created work is a work of fine art, as opposed to fiction? The next chapter addresses that question.

30. *Id.* at 504–05.
31. *Id.* at 511.

CHAPTER 8

Fan Art

Black Panther & Storm, original fan art by Paul Downs, © 2019

Fan art intersects with the law in a few different ways. A key factor that affects the scope of that intersection is whether the fan art reproduces the image of living or dead actor(s) who have a role in the subject matter of the artwork (fan art of Wonder Woman depicting actress Gal Gadot in her performance of the role is an example), or whether the artwork is based on another artist's version of the character (Jack Kirby's Silver Surfer, for example), or if the art is created solely from a text description of a character (Phillip Pullman's Lyra Belacqua Silvertongue, for example).

The first example, fan art that reproduces the image of the actor who plays a character, is likely to involve a potential issue arising from the right of publicity that the actor/actress owns in his or her name, image, likeness, and elements of identifiability, as well as a violation of the copyright the creator holds in the character. And this copyright may also be held by more than one party, for example if the artwork is based on a prior artist's take on the character or if the character copyright is owned by a production company (as DC owns the Wonder Woman character). Finally, in some cases the original creator owns both the copyright in the character and the artwork depicting that character, either through having licensed other artists to create the character or because the creator is also the artist (Todd McFarlane as creator and artist on Spawn is one example; Robert Crumb's Mr. Natural is another, as is Matt Groening's Homer Simpson).

In the Spawn example, a feature motion picture about the character was released in 1997, starring Michael Jai White in the lead role. So fan art depicting White's version of McFarlane's Spawn could bring claims of violation of White's right of publicity, McFarlane's artistic rendering of the character in graphic novels, and McFarlane's creator ownership rights as the owner of the copyright in the character. Whew! That's a lot to be paying attention to for the fan-art creator.

In the second example, the fan artist is creating a work inspired by the work of another artist, which implicates the copyrights in both the original artwork and the ownership interest in the character itself. And here again, it is necessary to investigate if the artist you are inspired by owns the rights to his or her version of the character or if his or her version was a work for hire for a third party.

In the last example, where the fan art is created based solely on a written description of the character or scene, there is much less risk for fan-art creators, as they are free from liability claims as to violation of rights of publicity or from copyright infringement claims based on the similarity of the artwork to the original or a prior version of the character. There may still, in this context, be a possible copyright violation if the text description of the character is distinctive enough to support an infringement claim.

A. Fan Art and the Right of Publicity

The right of publicity was not originally based on legislative statutes. Rather, it was first discussed in a law review article in 1890 written by Samuel Warren and Louis Brandeis, two Chicago lawyers.[1] Seventy years later, another law review article, this time by noted torts law professor William Prosser, laid out four separate and specific rights that he asserted emerged from the general right of privacy Brandeis and Warren had written about.

1. Samuel D. Warren & Louis D. Brandeis, *The Right to Privacy*, 4 HARV. L. REV. 193 (1890). Mr. Brandeis would go on to become an associate justice on the U.S. Supreme Court.

Professor Prosser described those four rights of privacy, and their violation, as follows:

1. Intrusion upon the plaintiff's seclusion or solitude, or into his private affairs;
2. Public disclosure of embarrassing private facts about the plaintiff;
3. Publicity which places the plaintiff in a false light in the public eye;
4. Appropriation, for the defendant's advantage, of the plaintiff's name or likeness.[2]

For lawyers and legal scholars alike, the fourth right was always problematic—it didn't really seem to fit well with the other three. These first three rights all dealt with forms of intrusion on a person's private life and activities. The fourth right, however, sounded more like a property right—a right to control an asset an individual had (his or her name and/or likeness). Another problem that arose in trying to enforce this fourth right is that in many cases, an individual's fame or notoriety came only after he or she died, and tort law, which was the legal base upon which these rights of privacy were based, did not apply after death—for example, the estate of a person who died in an accident cannot recover for the pain and suffering of the decedent.

The limitations of the tort right to be free from appropriation of one's name or likeness led a number of states to adopt statutes establishing penalties for these kinds of appropriations. As of the date of this writing, only 24 states have adopted right-of-publicity (ROP) statutes.[3] States that do have these laws, like New York, California, Illinois, and Texas, tend to also be states with large urban centers and active entertainment industries—in short, states where a lot of well-known celebrities work and/or are based.

Each state's laws are different, and creators of fan works are cautioned to check whether their state has an ROP law and what its provisions are before creating works based on living or dead celebrities. It is also important to consider whether works created in a state that does not have an ROP law will find their way, through interstate commerce, into a state with such a law, which could then create a basis for liability for the creator.

By way of illustration, and as a means to discuss the requirements these laws impose, here are California's ROP laws. The first statute, section 3344, applies to the use of the ROP of a living person. The second statute, section 3344.1, pertains to dead persons. Here is what section 3344 provides:

---

2. William L. Prosser, *Privacy*, 48 CAL. L. REV. 383, 388–89 (1960).

3. *Statutes & Interactive Map*, RIGHT OF PUBLICITY, https://rightofpublicity.com/statutes (last visited Jan. 26, 2021).

(a) Any person who ***knowingly uses another's name, voice, signature, photograph, or likeness, in any manner, on or in products, merchandise, or goods,*** or for purposes of advertising or selling, or soliciting purchases of, products, merchandise, goods or services, without such person's prior consent, or, in the case of a minor, the prior consent of his parent or legal guardian, shall be liable for any damages sustained by the person or persons injured as a result thereof. In addition, in any action brought under this section, the person who violated the section ***shall be liable to the injured party or parties in an amount equal to the greater of seven hundred fifty dollars ($750) or the actual damages suffered by him or her as a result of the unauthorized use, and any profits from the unauthorized use that are attributable to the use and are not taken into account in computing the actual damages.*** In establishing such profits, the injured party or parties are required to present proof only of the gross revenue attributable to such use, and the person who violated this section is required to prove his or her deductible expenses. Punitive damages may also be awarded to the injured party or parties. ***The prevailing party in any action under this section shall also be entitled to attorney's fees and costs.***

(b) As used in this section, "photograph" means any photograph or photographic reproduction, still or moving, or any videotape or live television transmission, of any person, such that the person is readily identifiable.

(1) A person shall be deemed to be readily identifiable from a photograph when one who views the photograph with the naked eye can reasonably determine that the person depicted in the photograph is the same person who is complaining of its unauthorized use.

(2) If the photograph includes more than one person so identifiable, then the person or persons complaining of the use shall be represented as individuals rather than solely as members of a definable group represented in the photograph. A definable group includes, but is not limited to, the following examples: a crowd at any sporting event, a crowd in any street or public building, the audience at any theatrical or stage production, a glee club, or a baseball team.

(3) A person or persons shall be considered to be represented as members of a definable group if they are represented in the photograph solely as a result of being present at the time the photograph was taken and have not been singled out as individuals in any manner.

(c) Where a photograph or likeness of an employee of the person using the photograph or likeness appearing in the advertisement or other publication prepared by or in behalf of the user is only incidental, and not essential, to the purpose of the publication in which it appears, there shall arise a rebuttable presumption affecting the burden of producing evidence that the failure to obtain the consent of the employee was not a knowing use of the employee's photograph or likeness.

(d) ***For purposes of this section, a use of a name, voice, signature, photograph, or likeness in connection with any news, public affairs, or sports broadcast or account, or any political campaign, shall not constitute a use for which consent is required under subdivision (a).***

(e) The use of a name, voice, signature, photograph, or likeness in a commercial medium shall not constitute a use for which consent is required under subdivision (a) solely because the material containing such use is commercially sponsored or contains paid advertising. Rather it shall be a question of fact whether or not the use of the person's name, voice, signature, photograph, or likeness was so directly connected with the commercial sponsorship or with the paid advertising as to constitute a use for which consent is required under subdivision (a).

(f) Nothing in this section shall apply to the owners or employees of any medium used for advertising, including, but not limited to, newspapers, magazines, radio and television networks and stations, cable television systems, billboards, and transit ads, by whom any advertisement or solicitation in violation of this section is published or disseminated, unless it is established that such owners or employees had knowledge of the unauthorized use of the person's name, voice, signature, photograph, or likeness as prohibited by this section.

(g) The remedies provided for in this section are cumulative and shall be in addition to any others provided for by law.[4]

California separately deals with the rights of publicity held by deceased persons, which are addressed in the next section of the law, section 3344.1, as follows:

(a)(1) ***Any person who uses a deceased personality's name, voice, signature, photograph, or likeness, in any manner, on or in products, merchandise, or goods, or for purposes of advertising or selling, or soliciting purchases of, products, merchandise, goods, or services, without prior consent from the person or persons specified in subdivision (c), shall be liable for any damages sustained by the person or persons injured as a result thereof.*** In addition, in any action brought under this section, the person who violated the section ***shall be liable to the injured party or parties in an amount equal to the greater of***

4. CAL. CIV. CODE § 3344 (emphasis added).

seven hundred fifty dollars ($750) or the actual damages suffered by the injured party or parties, as a result of the unauthorized use, and any profits from the unauthorized use that are attributable to the use and are not taken into account in computing the actual damages. In establishing these profits, the injured party or parties shall be required to present proof only of the gross revenue attributable to the use, and the person who violated the section is required to prove his or her deductible expenses. ***Punitive damages may also be awarded to the injured party or parties. The prevailing party or parties in any action under this section shall also be entitled to attorney's fees and costs.***

(2) For purposes of this subdivision, a play, book, magazine, newspaper, musical composition, audiovisual work, radio or television program, single and original work of art, work of political or newsworthy value, or an advertisement or commercial announcement for any of these works, shall not be considered a product, article of merchandise, good, or service if it is fictional or nonfictional entertainment, or a dramatic, literary, or musical work.

(3) If a work that is protected under paragraph (2) includes within it a use in connection with a product, article of merchandise, good, or service, this use shall not be exempt under this subdivision, notwithstanding the unprotected use's inclusion in a work otherwise exempt under this subdivision, if the claimant proves that this use is so directly connected with a product, article of merchandise, good, or service as to constitute an act of advertising, selling, or soliciting purchases of that product, article of merchandise, good, or service by the deceased personality without prior consent from the person or persons specified in subdivision (c).

(b) The rights recognized under this section are property rights, freely transferable or descendible, in whole or in part, by contract or by means of any trust or any other testamentary instrument, executed before or after January 1, 1985. The rights recognized under this section shall be deemed to have existed at the time of death of any deceased personality who died prior to January 1, 1985, and, except as provided in subdivision (*o*), shall vest in the persons entitled to these property rights under the testamentary instrument of the deceased personality effective as of the date of his or her death. In the absence of an express transfer in a testamentary instrument of the deceased personality's rights in his or her name, voice, signature, photograph, or likeness, a provision in the testamentary instrument that provides for the disposition of the residue of the deceased personality's assets shall be effective to transfer the rights recognized under this section in accordance with the terms of that provision. The rights established by this section shall also be freely transferable or descendible by contract, trust, or any other testamentary instrument by any subsequent owner of the deceased personality's rights as recognized by this section. ***Nothing in this section shall be construed to render invalid or unenforceable any contract entered into by a deceased personality during his or her lifetime by which the deceased personality assigned the rights, in whole or in part, to use his or her name, voice, signature, photograph, or likeness, regardless of whether the contract was entered into before or after January 1, 1985.***

(c) The consent required by this section shall be exercisable by the person or persons to whom the right of consent, or portion thereof, has been transferred in accordance with subdivision (b), or if no transfer has occurred, then by the person or persons to whom the right of consent, or portion thereof, has passed in accordance with subdivision (d).

(d) ***Subject to subdivisions (b) and (c), after the death of any person, the rights under this section shall belong to the following person or persons and may be exercised, on behalf of and for the benefit of all of those persons, by those persons who, in the aggregate, are entitled to more than a one-half interest in the rights:***

(1) The entire interest in those rights belongs to the surviving spouse of the deceased personality unless there are any surviving children or grandchildren of the deceased personality, in which case one-half of the entire interest in those rights belongs to the surviving spouse.

(2) The entire interest in those rights belongs to the surviving children of the deceased personality and to the surviving children of any dead child of the deceased personality unless the deceased personality has a surviving spouse, in which case the ownership of a one-half interest in rights is divided among the surviving children and grandchildren.

(3) If there is no surviving spouse, and no surviving children or grandchildren, then the entire interest in those rights belongs to the surviving parent or parents of the deceased personality.

(4) The rights of the deceased personality's children and grandchildren are in all cases divided among them and exercisable in the manner provided in Section 240 of the Probate Code according to the number of the deceased personality's children represented. The share of the children of a dead child of a deceased personality can be exercised only by the action of a majority of them.

(e) If any deceased personality does not transfer his or her rights under this section by contract, or by means of a trust or testamentary instrument, and there are no surviving persons as described in subdivision (d), then the rights set forth in subdivision (a) shall terminate.

(f)(1) A successor in interest to the rights of a deceased personality under this section or a licensee thereof shall not recover damages for a use prohibited by this section that occurs before the successor in interest or licensee registers a claim of the rights under paragraph (2).

(2) ***Any person claiming to be a successor in interest to the rights of a deceased personality under this section or a licensee thereof may register that claim with the Secretary of State on a form prescribed by the Secretary of State and upon payment of a fee as set forth in*** subdivision (d) of Section 12195 of the Government Code. ***The form shall be verified and shall include the name and date of death of the deceased personality, the name and address of the claimant, the basis of the claim, and the rights claimed.***

(3) ***Upon receipt and after filing of any document under this section, the Secretary of State shall post the document along with the entire registry of persons claiming to be a successor in interest to the rights of a deceased personality or a registered licensee under this section upon the Secretary of State's Internet Web site.*** The Secretary of State may microfilm or reproduce by other techniques any of the filings or documents and destroy the original filing or document. The microfilm or other reproduction of any document under this section shall be admissible in any court of law. The microfilm or other reproduction of any document may be destroyed by the Secretary of State 70 years after the death of the personality named therein.

(4) Claims registered under this subdivision shall be public records.

(g) An action shall not be brought under this section by reason of any use of a deceased personality's name, voice, signature, photograph, or likeness occurring after the expiration of 70 years after the death of the deceased personality.

(h) As used in this section, ***"deceased personality" means any natural person whose name, voice, signature, photograph, or likeness has commercial value at the time of his or her death,*** or because of his or her death, whether or not during the lifetime of that natural person the person used his or her name, voice, signature, photograph, or likeness on or in products, merchandise, or goods, or for purposes of advertising or selling, or solicitation of purchase of, products, merchandise, goods, or services. A "deceased personality" shall include, without limitation, any such natural person who has died within 70 years prior to January 1, 1985.

(i) As used in this section, "photograph" means any photograph or photographic reproduction, still or moving, or any videotape or live television transmission, of any person, such that the deceased personality is readily identifiable. A deceased personality shall be deemed to be readily identifiable from a photograph if one who views the photograph with the naked eye can reasonably determine who the person depicted in the photograph is.

(j) For purposes of this section, the use of a name, voice, signature, photograph, or likeness in connection with any news, public affairs, or sports broadcast or account, or any political campaign, shall not constitute a use for which consent is required under subdivision (a).

(k) The use of a name, voice, signature, photograph, or likeness in a commercial medium shall not constitute a use for which consent is required under subdivision (a) solely because the material containing the use is commercially sponsored or contains paid advertising. Rather, it shall be a question of fact whether or not the use of the deceased personality's name, voice, signature, photograph, or likeness was so directly connected with the commercial sponsorship or with the paid advertising as to constitute a use for which consent is required under subdivision (a).

(*l*) Nothing in this section shall apply to the owners or employees of any medium used for advertising, including, but not limited to, newspapers, magazines, radio and television networks and stations, cable television systems, billboards, and transit advertisements, by whom any advertisement or solicitation in violation of this section is published or disseminated, unless it is established that the owners or employees had knowledge of the unauthorized use of the deceased personality's name, voice, signature, photograph, or likeness as prohibited by this section.

(m) The remedies provided for in this section are cumulative and shall be in addition to any others provided for by law.

(n) This section shall apply to the adjudication of liability and the imposition of any damages or other remedies in cases in which the liability, damages, and other remedies arise from acts occurring directly in this state. For purposes of this section, acts giving rise to liability shall be limited to the use, on or in products, merchandise, goods, or services, or the advertising or selling, or soliciting purchases of, products, merchandise, goods, or services prohibited by this section.

(*o*) Notwithstanding any provision of this section to the contrary, if an action was taken prior to May 1, 2007, to exercise rights recognized under this section relating to a deceased personality who died prior to January 1, 1985, by a person described in subdivision (d), other than a person who was disinherited by the deceased personality in a testamentary instrument, and the exercise of those rights was not challenged successfully in a court action by a person described in subdivision (b), that exercise shall not be affected by subdivision (b). In that case, the rights

> that would otherwise vest in one or more persons described in subdivision (b) shall vest solely in the person or persons described in subdivision (d), other than a person disinherited by the deceased personality in a testamentary instrument, for all future purposes.
>
> (p) The rights recognized by this section are expressly made retroactive, including to those deceased personalities who died before January 1, 1985.[5]

There are several important points to understand that are common to both of these statutes and that are likely going to be present in other statutes in the other states that allow for and enforce ROPs, as well as elements unique to each of these statutes. It is also important to note that not all states have adopted ROPs for both living and dead persons, and at various times in various states, such as New York, heirs of a deceased person could not claim violation of ROPs unless the subject of those rights had claimed and enforced them during his or her lifetime. New York State no longer imposes that limitation; however, practitioners and creators should be careful to check their individual state laws to see if the law protects the ROP of dead persons, and if so, if the protection is afforded only to deceased persons who claimed and exercised their rights during their lifetimes.

One important element of both of these sections is the scope of what ROPs are covered—the original formulation was limited to name, image, and likeness, and subsequent cases led the legislature to add protection for voice, signature, and photograph, while dropping "image," which was vague and largely duplicative of "likeness."

An interesting distinction between these sections is that under section 3344, the unauthorized use must be made "knowingly"—a restriction not found in the use of a deceased person's ROP. Yet in both cases, punitive damages may be recovered—which differs from usual practice, which frowns on punitive damages being recoverable in situations where the conduct occurs through negligence as opposed to intentional conduct.

Creators and practitioners should also note that each of these sections also contains key limitations to the exercise of the ROP, which are not found in the other section. So in section 3344, the use of a person's publicity rights "in connection with any news, public affairs, or sports broadcast or account, or any political campaign, shall not constitute a use for which consent is required under subdivision (a)." This limitation does not exist in section 3344.1.

---

5. Cal. Civ. Code § 3344.1 (emphasis added). California's ROP statutes used to be located in different sections of the Civil Code, which led to all kinds of confusion. The legislature remedied the problem by moving the deceased person's statute to follow right after section 3344 for living persons.

Conversely, section 3344.1 has a single-work limitation, which reads: "[A] play, book, magazine, newspaper, musical composition, audiovisual work, radio or television program, single and original work of art, work of political or newsworthy value, or an advertisement or commercial announcement for any of these works, shall not be considered a product, article of merchandise, good, or service if it is fictional or nonfictional entertainment, or a dramatic, literary, or musical work."

This last exception is an important one, which allows fan-art creators to create a "single and original work of art" depicting the image or likeness of the celebrity they admire, without penalty. To give you an example of how this clause works in actual practice, some years ago I was retained by an artist who created an original oil painting of his favorite Bay Area football team. The painting showed the team in a huddle, with the quarterback facing the team and with his back to the viewer. His name and number were clearly visible, so the elements of identifiability were clear.

The artist had traveled from his native Oregon, a state that does not have a statutory ROP, to the Bay Area and had an opportunity to give the original painting to the quarterback, who so liked the work that he hung it in his workout room. The artist returned to Oregon and later licensed rights to the painting to a printer who printed up posters of the image. The posters were sold to sports fans at conventions, and the quarterback's representatives, seeing this, filed suit in California for breach of the athlete's ROP. They had a valid claim, because even though the quarterback had impliedly liked and accepted the original work of art, that wasn't consent to allowing multiple copies to be made—which is precisely the scope and point of this carved-out exception in the statute.[6]

Two other subsections of section 3344.1 bear mention. The first is subsection 3344.1(h), which defines a "deceased personality" as "any natural person whose name, voice, signature, photograph, or likeness has commercial value at the time of his or her death." Fan-art creators should note that this definition is not limited to celebrities—it applies literally to anyone whose elements of identifiability have commercial value. What exactly does "commercial value" mean in this context? Of course it means those activities we connect with celebrities—allowing their name or image to be used in endorsements of goods and services (this includes online influencer roles). However, it can also mean a business owner who uses his or her name in the business. In one case I handled, I was able to successfully claim the statutory ROP in California for the

6. The case settled, and by its terms, the parties were limited in what they could say about it in public, which is why I haven't identified the parties. The resolution of the case was affected by the fact that the athlete's original signature appeared on a number of the posters, which arguably was a waiver of his ROP violation claims.

partner in an accounting firm whose name was a part of the firm name and whose public reputation added value to the firm.

The second subsection fan-art creators should be aware of is subsections 3344.1(f)(1)–(4), which provide a system by which one heir of a deceased personality may register his or her name as the designated representative of the estate of that person, which allows people seeking to license the personality's ROP for use in commercial contexts to know whom they have to contact to obtain that permission. This is useful information for fan artists who may want to create their version of that personality's image—checking the state's records to determine if there is a designated representative of the estate will allow you to know whom you have to contact to license the ROP, which is very helpful, and if there is no such registration, that tells you the heirs may not know of their rights under the law or may have chosen not to pursue those rights. Either way, you meet your good-faith, due-diligence obligations by conducting that investigation.

Although my focus here is on how ROPs affect the creation of fan art, that effect is not limited to fan art. ROP laws also apply with equal force to fan fiction, to film, and possibly even to cosplay.

Shifting our focus, let's look at the case of the fan artist who wants to create a work of art inspired by, or in homage to, the original work done by a different artist. A number of different legal issues are presented in that context. Before going through those issues, it is important to talk about how and where fan art is seen by the public.

Although exhibitions of fan art can be sometimes seen in galleries and museums, fan art is also, and primarily, seen at fandom conventions and on websites devoted to it. Each of these locations offers different benefits and legal challenges for the fan artist as well as for the original artist whose work is the source of the fan artist's inspiration and admiration.

Fan art at conventions is seen primarily in two contexts—in the exhibitor's area and in portfolio review sessions with major publishing companies. Let's start with the portfolio review process.

Portfolio reviews are done by representatives from major publishing companies who are looking for artists to illustrate upcoming publications. These reviews can lead the fan artist to a part-time or even full-time job working as a graphic artist, inker, colorist, or letterer, or they can lead to being hired in one of these capacities as an independent contractor to do a single graphic or a series of them.

At many smaller fan conventions, which include niche fandoms like *Star Trek* conventions, Xena conventions, etc., publishers may send their art directors, or art department staffers, to work in a booth or at a table with the publisher's logo displayed to meet with fan artists to review a portfolio of their work, with the idea that they can recruit new artists to illustrate their graphic novels, comic books, or other products, such as video games. It is a great way to find new artists for these companies, since live in-person interviews are a much better way to evaluate whether the artist will be a good fit for the company's needs. Fan artists participating in portfolio reviews for particular publishing companies in the comics business, for example, may prepare work done in the style of existing artists who have made their name working on those same characters. For example, comic artist Alex Ross is well known for a painterly style of graphic illustration and has done a great deal of work for DC Comics. A fan artist hoping to get a job with DC might submit for portfolio review a series of illustrations of DC superhero characters (Superman, Batman, Wonder Woman, Green Lantern, Aquaman, etc.) done in the Alex Ross style.

Whether this is the best path to a job with one of these companies depends on the reviewer who sees the work and how the company feels about this kind of copying. Some reviewers feel that graphics done of their stable of heroes are helpful—they tell the reviewer that the artist can reproduce, with skill and talent, those heroes, which would be a part of his or her job if hired. Other reviewers and companies, particularly what are known as creator-owned companies, which are looking for new characters and stories, are more interested in artists who have their own original characters to display. Often, fan artists can find out the preferences of the reviewing companies by following online discussions about those companies' portfolio review processes.

On the legal side, artists preparing work for a portfolio review do not have to worry about the publishing companies threatening copyright infringement claims against portfolios submitted to them depicting their major characters. Although all portfolio reviewers want you to give them copies of your work as opposed to the originals, so they can bring the portfolios back to their companies for further review, the making of one such copy isn't the same thing as making, distributing, and selling multiple copies of the work, and so the fan artist can create these kinds of derivative works without fear of prosecution. And since in this case, the graphics generally depict characters, as opposed to the actors/actresses who portray them, there are no ROP issues presented in these reviews either.

Fan artists who wish to participate in portfolio reviews at larger conventions, like the San Diego Comic-Con International or the New York Comic Con, are cautioned to carefully review the process for participating in portfolio reviews at these cons. In these cases, artists often have to fill out participation request forms and submit to random ticket drawing processes in order to get a place in the line for review by a company. These processes are necessary because these large cons draw more applicants for portfolio review than the company representatives can possibly see over the day(s) they spend at the con doing the reviews.

The other place fan artists' work is shown at conventions is in what most cons call their Exhibitors Hall, which is usually a large hall or other open space at the convention, where artists show and sell original art, posters, and other copies of their artwork. Often, conventions feature an Artist's Alley within the Exhibitors Hall, which is where individual artists can rent table space at a price much lower than other convention exhibitors who rent larger booths or exhibits in the hall.

Fan artists, like fan-fiction writers, are found along a broad spectrum. Some are very amateurish in their work, just create their art out of their passion for their subjects, and aren't very concerned with honing their level of craftsmanship or with making any money selling their work. At the other end of the spectrum are trained, highly talented artists, who see creating fan art as a path toward a successful, reasonably well-paid job as a professional artist.

And so it is not uncommon for fan artists with mid-level to higher-level artistic skills to develop a catalog of illustrations in the style of their favorite well-known professional artists and to produce posters and prints of those works for commercial sale. Some of these artists then choose to sell these posters and prints at the many pop-culture conventions that now crisscross the country. And it is in the Artist's Alleys of those conventions that a real problem emerges. Two tables down from the fan artist in Artist's Alley sits the original artist whose work the fan artist is emulating. The original artist may even be selling posters or prints of the same work the fan artist is selling.

Needless to say, sparks fly in this situation. Making a living as an artist is a difficult path for most—and it is particularly galling for those artists to find themselves in competition with fan artists who are emulating their original work. Is this illegal? Maybe. It depends on whether the work is so much a copy that a judge or jury would not find the fan art to be transformative enough to avoid an infringement claim, as discussed previously.

For both the original artist and the pop-culture convention, this situation, which I am told by a number of original artists is happening more often in recent years, presents several real-world problems. For the original artist, after their fury at seeing someone else profiting off copies of their original work, the question remains—what can they do about it? Lawsuits are prohibitively expensive, and the recoverable damages are both hard to prove and, in many cases, even harder to collect. More importantly, since these aren't contractual relationships, attorney fees are recoverable only if you prove statutory copyright infringement, and not all fees are likely to be recovered.[7]

---

7. It is a little-known fact that the recovery of attorney fees in a litigation case is largely up to the discretion of the judge. Even if fees are recoverable in the case because there is a contract that provides for their recovery, all such contracts are interpreted by the courts as allowing recovery of "reasonable legal fees"—and many judges reduce the amount sought by a party by as much as 50 percent, having concluded that what the attorney charged was more than what the judge thinks is a reasonable amount. So attorneys should be very careful to explain to clients that seeking recovery of legal fees in a case is not a guarantee that they will be recovered or in what amount.

And for the convention itself, this situation also puts it between the proverbial rock and a hard place. On the one hand, conventions get an important set of benefits by having well-known artists in their Artist's Alley—they often spotlight those artists in their publicity for the event and in some instances even comp the artists the cost of their table in the alley. On the other hand, the convention promoters need the income the fan artists bring in through their table rentals. So the outcome of this depends on how much clout the complaining original artist has and how egregious the fan artist's imitation is, as well as how close the artists are to each other on the convention floor. There is no right or good answer here, and outcomes vary from convention to convention.

The importance convention sales have for fan artists was the subject of a *New York Times* article—a fact that in itself is reflective of how important these convention sales have become to the lives of fan artists. In the article, *Fan Artists Scramble for Sales,* writer Paige Lyman interviews fan artists who were adversely affected by the shuttering of most fan conventions during the 2020 COVID-19 pandemic. Freelance fan artist Karen Hallion is quoted, describing the situation: "It's been tough. From a business perspective, conventions represent a significant portion of our income stream, so it has made me feel less secure generally."[8]

The extent to which fan art is becoming a commercial activity calls into question whether the art these artists are creating is still "fan art." As we saw in the Omegaverse fan fic, it may have started out as fan art, but it has crossed over into the commercial realm. To the extent that these artists see convention sales as a "significant portion" of their income, it can certainly be argued that despite the "fan" nature of the art they are doing, it is either fully professional art now or very close to that characterization.

Fan artists who aren't necessarily looking for work that they might get via a portfolio review, and who aren't looking to make money selling prints at conventions, have another huge venue to display their works—the Internet. And for fan artists, one important forum for displaying their fan art is the DeviantArt website, found at www.deviantart.com.

DeviantArt, launched in August 2000, is a website-based community where members can upload artwork, photography, and videos primarily, as well as literature and skins for applications, and can add or view tutorials, participate in group activities, and archive their portfolios. The company incorporated shortly after its launch and went on to become one of the largest websites on the Internet, currently hosting over 358 million images posted by over 35 million registered members as of 2015. In 2017, the company was acquired for $36 million by Wix, Inc.

---

8. Paige Lyman, *Fan Artists Scramble for Sales,* N.Y. Times, Aug. 2, 2020, Styles sec. at 3.

DeviantArt was not the only online platform for fan art. Other sites, like Conceptart.org and WetCanvas, soon followed. With increased size, however, came concerns about the loss of the "artist community" feeling that these sites had when they were small. New small sites, like Nasty Nets, which launched in 2006, tried to fill that sense of community loss. And the rise of social media platforms, such as Instagram, Tumblr, YouTube, and Facebook, also took the place of the more "limited to art" sites—following the pattern of many online communities that prove to have only a fragile loyalty from their user base.[9]

So while sites like DeviantArt have lost some of their more underground or rebel appeal due to their substantial growth, they are still important, and large, depositories of fan art—large enough to warrant a deeper look to understand how their operations benefit the fan-art community, as well as to expose some of the pitfalls and traps for the unwary, both legal and otherwise, that can arise when artwork is uploaded to the site.

We begin that inquiry by reviewing the principal agreements and governing documents that comprise the rules of the road for members of DeviantArt. The first of these is the Terms of Service (TOS) agreement. These TOS agreements are written by lawyers and are often a dense thicket of legalese, going on for far too many pages to be understandable to most members. TOS agreements are also, as is true for the one governing members of DeviantArt, subject to revision by the company at any time. And while registered members get an e-mail letting them know the terms have changed, casual visitors to the site, who by accessing the site agree to be bound by those TOS, do not get notice of changes. So the better practice in all such fan art sites is to periodically review the TOS to make sure changes that might impact you have not been made without your knowledge.

A few of these TOS terms warrant special mention here. By doing so, however, I am not advising you to skip reading the rest of the terms or, if you are not an attorney, having a lawyer read them and help you understand them all. I just highlight a few that have a direct bearing on the activities of fan artists who are interested in uploading their artwork to the site. It is also important to note that while the DeviantArt pages that apply to the user experience are pretty standard in their approach, every TOS and related set of documents are different and may contain unique terms that impact fan-art creators' efforts and rights, so it is important to review these terms before using these services and to periodically reread them, as they change often.

The first of the TOS terms DeviantArt sets forth is in the initial section, where it explains that there are actually two sets of TOS—one for people who just visit the site to look at images and a second set, the Additional Terms,

9. *See* Kelsey Ables, *The Rise and Fall of Internet Art Communities*, Artsy.net (Apr. 19, 2019), https://www.artsy.net/article/artsy-editorial-rise-fall-internet-art-communities.

which applies to members who upload content or visitors who are also buyers of artwork from members via the DeviantArt Shop:

> By using our Service, you agree to be bound by Section I of these Terms ("General Terms"), which contains provisions applicable to all users of our Service, including visitors to the DeviantArt website (the "Site"). If you choose to register as a member of our Service or purchase products from the DeviantArt Shop, you will be asked to check a box indicating that you have read, and agree to be bound by, the additional terms set forth in Section II of these Terms ("Additional Terms").[10]

Note here that while DeviantArt is comfortable using the "by using our service" language to bind casual users to its TOS, it is not relying on that use when it comes to members or purchasers at its online store—those users are required to sign off on a check box accepting those terms.

Next up is the policy DeviantArt holds with respect to copyright ownership of content that artists upload to the site. Note here that while DeviantArt makes it clear that it does not own the copyright in the content you upload, it retains the right, along with the owner, to grant third parties the right to distribute, publicly display, perform, or create derivative works based on that content! Here is the language:

> **4. Copyright**
>
> DeviantArt is, unless otherwise stated, the owner of all copyright and data rights in the Service and its contents. Individuals who have posted works to DeviantArt are either the copyright owners of the component parts of that work or are posting the work under license from a copyright owner or his or her agent or otherwise as permitted by law. ***You may not reproduce, distribute, publicly display or perform, or prepare derivative works based on any of the Content including any such works without the express, written consent of DeviantArt or the appropriate owner of copyright in such works.*** DeviantArt does not claim ownership rights in your works or other materials posted by you to DeviantArt (Your Content). You agree not to distribute any part of the Service other than Your Content in any medium other than as permitted in these Terms of Service or by use of functions on the Service provided by us. You agree not to alter or modify any part of the Service unless expressly permitted to do so by us or by use of functions on the Service provided by us.[11]

---

10. *DeviantArt Terms of Service: Introduction,* https://deviantart.com/policy/service (last visited Aug. 4, 2020).
11. *Id.* sec. 4 (emphasis added).

DeviantArt is also very careful to make it expressly clear that it disclaims any liability for any claims that may arise from the use of the site—a section in the general terms that is in full caps to make sure it is conspicuous and to defeat any claims that a person didn't see these limitations. Here's what they look like:

> **9. Disclaimer of Warranty and Limitation of Liability**
>
> DEVIANTART MAKES NO REPRESENTATIONS OR WARRANTIES OF ANY KIND, EXPRESS OR IMPLIED AS TO THE OPERATION OF THE SERVICE, OR THE CONTENT OR PRODUCTS, PROVIDED THROUGH THE SERVICE. ***YOU EXPRESSLY AGREE THAT YOUR USE OF THE SERVICE IS AT YOUR SOLE RISK. DEVIANTART DISCLAIMS ALL WARRANTIES, EXPRESS OR IMPLIED, INCLUDING WITHOUT LIMITATION, IMPLIED WARRANTIES OF MERCHANTABILITY, FITNESS FOR A PARTICULAR PURPOSE, AND NON-INFRINGEMENT, TO THE FULLEST EXTENT PERMITTED BY LAW. DEVIANTART MAKES NO WARRANTY AS TO THE SECURITY, RELIABILITY, TIMELINESS, AND PERFORMANCE OF THIS SERVICE. YOU SPECIFICALLY ACKNOWLEDGE THAT DEVIANTART IS NOT LIABLE FOR YOUR DEFAMATORY, OFFENSIVE OR ILLEGAL CONDUCT, OR SUCH CONDUCT BY THIRD PARTIES, AND YOU EXPRESSLY ASSUME ALL RISKS AND RESPONSIBILITY FOR DAMAGES AND LOSSES ARISING FROM SUCH CONDUCT. EXCEPT FOR THE EXPRESS, LIMITED REMEDIES PROVIDED HEREIN,*** AND TO THE FULLEST EXTENT ALLOWED BY LAW, DEVIANTART SHALL NOT BE LIABLE FOR ANY DAMAGES OF ANY KIND ARISING FROM USE OF THE SERVICE, INCLUDING BUT NOT LIMITED TO DIRECT, INDIRECT, INCIDENTAL, CONSEQUENTIAL, SPECIAL, EXEMPLARY, OR PUNITIVE DAMAGES, EVEN IF DEVIANTART HAS BEEN ADVISED OF THE POSSIBILITY OF SUCH DAMAGES. THE FOREGOING DISCLAIMERS, WAIVERS AND LIMITATIONS SHALL APPLY NOTWITHSTANDING ANY FAILURE OF ESSENTIAL PURPOSE OF ANY LIMITED REMEDY. SOME JURISDICTIONS DO NOT ALLOW THE EXCLUSION OF OR LIMITATIONS ON CERTAIN WARRANTIES OR DAMAGES. THEREFORE, SOME OF THE ABOVE EXCLUSIONS OR LIMITATIONS MAY NOT APPLY TO YOU. IN NO EVENT SHALL DEVIANTART'S AGGREGATE LIABILITY TO YOU EXCEED THE AMOUNTS PAID BY YOU TO DEVIANTART PURSUANT TO THIS AGREEMENT.[12]

12. *Id.* sec. 9 (emphasis added).

When the DeviantArt TOS moves from its General Terms to its Additional Terms, the focus becomes more restrictive, with a number of specific elements required of members. First among them is an age limit, and notice that uploading work to the site is governed by a separate policy, the Submission Policy, whose terms must also be complied with:

Section II: Additional Terms

13. Registration

To register as a member of the Service or purchase products, you must be 13 years or lawfully permitted to enter into and form contracts under applicable law. In no event may minors submit Content to the Service.

Artist Materials - ***As a registered member of the Service, you will also be granted the privilege of submitting certain types of Your Content, known as "Artist Materials," for display on your user page. Prior to submitting Artist Materials, you must accept the additional terms and conditions of the Submission Policy, which is incorporated into, and forms a part of, the Terms.***[13]

Section 16 of the Additional Terms, which focuses on Copyright in Your Content, is somewhat duplicative of section 4 in the General Terms, although it contains one interesting change that may create a conflict between the two sections. Section 4 states that third-party visitors or other users of the site may not reproduce, distribute, or create derivative works based on the art on the site without the consent of DeviantArt **or** the owner of the artwork. However, when you get to section 16, it tells you that third-party use made without the permission of the owner of the art may be a violation of section 4. These sections appear to be in conflict, as it isn't clear if a member has any recourse if DeviantArt grants consent to a use by a third party of content on the site. Creators are advised to obtain clarification of this point before uploading content to the site.

16. Copyright in Your Content

DeviantArt does not claim ownership rights in Your Content. For the sole purpose of enabling us to make your Content available through the Service, you grant to DeviantArt a non-exclusive, royalty-free license to reproduce, distribute, re-format, store, prepare derivative works based on, and publicly display and perform Your Content. **Please note that when you upload Content, third parties will be able to copy, distribute and display your Content using readily available tools**

13. *Id.* sec. 13 (emphasis added).

> **on their computers for this purpose although other than by linking to your Content on DeviantArt any use by a third party of your Content could violate paragraph 4 of these Terms and Conditions unless the third party receives permission from you by license.**[14]

Companies that provide an opportunity for third parties using their site to access the Internet were, in the early days of online communications, concerned that they might be held liable for content that was posted on their site but that they otherwise did not have any control over—they didn't exercise editorial control, nor did they create any of the content uploaded. In answer to those concerns, the U.S. Congress, in enacting the Digital Millennium Copyright Act of 1999 (the DMCA), enacted section 230 of the Act, which creates an absolute immunity from liability for these companies, known as Internet service providers (ISPs), so long as they can establish that they don't exercise any control over the content at issue. So it is not surprising to find in DeviantArt's TOS, and in similar terms for other fan-art sites, the following notice to uploading members:

> **17. Monitoring Content**
>
> ***DeviantArt has no ability to control the Content you may upload, post or otherwise transmit using the Service and does not have any obligation to monitor such Content for any purpose. You acknowledge that you are solely responsible for all Content and material you upload, post or otherwise transmit using the Service.***[15]

One of the benefits of uploading artwork to a site like DeviantArt is that you can store, organize, and archive your body of work in one conveniently accessible location. However, there are limits to how much you can store, and importantly, DeviantArt can delete your stored files if you are not an active member of the site—and there is no definition of what constitutes inactivity, leaving this important issue solely in the discretion of the site owner. Here's the specific term:

> **18. Storage Policy**
>
> At this time, DeviantArt provides free online storage of Your Content to registered members of the Service. However, you acknowledge and agree that ***DeviantArt may, at its option, establish limits concerning your use of the Service, including without limitation the maximum number of days that Your Content will be retained by the Service,*** the maximum size of any Content files that may be stored on the Service,

---

14. *Id.* sec. 16 (emphasis added).
15. *Id.* sec. 17 (emphasis added).

> the maximum disk space that will be allotted to you for the storage of Content on DeviantArt's servers. Furthermore, you acknowledge that ***DeviantArt reserves the right to terminate or suspend accounts that are inactive, in DeviantArt's sole discretion, for an extended period of time (thus deleting or suspending access to your Content). Without limiting the generality of Section 9, DeviantArt shall have no responsibility or liability for the deletion or failure to store any Content maintained on the Service and you are solely responsible for creating back-ups of Your Content.*** You further acknowledge that DeviantArt reserves the right to modify its storage policies from time to time, with or without notice to you.[16]

Fan-art creators who upload to DeviantArt expecting to be able to leave their content on the site indefinitely are advised to keep a backup copy of all artworks they upload and should also establish a regular pattern of using the site, so they aren't found to be inactive, triggering a deletion of their archive. Caveat emptor, members!

The Additional Terms also introduce two other policies that govern your use of the DeviantArt site: the Etiquette Policy and the Copyright Policy. Here's how these additional policies are introduced, followed by an exhaustive, and somewhat exhausting, list of conduct rules binding on members:

> **19. Conduct**
>
> You agree to be subject to and to conduct yourself in accordance with the DeviantArt Etiquette Policy. You are responsible for all of Your Content you upload, download, and otherwise copy, distribute and display using the Service. You must have the legal right to copy, distribute and display all parts of any content that you upload, download and otherwise copy, distribute and display. Content provided to you by others, or made available through websites, magazines, books and other sources, are protected by copyright and should not be uploaded, downloaded, or otherwise copied, distributed or displayed without the consent of the copyright owner or as otherwise permitted by law. Please refer to DeviantArt's Copyright Policy for further details.
>
> You agree not to use the Service:
>
> 1. for any unlawful purposes;
> 2. to upload, post, or otherwise transmit any material that is obscene, offensive, blasphemous, pornographic, unlawful, threatening, menacing, abusive, harmful, an invasion of privacy or publicity rights, defamatory, libelous, vulgar, illegal or otherwise objectionable;

16. *Id.* sec. 18 (emphasis added).

3. to upload, post, or otherwise transmit any material that infringes any copyright, trade mark, patent or other intellectual property right or any moral right or artist's right of any third party including, but not limited to, DeviantArt or to facilitate the unlawful distribution of copyrighted content or illegal content;
4. to harm minors in any way, including, but not limited to, uploading, posting, or otherwise transmitting content that violates child pornography laws, child sexual exploitation laws or laws prohibiting the depiction of minors engaged in sexual conduct, or submitting any personally identifiable information about any child under the age of 13;
5. to forge headers or otherwise manipulate identifiers in order to disguise the origin of any Content transmitted through the Service;
6. to upload, post, or otherwise transmit any material which is likely to cause harm to DeviantArt or anyone else's computer systems, including but not limited to that which contains any virus, code, worm, data or other files or programs designed to damage or allow unauthorized access to the Service which may cause any defect, error, malfunction or corruption to the Service;
7. for any commercial purpose, except as expressly permitted under these Terms;
8. to sell access to the Service on any other website or to use the Service on another website for the primary purpose of gaining advertising or subscription revenue other than a personal blog or social network where the primary purpose is to display content from DeviantArt by hyperlink and not to compete with DeviantArt.[17]

There are risks for fan-art creators in agreeing to these conduct terms. The primary problems lie in the first four items on this list. By agreeing, for example, that you won't use the service for any "unlawful purpose" (item 1), you are agreeing to a vague and undefined term. What exactly is an "unlawful purpose" as used in this context? The vagueness allows great discretion to DeviantArt to remove or alter content at its discretion, without recourse for the creator.

Similarly, in item 2, the member/user is agreeing that he or she will not post or upload any content that falls under the laundry list of content described by incredibly vague terms, such as "obscene, offensive, blasphemous, pornographic, unlawful, threatening, menacing, abusive, harmful, an invasion of privacy or publicity rights, defamatory, libelous, vulgar, illegal or otherwise objectionable." The U.S. Supreme Court can't figure out what is obscene, and terms like "offensive" and "blasphemous" are similarly impossible to define. Requiring that members/users figure out in advance of posting work whether

---

17. *Id.* sec. 19.

the work fits into one of these categories is an impossible task—once again meaning that fan-art creators are entirely at the mercy of DeviantArt's staff as to whether their postings will be allowed at all or will be taken down without notice.

Item 3 attempts to limit postings that violate copyright law . . . once again a difficult thing to understand and determine, and even more problematic, creators agree not to post anything that violates another's "moral rights"—a legal standard that applies throughout the European Union but that has never been fully adopted in the United States, except for a very limited version that applies only to fine arts. That law, found in section 106(a) of the Copyright Act, known as the Visual Artists Rights Act, only protects against acts affecting the integrity or attribution of a work and has proven very difficult to enforce. Defining a moral rights violation is also hard to do and likely impossible for creators to do without the help of legal counsel.

Lastly, item 4 attempts to prevent users from posting or uploading any material harmful to minors, such as "content that violates child pornography laws, child sexual exploitation laws or laws prohibiting the depiction of minors engaged in sexual conduct." Even more so than the other items, this leads the fan-art creator into the morass of child pornography laws, an area rife with ill-defined standards and that has led to terrible results, putting artists in jail for drawing fictional creatures, whose age and species are undefined but whose apparently youthful appearance justifies the sentences imposed. I have written at length about these problems in my prior book, *Comic Art, Creativity and the Law*.[18]

Once a fan-art creator decides to upload content to the DeviantArt site, compliance with the site's Submission Policy[19] is required. This policy makes it clear that by submitting work to the site, the fan-art creator grants to DeviantArt a broad array of rights to use his or her content:

Submission Policy

AGREEMENT

3. License To Use Artist Materials. As and when Artist Materials are uploaded to the DeviantArt Site(s), Artist grants to DeviantArt a worldwide, royalty-free, non-exclusive license to do the following things during the Term:

b) to display, copy, reproduce, exhibit, publicly perform, broadcast, rebroadcast, transmit, retransmit, distribute through any electronic

18. Marc H. Greenberg, Comic Art, Creativity and the Law 126–172 (Edward Elgar Publ'g 2014).

19. *Submission Policy*, DeviantArt, https://about.deviantart.com/policy/submission/ (last visited Jan. 27, 2021).

> *means (including analog and digital) or other means, and electronically or otherwise publish any or all of the Artist Materials, including any part of them, and to include them in compilations for publication, by any and all means and media now known or not yet known or invented;*
>
> *c) to modify, adapt, change or otherwise alter the Artist Materials (e.g., change the size) and use the Artist Materials as described in Section 3(b); and*
>
> d) the right to sublicense to any other person or company any of the licensed rights in the Artist Materials, or any part of them, subject to the terms and conditions of this Agreement.[20]

Submitted artwork also may be used by DeviantArt to promote its own website:

> *f) During the Term, DeviantArt's licenses under this Agreement include the right to use any part of the Artist Materials in the promotion, advertising or marketing of the DeviantART Sites.*
>
> *g) As used in this Agreement, the term "Artist Materials" means any content uploaded to the DeviantArt Site(s) which may include without limitation Artist's name(s) (including professional names), trademarks, trade names, likenesses, photographs, biographical materials, audio-visual materials, artwork, liner notes, and other graphical, textual, video, film or audio materials and any and all "skins," computer-generated images or other artwork or images that Artist submits to DeviantArt in any medium or format whatsoever.*[21]

And the rights creators grant to DeviantArt don't stop there. They also include a license of ROP from the creator to the site, as well as a waiver of the creator's rights of privacy and moral and similar rights—a very broad immunity grant:

> *4. Name and Likeness. Artist also grants to DeviantArt:*
>
> *a) a worldwide, royalty-free, non-exclusive license to use Artist's name(s), group name, photograph and/or likeness(es) and biographical materials in connection with the distribution, exploitation, promotion, marketing and advertising of the Artist Materials, and the DeviantArt Site(s) as described hereunder, during the Term;*
>
> *b) Artist also agrees not to assert against DeviantArt any privacy, publicity, moral or similar rights held by Artist and on behalf any other person(s) whose name(s), photographs and/or likeness(es) and/or*

---

20. *Id.* at 3 (emphasis added).
21. *Id.* (emphasis added).

> ***performances are embodied in the Artist Materials. Artist also agrees that any persons other than Artist appearing recognizably or otherwise in Artist Materials will not assert of [sic] any privacy, publicity, moral or similar rights) under the laws of the United States and any other country in connection with the exploitation of the materials as described in this Agreement[.]***[22]

Lastly, DeviantArt makes it clear that the license to make the kind of extensive uses granted to the company by the submitting artist is granted to the company without any expectation of any fee or royalty being paid to the artist, a condition that is standard for such sites—and that allows it to generate advertising and other revenue based on the content on the site, without having to pay anything to the artists who create that content.

> 6. ***Payment. Unless otherwise agreed between Artist and DeviantArt in a writing from DeviantArt, the license granted to DeviantArt under this Agreement is royalty-free.***[23]

Which brings us to the last of the key policies DeviantArt imposes—a policy governing behavior in ways not usually seen in sites like this—a policy named the "Etiquette Policy," a throwback term rarely used in contemporary society, other than its reformulation as "netiquette" during the early years of the Internet, when conduct like "flaming" (SENDING MESSAGES IN ALL CAPS) was called out and derided as a violation of netiquette.

It turns out that the Etiquette Policy is a catchall for a variety of conduct concerns that include limitations on free-speech commentary, mature content, and the use of models, in particular underage models, in materials posted to the site.

The Etiquette Policy begins by confronting the uncomfortable reality, in a subsection titled "Guidelines for Deviants: Quality and Placement," that at least some of the artwork submitted for uploading may not be of very good quality, and DeviantArt needs a way to screen that content out and to refuse to allow it to be uploaded to the site. Here's how it navigates this delicate matter:

Etiquette Policy

Introduction

> DeviantArt is an expansive, worldwide community of artists of every age, and every nationality who create works spanning every medium, every subject and every level of talent and skill.

---

22. *Id.* at 4 (emphasis added).
23. *Id.* at 6 (emphasis added).

> *As the guiding force of this large and vibrant community we have two primary and often conflicting goals in the service we provide for you, the members of the community; the first being to ensure that members are free to express themselves within reason with as few restrictions as possible while nurturing an environment of creativity, learning, and talent and the second is to protect the members of the community, to the best of our abilities, from infringement of copyright, discrimination, harassment, and prejudice.*
>
> . . . .
>
> *It is our policy to welcome artists of all levels from amateur to professional and to that end we do not attach any minimum standards of quality to deviations submitted by our membership; all manner of artworks are welcome providing they meet with our etiquette and copyright policies. While we do not impose quality standards we do ask that you practice self-moderation in what you choose to submit and that you submit your works into the most appropriate gallery. While we encourage the submission of only your very best works we have provided an area for those submissions which may fall short of that 'top quality' mark; this is your "Scrapbook" gallery and we highly encourage its use.*
>
> *Our community volunteers may elect to move one or more of your deviations from the Gallery categories into a different, more appropriate, section or into the Scrapbook category; we ask that you accept this decision gracefully and with a mature attitude. If you desire a full explanation for this action, or if you feel the administrative action was performed in error, you should submit an inquiry to the official DeviantArt Helpdesk and include a link to the relevant deviation. Please do not bring these issues into the Forums, userpages, or other areas of DeviantArt.*[24]

When someone wants to insult you, they are likely to begin by saying, "I don't want to insult you, but. . . ."; in a similar vein, you might hear "with all due respect" right before the speaker goes on to insult you. So too, in the *Cariou v. Prince* case,[25] the Court notes that it is not trying to act as an art critic right before it does precisely that. Here, DeviantArt tells the prospective uploader artist that it doesn't impose quality standards on the art posted but that it does have a "Scrapbook" gallery where users are encouraged to post work "which

24. *Etiquette Policy*, DEVIANTART, https://about.deviantart.com/policy/etiquette/ (last visited Jan. 27, 2021).

25. Cariou v. Prince, 714 F.3d 694 (2d Cir. 2013).

may fall short of that 'top quality' mark"—which sure sounds like a subjective quality ranking process to me.

Next on the list of what the site views as etiquette are rules governing a variety of forms of commentary and guidelines for what kind of release artists need to get from models, particularly underage models, if they want to post content depicting those models. Commentary that is problematic includes commentary that is "prohibited," "discouraged," or "exploitive" or content that is "mature."

Once again as we look at these categories and how they are defined, we are confronted with significant amounts of vagueness and ambiguity in the definitions of these categories, as will become evident as you review them:

> **Prohibited Commentary**
>
> *Prohibited commentary is typically considered to be* ***inherently disrespectful, aggressive, or otherwise abusive.***
>
> ***We must insist that you refrain from comments which are racist, bigoted, or which otherwise offensively target a philosophy or religion. In addition we ask that our members avoid making offensive remarks based on gender or sexual preference and that you do not make any remark, comment or critique which is intended to be a direct insult to an individual, group, or genre of artwork. Hate propaganda is met with zero tolerance. Comments which are overly aggressive, personally insulting or needlessly abusive are also prohibited.***
>
> ***If you feel that you have been the target of harassment, personal insults or other severe behavior please notify the staff by using the official DeviantArt helpdesk. Please be aware that the staff will only directly intervene in cases which are considered severe; minor situations may be dealt with using tools made available to all registered members.***[26]

So what commentary is "typically considered to be inherently disrespectful, aggressive, or otherwise abusive"? And who is the audience that decides that a given piece of commentary is inherently disrespectful? Hate speech is a vague term, and one person's hate speech is another's protected free expression. So these terms are vague and poorly defined, making enforcement of them an exercise laden with minefields for the unwary site operator or uploader.

Next, as we look at the content limitations regarding what the site labels "mature content," you will see a repetition of the limitations found in subsections 2 and 4 of the Additional Terms, with the same problems of unenforceable vague and uncertain terms, such as "offensive," "distasteful," or "otherwise

---

26. *Etiquette Policy*, *supra* note 24 (emphasis added).

undesirable to view or read." According to whose standards? We aren't told—there is no transparency as to how these criteria are determined and who both makes that determination and enforces it. Despite that ambiguity, here is the standard:

> **Mature Content**
>
> When we discuss *mature content* we are specifically referring to deviations which contain ***images, subject matter, or other themes which some viewers may find offensive, distasteful, or otherwise undesirable to view or to read. The most common 'undesired' viewing material may include, but is not limited to, images containing artistic nudity (see details below), large amounts of simulated blood and gore, or generally violent themes.***
>
> ***DeviantART strictly prohibits the submission of materials classified as pornographic or obscene. There is no exception to this prohibition.***
>
> ***Certain content may be deemed obscene by the administration and as such the staff reserves the right to remove such content immediately upon discovery. The administration reserves the sole right to review and classify questionable material as obscene or not obscene.***[27]

And finally, the Etiquette section of the DeviantArt set of policies deals with an issue not presented in fan fiction—the need to secure a release from any model used in creating your artwork, including but not limited to photographic work. This section also deals with the problem of working with models who are under the legal age of consent (in the United States, this is generally set at either 18 or 21 years of age). DeviantArt points out that it is for both the site's protection and the protection of the creator that appropriate releases be obtained. For creators, there are free examples of model releases available online—and if you hope to transition from an amateur to a professional artist working with models, it is a good plan to consult with experienced legal counsel to create a tailored, effective model release. Here's what DeviantArt requires for model releases:

> **Model release forms**
>
> ***The DeviantArt administrative staff reserves the right to demand a Model Release form be provided for any photography (nude or otherwise) located within either your Gallery or Scrapbook areas. In the event that you receive such a request an appropriate link will be included in the notification you received. Failure to properly respond***

27. *Id.* (emphasis added).

to a Model Release form demand within seven (7) days will result in the automatic removal of the associated photograph.

For your own protection it is highly recommended that you have any model who poses for you sign a release form giving you the explicit permission to publish, share, distribute, and otherwise display the associated images. It is highly recommended that you provide this form immediately after submitting your photograph, especially if your subject is depicted nude. Details of this process may be found in the official DeviantArt FAQ.[28]

And the knotty problem of dealing with underage models, particularly if the subject of the artwork involves nudity or sexually explicit materials, is dealt with in no uncertain terms by DeviantArt:

Underage models

We cannot allow any nude works featuring individuals under the age of 18, nor may the works depict these individuals in a 'sexually driven' manner such as posing in lingerie or displaying a sexually suggestive or provocative pose.

This prohibition is for legal reasons; the laws in the United States are the governing laws in regards to all submissions regardless of the deviant's country of origin. Photographs which are suspected of depicting a minor in this manner will be temporarily suspended from public view and proper legal documentation (as outlined above) will be demanded while photographs which clearly depict a minor (including toddlers, preteens, and teenagers) in this manner will be removed without notice.

Submissions of a non-photographic nature which clearly depict a minor, fictional character or otherwise, either nude or in a sexually driven manner will be removed and deleted without notice as they come to the attention of the staff.[29]

So it is fair to say that between fan fiction and fan art, the number of legal issues involved in fan art is greater than is the case with fan fiction—we don't see claims of violation of ROP in fan fiction, nor are fan-fiction sites like AO3 as restrictive or extensive in their terms and conditions. And yet even this number of legal issues is dwarfed by the issues presented by the next area we examine, which is fan films.

---

28. *Id.* (emphasis added).
29. *Id.* (emphasis added).

CHAPTER 9

Fan Film

Film, by its nature, is generally a collaborative effort. It is the rare film that is created, directed, filmed, acted, written, and musically scored by the same solo auteur. Rather, most film productions involve a number of people—and in some of the tent-pole popular-culture films, like the *Avengers* series, the number of people involved gets up into the thousands.

Fan films don't usually require such a huge cast and crew, but they do typically involve a dozen or more participants, often contributing different elements to the filmmaking process—from sound engineering to actual filming, set design and creation, fashion design and creation, scriptwriting, etc. Each stage of the process, if done with an eye to making sure the filmmaker is protected on the legal front, may require dozens of contracts to be drafted, negotiated, and put into effect.[1]

Another legal hurdle you can encounter in creating a fan film is that you may find that the best people to hire to work on your film may be members of one of the many unions involved in the filmmaking process, such as the Screen Actors Guild or the International Association of Theatrical and Stage Employees. Members of these unions may, depending on the size of the production, be required to work only on projects that adhere to the unions' labor policies—which, while they have the laudable effect of protecting those workers and guaranteeing fair wages, also in some instances render a project too expensive to complete.

1. In a case I handled some years ago, dealing with a mainstream feature film in the sci-fi/horror genre, the request I made in the litigation for any and all documents related to the making of the film yielded some 17 boxes, totaling over 8,500 pages of contracts!

It is beyond the scope of this book to delve into the intricacies of these film production contracts—that is a book-sized subject on its own. I will instead encourage readers to look to online sources for sample contract forms and to recognize that putting together an independent fan film is a venture you should not undertake without the help of knowledgeable legal counsel—there are far too many problems you can encounter that can derail the project if not properly anticipated and handled.

What is within the scope of this book is an examination of the legal issues that arise in the creation of fan films when they are based on pop-culture programs and how the original programs deal with fan-film creations. In order to better understand these relationships, it helps to understand a bit about the genres where most fan films get their inspiration.

The Internet Movie Data Base (IMDb) is a well-known website with a deep database of information about movies, actors, directors, and other key players in the motion-picture business. A page on the site catalogs fan films, carrying a listing of the most popular fan-film movies and TV shows. The list tells us something about the general subject matter of fan films. Here are the top 20 films on its list:

1. **Spider-Man 4: Fan Film (2020)**
   Action, Adventure, Drama | **Pre-production**
2. **Star Trek Continues (2013–2017)**
   45 min | Action, Adventure, Sci-Fi
3. **Vengeance (I) (2019)**
   95 min | Horror
4. **Uncharted: Live Action Fan Film (2018 Video)**
   Not Rated | 15 min | Short, Action, Adventure
5. **Kenobi: A Star Wars Story (2019)**
   19 min | Short, Adventure, Fantasy
6. **Star Trek New Voyages: Phase II (2004–)**
   TV-PG | 45 min | Action, Adventure, Sci-Fi
7. **Stab 7: Knife of the Hunter (2013)**
   52 min | Comedy, Horror, Thriller
8. **Percy Jackson and the Titan's Curse**
   90 min | Action, Adventure, Fantasy | **Filming**
9. **Power Rangers (2015)**
   Not Rated | 14 min | Short, Action, Sci-Fi
10. **The Hunt for Gollum (2009)**
    Unrated | 38 min | Short, Action, Adventure

11. **Jurassic Park: Island Survival**
    Action, Adventure | **Pre-production**

12. **Born of Hope (2009)**
    71 min | Action, Adventure, Fantasy [based on *Lord of the Rings*]

13. **The Punisher: Dirty Laundry (2012)**
    Not Rated | 10 min | Short, Action, Crime

14. **Moon Knight (2019)**
    17 min | Short

15. **Knight Rider (2019)**
    7 min | Short, Action

16. **Star Trek: Hidden Frontier (2000–2007)**
    30 min | Short, Action, Sci-Fi

17. **Batman Beyond**
    Action | Post-production

18. **The Last of Us (2013)**
    14 min | Short, Action, Adventure

19. **Sonic (2013)**
    18 min | Short, Action, Adventure

20. **Star Trek: Odyssey (2007–2011)**
    Short, Sci-Fi[2]

Two important items to note about this list—most of the films are about well-known genre works, with *Star Wars, Star Trek,* and comic-book superheroes holding a high number of listings; and most of the films are short in length, many less than 30 minutes long and some even less than 20 minutes.

Before delving into the legal issues between these fan filmmakers and the original films and television shows they are based on, a little history of fan films is in order. As we've seen with fan fiction and fan art, fan films trace their origin back primarily to the early days of media technology—in this case, to the early days of the video revolution ushered in by videotape recorders and cassettes. This history is ably chronicled in Lucas Hilderbrand's 2009 book, *Inherent Vice: Bootleg Histories of Videotape and Copyright*.[3]

A key reason fan films weren't prevalent prior to the videocassette era is that there was simply no place for fan filmmakers to show their films to other

2. *Most Popular Movies and TV Shows Tagged with Keyword "Fan-Film"*, IMDb, https://www.imdb.com/search/keyword/?keywords=fan-film (last visited Jan. 27, 2021).

3. Lucas Hilderbrand, Inherent Vice: Bootleg Histories of Videotape and Copyright (Duke Univ. Press 2009).

fans. Motion pictures were pretty exclusively shown either in movie theaters or on commercial, public television. Fan films had no access to these exhibition venues. It wasn't until the mid-1970s, with the development of videocassette tapes, Beta and VHS recorders, and playback machines, that the technology came into existence to allow the creation of videotapes, edited and with newly created soundtracks, making fan films possible and then popular.[4]

As Hilderbrand points out, "[M]agnetic tape allowed people to record their own voices, their own lives, the media, and the world around them to an unprecedented degree."[5] One of the other things videotape allowed was for fan creators to create what were at the time called "mashups"—the process whereby fans could tape a television show and then edit the tape by adding their own soundtrack and editing clips from the show with other material, all for the purpose of creating a video mashup that celebrated their favorite characters.

A popular example of this approach came from watchers of the action/adventure show *Xena, Warrior Princess,* many of whom wanted the thinly veiled romantic attraction of the two female leads, Lucy Lawless (Xena) and Renee O'Connor (Gabrielle), to become more explicit and who created mashup videos depicting that ideal relationship. Fans of the show traded videos by mail and at conventions.

Communities of fans sprang up around the making and trading of these videos. Although social media as we know it today did not exist in the mid-1980s, the informal networks of fan videos grew more popular, aided by a venue, the pop-culture convention, that gave fan-film creators a place where they could display their works.

Change came again to the television industry—in 1997, Warner announced its first 30 DVD titles. Consumers no longer had to fiddle with bulky, storage dense videocassettes and boxes—instead, the sleek jewel box that had been in use for years for compact discs could be slightly enlarged and repurposed to serve as DVD containers. The entertainment industry touted the DVDs for their sleek look and better overall performance capabilities and durability compared with videocassettes. What they didn't discuss was the far more important element of this switch—videocassettes were a recordable medium, and DVDs are not recordable. So this meant that to the extent buyers shifted to DVDs, they gave up the ability to record, edit, and create their own content. And so the period of a decade or so when videocassettes gave fan creators the opportunity to create their own mashups in this early form of fan films came to an end.

But that ending proved short-lived. On February 14, 2005, Steve Chen, Chad Hurley, and Jawed Karim, three former employees of e-commerce company

4. *Id.* at 46.
5. *Id.* at 7.

PayPal, gave the world a Valentine's present when they registered their new company, YouTube, as a corporation. The goal of YouTube was to provide an online platform for people to share their home videos. Within a year, over 25 million videos had been uploaded. The intersection of cats and Roombas was born. And at least one company thought that YouTube's ad revenue, comprised of ad buys made by companies hoping to catch the eyes of those viewers of millions of videos, was worth something—in November 2006, YouTube was purchased by Google for $1.65 billion in stock.[6]

YouTube offered the perfect venue for the presentation of fan films. Easy to navigate and upload films to, and with millions of users watching short films on a regular basis, YouTube became the host of choice for thousands of fan films. The creators of these films were largely left alone by the major film production companies. The fan films were generally short in duration, with amateurish sets, weak writing, and hokey special effects and featuring casts of unknown, largely amateur actors. Existing fan communities, comprised mostly of fan-fic writers, discovered and supported these fan films as exciting new contributions to their communities. Scanning for fan films on YouTube, you will find countless films inspired by *Star Trek*, *Star Wars*, *Lord of the Rings*, *Harry Potter*, *Raiders of the Lost Ark*, *Toy Story*, and other works that have received the fan-film treatment.

The badge of the USS Federation Starship *Ares*, from the *Battle of Axanar* series.[7]

Two such works, a short film and a longer film, both set in the *Star Trek* universe, gave rise to a lawsuit, and its settlement, that has had a huge impact on the fan-film genre—this is the *Battle of Axanar* case.

The *Star Trek* universe is a genuine pop-culture phenomenon. Launched as a television series by CBS in 1966, the original series ran for three years, from 1966 to 1969. Its cast, comprised of William Shatner (as Captain James T. Kirk), Leonard Nimoy (as the alien Vulcan First Officer, Dr. Spock), DeForest Kelly (as ship's doctor Leonard McCoy), Nichelle Nichols (as Communications Officer Nyota Uhura), George Takei (as Pilot and Lieutenant Hikaru Sulu), and James Doohan (as Chief Engineer Montgomery Scott), represented the ethnic and gender diversity of the 23rd century when the series takes place.

---

6. William L. Horsch, *YouTube*, BRITTANICA, https://www.britannica.com/topic/YouTube (last visited Jan. 27, 2021).

7. *Axanar*, YOUTUBE, https://www.youtube.com/user/startrekaxanar (last visited Jan. 27, 2021).

After the initial run ended with the series' cancellation in 1969, fans demanded more. They got what they wished for, as the series went on to spawn seven more television shows to date, plus 13 feature films. The fan base is deeply devoted to the series, and appearances of the remaining few living cast members of the original television show, now mostly in their mid-80s, still draw a loyal crowd.

In one of those episodes from the original television series, Captain Kirk meets Garth, a ship's captain from the planet Izar. They discuss Garth's recent success in the Battle of Axanar. This is a classic literary trope, to mention an event that has happened outside of the content of the series. A well-known example of this trope is the reference, in Arthur Conan Doyle's Sherlock Holmes story "The Sussex Vampire," to the case of the Giant Rat of Sumatra—an unrecorded Sherlock Holmes story that Conan Doyle never wrote about.[8] The Battle of Axanar was a similar throwaway reference—destined to become a part of *Star Trek* lore that would tantalize fans for decades.

And then along came Alec Peters, a *Star Trek* fan (fans are often referred to as Trekkies). Peters decided that in this YouTube era, he could do a fan film about the Battle of Axanar and give fans a long-awaited view of this never-filmed story. He began by using crowdfunding sites to raise money—at first to produce a short film, called *Star Trek: Prelude to Axanar,* to introduce fans to his concept. The short film was fully funded through Kickstarter and became very popular on YouTube. Here is how Peters described the *Prelude* project:

> Prelude to Axanar is a short film that will give viewers a historical look at the events leading up to the Battle of Axanar, the central event of the film Axanar, to be filmed later this year. Shot like a History Channel special, Prelude to Axanar will be Star Trek like you have never seen it before, showing the central characters of Axanar giving both a historical and personal account of the war. How did they hold off a Klingon fleet that had been conquering star systems for centuries? What role did the various founding planets play in Starfleet? Why were the Constitution class ships so important to Starfleet? How did Garth of Izar come to be regarded as the greatest Starfleet Captain of his time?[9]

At some point during or after producing and releasing *Prelude* on YouTube, to considerable success, Peters formed Axanar Productions, Inc., and set about the process of producing a feature-length film, *The Battle of Axanar,* seeking to

---

8. Scott Monty, *The Giant Rat of Sumatra,* I Hear of Sherlock Everywhere (Dec. 17, 2007), https://www.ihearofsherlock.com/2007/12/giant-rat-of-sumatra-suss_17.html#.XziUnhJlCM8.

9. Plaintiff Paramount Pictures' Amended Complaint (Mar. 11, 2016) [hereinafter PAC], 29:3-9, at 7 (on file with author) (emphasis added by plaintiff's counsel).

raise at least $1 million to fund the film. A full-length script was written, and at least one scene for the movie, known as the Vulcan Scene, was shot and posted on a newly created website for the production. The website featured the following description of the plot of the proposed movie:

> Axanar takes place 21 years before the events of "Where No Man Has Gone Before", the first Kirk episode of the original Star Trek. Axanar is the story of Garth of Izar, the legendary Starfleet captain who is Captain Kirk's hero. We met Garth in the third season TOS [*The Original Series*] episode Whom Gods Destroy. Kirk called Garth the role model for all future Starfleet Officers. Garth charted more planets than any other Captain and was the hero of the Battle of Axanar, the story of which is required reading at the academy. This is that story. Axanar tells the story of Garth and his crew during the Four Years War, the war with the Klingon Empire that almost tore the Federation part. Garth's victory at Axanar solidified the Federation and allowed it to become the entity we know in Kirk's time. It is the year 2245 and the war with the Klingons ends here.[10]

These descriptions would be cited by Paramount and CBS as evidence of copyright infringement in the lawsuit they subsequently filed, and it is difficult to argue with that characterization. The descriptions include references to a number of elements of the *Star Trek* universe, including references to Captain Kirk, Garth of Izar, Starfleet, the Klingon Empire, the Four Years War, and the name of a specific episode of the original series from which most of this is drawn. Plaintiffs were even able to allege that Alec Peters, in an interview, admitted that *Axanar* violates plaintiff's copyright, excusing that violation by saying, "We violate CBS copyright less than any other fan film."[11] While that comparison may be accurate, admitting liability while arguing that you didn't infringe as much as others isn't a compelling defense position.

So faced with a situation where their infringing activity seems clear, Peters and company looked to other defenses to the Paramount/CBS lawsuit. After the original suit was filed, an amended version was later filed by the plaintiffs. Although the record isn't clear why this happened, generally speaking a plaintiff is entitled as a matter of law to file an amended complaint at any time after the original suit is filed, until the defendant files its answer to the complaint. At that point, a plaintiff who wants to file an amended complaint is required to obtain court approval in order to file that amended pleading. While courts

10. *Id.* at 40:9-15 at 9.
11. *Id.* at 43:23-26 at 9.

generally grant leave to amend, it isn't guaranteed, and depending on the status of the lawsuit when the request is made, the court could impose monetary or other sanctions as a condition of granting that leave.

In the *Axanar* case, the likely scenario was that in response to the original complaint, counsel for Peters et al. may have written to Paramount/CBS's counsel, threatening to file a motion to dismiss the complaint for failure to state a valid claim for relief, a motion allowed under Rule 12b(6) of the Federal Rules of Civil Procedure. Before a party is allowed to file such a motion, counsel is required to first "meet and confer" with opposing counsel to see if any disagreements about the validity of the complaint can be amicably worked out without the necessity of a hearing on a motion to dismiss.

The meet-and-confer requirement doesn't mean the parties must actually meet in person to try to solve the dispute—a letter setting out the position of the party and demanding changes or clarification of the claims involved is usually sufficient. When I teach students about 12b(6) motions, I point out that unless you have a surefire basis for the motion (like the statute of limitations on the claim expired before the suit was filed), it isn't a good strategy to file these motions. The reason is that even if the court is likely to grant the motion to dismiss, it is usually accompanied by the court allowing the losing party an opportunity to amend the complaint to try to cure the defects in the document. So in effect, by filing the motion, all the moving party has done is give the other side a tutorial in what is wrong with its lawsuit and an opportunity to cure those defects at this early stage in the case. Unless you truly don't understand the basis of the case against you, it may be better to leave the other side with a poorly drafted complaint that you can attack at trial, rather than educate the other side and allow it to redraft the complaint to make it stronger.

Counsel for Alec Peters didn't follow this advice and instead responded to the amended complaint Paramount/CBS filed with a motion to dismiss that pleading. Defendants presented an array of arguments attacking the merits of the amended complaint.

They first argued that Paramount/CBS failed to plead copyright infringement with enough specificity—they argued that the plaintiffs should be required to identify each episode of the television or movie series they allege was infringed and each scene and element of the series that was allegedly infringed. Without that specificity, they argued, they cannot defend the lawsuit, because they don't know what they are being sued for.

The Court rejected this argument, noting that neither copyright law cases nor the language of the statute requires that level of detail in the pleadings of a complaint and that what Paramount/CBS are suing for is infringement "as to the Star Trek universe as a whole" and that the plaintiffs had gone to "great lengths to compare and contrast allegedly infringing elements of the Star Trek franchise through photographs and vivid descriptions."[12]

Great lengths indeed. Of the 45 pages of the amended complaint, 28 pages are devoted to minutely detailed descriptions of 53 "copied copyrighted Star Trek elements" ranging from the appearance of, and use of the names of, Vulcan and Klingon characters to terms like the dilithium crystals that power Starfleet ships.[13] Given the degree of detail provided, defendants' claim that the complaint doesn't give them enough information to understand the nature of the claims made against them is a weak argument, properly rejected by the Court.

Defendants also argued that only CBS had the right to sue them, because Paramount only has copyrights in the original new material added by the motion pictures, and since the amended complaint doesn't identify elements specific to the motion pictures that are allegedly infringed, Paramount lacked standing to file the suit. This is a time-honored litigation tactic in intellectual property cases: if you can't defend an obvious infringement, attack the underlying basis for the infringement claim—argue that the plaintiff lacks the right or power to bring the claim, regardless of its underlying merits.

The Court made short shrift of this argument, noting that Paramount was in the case based on its status as a joint rights holder with CBS of the "Star Trek Copyrighted Works" as defined in the complaint.[14] A similar fate was in store for defendants' challenge to the complaint on the grounds that some of the allegations were made on "information and belief." This refers to a phrase used in pleadings where the filing party is referring to something that it lacks first-hand knowledge of but has a good-faith belief has happened—so for example, an allegation that Peters raised $1 million for the production of the feature-length *Axanar* film might be an instance where Paramount generally knew that Peters raised that much, but it might not be certain of the exact amount, so it would allege, "Plaintiffs are informed and believe that Defendants raised $1 million for the production costs. . . ." This is a perfectly valid way to allege this activity, and the Court again rightly rejected this defense claim.[15]

Defendants claim that many of the elements Paramount/CBS were suing on are nonprotectable elements of the Star Trek Copyrighted Works. This is the *scene a faire* defense described previously. They argued that the elements of a "science fiction action adventure" cannot be protected by copyright, therefore there is no copyright protection for those elements and no infringement

12. Paramount v. Axanar, Case No. CV 15-09938 RGE (EX), Civil Minute Order Denying Motion to Dismiss [hereinafter Minute Order], at 3 (C.D. Cal. May 9, 2016) (on file with author).

13. PAC at 10-38.

14. Minute Order at 4.

15. *Id.* at 5.

is possible. The Court rejected this argument as well, noting that it mischaracterizes the complaint—it is the entirety of the *Star Trek* universe that has been infringed, not minute and particular parts of that universe.[16]

Defendants' last two arguments in support of their motion to dismiss were that the claims of Paramount/CBS were premature because the movie wasn't yet completed and that the complaint operated as an unconstitutional prior restraint on their free-speech rights, preventing them from completing the full-length feature. The Court quickly rejected these arguments as well—noting that the completion of the full script and the filming of the Vulcan scene moved the *Axanar* film far enough along to give Paramount/CBS enough of a basis to bring the suit and that since Paramount/CBS did not seek an injunction to prevent the filming of *Axanar*, there was no prior restraint—although, as the Court noted, Peters and company would proceed with the certainty that if they completed the film, Paramount/CBS would seek to block its exhibition at that point.

So based on the foregoing, the Court denied Peters's motion to dismiss the complaint, meaning the case would now move into the expensive discovery process. Knowing that they were likely to lose on the merits of the infringement claims, and having lost all of their procedural arguments, the defendants faced a difficult, and likely unsuccessful, road ahead if they continued to litigate the case.[17]

And here it is appropriate to note, as a matter of understanding of the litigation process fan creators can sometimes find themselves ensnarled in, that hoping to rely on purely procedural defenses in copyright cases, which is the approach the defendants in this case relied on, is a risky strategy, as courts are reluctant, except in clear-cut cases, to throw out a case solely on procedural grounds. U.S. jurisprudence is based on a strong policy of allowing parties to have their day in court and cases to be resolved based on their substantive merits, rather than on procedure. This is not to say that in the right case a procedural argument cannot be made—rather it is to point out that such cases are the exception, rather than the rule.

Following their loss of the motion to dismiss, defendants realized they had limited options and weren't likely to win their defense. So they entered into settlement negotiations, and by January 2017, a little over eight months after losing the dismissal motion, a settlement of the case was reached and the parties then filed a Joint Stipulation of Voluntary Dismissal, ending the case.[18]

And this is where things got even more interesting, as the settlement of this case gave rise to a tactic that Paramount/CBS adopted and that has become a

---

16. *Id.* at 6.

17. *Id.* at 8.

18. Paramount v. Axanar, Case No. CV 15-09938 RGE, Joint Stipulation of Voluntary Dismissal (C.D. Cal. Jan. 31, 2017) (on file with author).

popular tactic now used by a number of other production companies to limit the scope of fan films. Paramount/CBS created a set of guidelines for fan filmmakers, in an effort to prevent future *Axanar*-style problems.

Reading these guidelines is an interesting exercise. They begin with restrictions that make perfect sense for the production companies—limiting the fan filmmaker's ability to make a competing product. But then they get a bit more problematic from a free-speech perspective, as they begin to restrict the content of the films—in ways that are likely unenforceable from that perspective.

Here are the Paramount/CBS guidelines—see if you can spot when they start to veer into what is arguably protected free speech:

Fan Films

CBS and Paramount Pictures are big believers in reasonable fan fiction and fan creativity, and, in particular, want amateur fan filmmakers to showcase their passion for *Star Trek*. Therefore, CBS and Paramount Pictures will not object to, or take legal action against, *Star Trek* fan productions that are non-professional and amateur and meet the following guidelines.

Guidelines for Avoiding Objections:

1. The fan production must be less than 15 minutes for a single self-contained story, or no more than 2 segments, episodes or parts, not to exceed 30 minutes total, with no additional seasons, episodes, parts, sequels or remakes.
2. The title of the fan production or any parts cannot include the name "*Star Trek*." However, the title must contain a subtitle with the phrase: "A *STAR TREK* FAN PRODUCTION" in plain typeface. The fan production cannot use the term "official" in either its title or subtitle or in any marketing, promotions or social media for the fan production.
3. The content in the fan production must be original, not reproductions, recreations or clips from any *Star Trek* production. If non-*Star Trek* third party content is used, all necessary permissions for any third party content should be obtained in writing.
4. If the fan production uses commercially-available *Star Trek* uniforms, accessories, toys and props, these items must be official merchandise and not bootleg items or imitations of such commercially available products.
5. The fan production must be a real "fan" production, i.e., creators, actors and all other participants must be amateurs, cannot be compensated for their services, and cannot be currently or previously employed on any *Star Trek* series, films, production of DVDs or with any of CBS or Paramount Pictures' licensees.

6. The fan production must be non-commercial:
   - CBS and Paramount Pictures do not object to limited fundraising for the creation of a fan production, whether 1 or 2 segments and consistent with these guidelines, so long as the total amount does not exceed $50,000, including all platform fees, and when the $50,000 goal is reached, all fundraising must cease.
   - The fan production must only be exhibited or distributed on a no-charge basis and/or shared via streaming services without generating revenue.
   - The fan production cannot be distributed in a physical format such as DVD or Blu-ray.
   - The fan production cannot be used to derive advertising revenue including, but not limited to, through for example, the use of pre or post-roll advertising, click-through advertising banners, that is associated with the fan production.
   - No unlicensed *Star Trek*-related or fan production-related merchandise or services can be offered for sale or given away as premiums, perks or rewards or in connection with the fan production fundraising.
   - The fan production cannot derive revenue by selling or licensing fan-created production sets, props or costumes.
7. The fan production must be family friendly and suitable for public presentation. Videos must not include profanity, nudity, obscenity, pornography, depictions of drugs, alcohol, tobacco, or any harmful or illegal activity, or any material that is offensive, fraudulent, defamatory, libelous, disparaging, sexually explicit, threatening, hateful, or any other inappropriate content. The content of the fan production cannot violate any individual's right of privacy.
8. The fan production must display the following disclaimer in the on-screen credits of the fan productions and on any marketing material including the fan production website or page hosting the fan production:

   "*Star Trek* and all related marks, logos and characters are solely owned by CBS Studios Inc. This fan production is not endorsed by, sponsored by, nor affiliated with CBS, Paramount Pictures, or any other *Star Trek* franchise, and is a non-commercial fan-made film intended for recreational use. No commercial exhibition or distribution is permitted. No alleged independent rights will be asserted against CBS or Paramount Pictures."

9. Creators of fan productions must not seek to register their works, nor any elements of the works, under copyright or trademark law.

10. Fan productions cannot create or imply any association or endorsement by CBS or Paramount Pictures

> CBS and Paramount Pictures reserve the right to revise, revoke and/or withdraw these guidelines at any time in their own discretion. These guidelines are not a license and do not constitute approval or authorization of any fan productions or a waiver of any rights that CBS or Paramount Pictures may have with respect to fan fiction created outside of these guidelines.[19]

For the fandom community, the issuance of these "guidelines" offered a mixed bag—on the one hand, they offered clarity and a road map for how to do fan films based on one of the most popular sources of fan creations, while on the other hand, they constituted limitations on expression that went beyond free-speech limits and significantly constrained what fans could create in this universe.

Henry Jenkins offered cogent insights, and echoed these concerns, in a blog post entitled *How the New Star Trek Guidelines May Change Fandom.*[20] Here's how he framed his concerns:

> Let's stipulate that CBS and Paramount have legitimate reasons to protect a top media franchise from being appropriated for commercial purposes, and we can understand why the studios felt a need to clarify where they might draw the line. That said, the new guidelines for *Star Trek* fan films also over-reach, going beyond what was needed to resolve ambiguities, doing damage to the fan community's good will, and potentially violating the public's fair use rights. While the producers insist that these guidelines apply only to fan films, they could have a chilling effect on all forms of grassroots fan culture and are apt to be mimicked by other franchise producers.[21]

He was right about his last point. Since the *Axanar* case settled and these guidelines were published, the major comic-book publishers, Marvel and DC, as well as other major production companies, have jumped on the "guidelines" bandwagon and issued similar rules. An important element of these guidelines is their attempt to control the creative narrative to fit their own needs and interests.

Voicing his support for fan films, Jenkins asserts that in at least three ways, fan films enhance the value of the original films they are based on: (1) they

---

19. *Fan Films*, STAR TREK, http://www.startrek.com/fan-films (last visited Jan. 27, 2021).

20. Henry Jenkins, *How the New Star Trek Fan Film Guidelines May Change Fandom*, CONFESSIONS OF AN ACA-FAN (Sept. 22, 2016), http://henryjenkins.org/blog/2016/09/how-the-new-star-trek-fan-film-guidelines-may-change-fandom.html.

21. *Id.*

represent a particularly active form of fan engagement; (2) they can be understood as a site of innovation, pointing out the contributions the filmmakers may make in shaping the ongoing works done by the original series creators; and (3) they are protected transformative works that add to and enhance the original works. He notes that the Organization for Transformative Works has argued for these and other reasons that fan filmmakers should be exempt, like documentary filmmakers, from violating "[t]he law by removing DVD copy protection software in the pursuit of their work. And the U.S. Copyright office agreed, a decision that many think indicates how courts would be apt to rule in a similar case . . . ."[22]

Notwithstanding those benefits, Jenkins acknowledges that the use of "guidelines" is a new approach that is likely to cause significant problems for fan-film creators:

> Some of the guidelines seem reasonable, such as a call to be even more explicit in distinguishing fan films from the official property. Fan filmmakers have historically been conscientious in signaling their unauthorized status; fans often make strong distinctions between canon (official texts) and fanon (grassroots responses). Everyone will be well served by lowering the ambiguity about what the rights holders see as commercial uses of their materials. We can debate what is or is not a reasonable policy towards the crowdfunding of production costs.
>
> But many other provisions are apt to have a chilling effect on all forms of fan production or will if fan artists read them as superseding fair use protections. For example, a provision against the use of clips seemingly targets fanvids and restrictions on the use of recreated costumes and props have implications for the maker culture and cosplay communities. The guidelines block the collaborations between professionals and amateurs that have been a hallmark of earlier *Star Trek* fan films, there are restrictions on how fan films can be distributed (streaming rather than DVD) that have implications for how these materials will be archived. There are new format restrictions that mean that fans can no longer produce continuing series. Constraints on the film's content designed to keep *Star Trek* "family friendly" amount to censorship over many forms of critical commentary (slash for example) that would fall squarely under transformative use.[23]

Jenkins concludes his blog post on a somber note, acknowledging that as fan films become more sophisticated, film production companies may view them as competitors and enforce more and more restrictions governing their

---

22. *Id.*
23. *Id.*

creation. This, he asserts, will have a chilling effect on the creative process and contribution to the fan community:

> If copyright law rests on a balancing of interests, we can all agree that current factors are out of whack. From the perspective of the rights holders, we are dealing here with a crisis in copyright as it becomes hard to distinguish amateur and commercial productions. As amateur works are reaching wider and wider audiences and impact public perceptions of their franchises, the studios may perceive them as commercial competitors. From the perspective of the public, we are dealing with there is a crisis in fair use, since forms of cultural expression commonplace in the past are now endangered by a legal culture that puts many advantages in the hands of media corporations. Under these circumstances, copyright enforcement can and does sometimes constitute a form of censorship. For a while, informal policies have created a space where *Star Trek*'s producers and fans could play and work together, producing films intended to pay tribute to the original, that are and [sic] valuable as forms of engagement, innovation, and transformative use. My fear is that the new guidelines back away from those collaborative practices and towards policies more antagonistic to fan participation and expression. As such, the guidelines can have a chilling effect on forms of cultural production that are a uniquely valuable aspect of contemporary culture.[24]

I agree with Professor Jenkins's concerns and add one of my own. The use of these guidelines, with restrictions that go far beyond what First Amendment freedoms would otherwise allow filmmakers to use in their work, is structured so that the production companies can get compliance from the filmmaker by their implicit, and in many instances explicit, warnings that violating the guidelines will result in a copyright infringement lawsuit.

Note that the companies do not assert that they will sue a filmmaker for violating the specific guidelines—only that they will sue for copyright infringement. In this way, the production companies are able to obtain a level of compliance with their guidelines that they could not enforce legally if they had to defend the specific overly restrictive guidelines themselves. And as the use of these guidelines as a tactic spreads, it may result in some significant limitations appearing in fan films and other fan works based on content controlled by these companies. What may arise to limit the use of these guidelines is an instance when a company sues for copyright infringement and the filmmaker pushes back by asserting a transformative-use defense. Such a case is more likely to succeed for the filmmaker if he or she can avoid the "infringement of the universe of these works" argument that succeeded in the *Axanar* case. Time will tell.

---

24. *Id.*

CHAPTER 10

Cosplay

Cosplay is, in many ways, the most ephemeral of all of the genres of fan-created works. Where fan fiction, art, and film produce works that exist separately from the lives of their creators and can be read, seen, and viewed by fans all over the world, costume players, or cosplayers as they are more familiarly named, create works that they wear on their bodies and, in many cases, as makeup on their faces and other parts of their bodies.

Cosplay is also one of the latest entries into the realm of fan-created works. While the other formats examined thus far date back to the 1960s, cosplay didn't really exist in any organized fashion until pop-culture conventions began to offer a venue for cosplayers to be seen by other fans and even to compete in onstage cosplay competitions. San Diego Comic-Con, Anime Expo (Los Angeles), Emerald City Comic Con (Seattle), DragonCon (Atlanta), and many other conventions now offer a venue, and a competition event with cash prizes, for cosplayers. There have even been two television series, each of which ran for a year, focused entirely on cosplayers—*Heroes of Cosplay* (2013–14) and *Cosplay Melee* (2017).

The range of expression, imagination, and artistry of cosplayers are a sight to be seen. And being seen is a significant goal of cosplayers. In my own acafan work, here are a few cosplayers I photographed at the 2014 San Diego Comic-Con:

Robot Chicken and the Mad Professor

Batman?

Olaf from Disney's *Frozen*

Cosplay is generally defined as the practice of wearing a costume similar to, or a direct copy of, that worn by a character from a fictional work—and can be accompanied by makeup, wigs, and related items to replicate the appearance of either the character or the actor/actress who plays that character in movies or on television. Like the other genres of fan-created works we have looked at, cosplay in the law is focused on its intersection with copyright law, right-of-publicity law, and, if the characters featured are also used as brands by their production company owners, trademark law as well.

A. Cosplay and Copyright

The intersection point between cosplay and copyright comes from the extent to which costumes and the look of a character may be protected by copyright law. And unlike in the case of fan fiction, art, and films, all of which are, in their own right, the valid subject of copyright protection under section 102 of the Copyright Act, costumes are granted much more limited protection, due to the limits of protection on fashion designs in general. As a policy matter, Congress has not extended copyright protection to fashion design, despite the concerted efforts of many in the fashion industry to obtain that protection.

One justification for this is that clothing is a functional item and does not, in its design, constitute an artistic expression. So while you can get copyright protection for a design or other graphic you add to, or print on, a garment, the utilitarian elements of the underlying garment may not be protected by copyright. So a man who wants to create a superhero costume may use elements consisting of a pair of tight-fitting boots, tights, shorts worn over the tights, a close-fitting body shirt, and a cap (and possibly a mask over parts of his face) and may do so without fear of an infringement claim. This is because those elements are *scene a faire* elements of most male superhero costumes.

However, if you choose red boots, blue tights, a dark red pair of shorts with a yellow belt, a blue body shirt, and a red cape, and you add a five-pointed shield pattern with a yellow background and a stylized red "S" in the center, now you may have infringed on the copyright-protected costume for Superman.

But wait, you cry. There are costumes for many of the DC and Marvel characters sold in every Halloween costume display all over the country and the world. How can they "get away" with this infringing activity? The answer is that the companies producing these costumes have licensed the right to duplicate the superhero costumes from the owners of those rights. And it is in this process that we can discern an important limit in the cosplay arena—one that tracks the fan-art world—the right of an individual to do a single work based on a pop-culture character versus the making, distributing, and selling of multiple copies of the image.

So cosplayers who create, sometimes in astonishingly identical workmanship, versions of their favorite characters' costumes, rarely face infringement claims unless they decide to try to go into the business of mass marketing of those costumes. And for most cosplayers, the quality of the mass-market Halloween costumes isn't good enough to truly celebrate their favorite characters, which is why you almost never see such costumes on the convention-hall floor—they are relegated to use by kids and adults at local home Halloween parties. And this is why if you go shopping for a *Star Wars* stormtrooper costume, you will find the low-end price to range from $19.99 to $59.99, whereas the high-end version of the same costume sells for between $899 and $1,299—quality comes at a cost. All of these costumes are the subject of license deals.

The nonprofit aspect of cosplay ties in with the availability of the fair-use defense for cosplayers. The nonprofit nature of the use of the costume and/or makeup by a cosplayer, and the absence of any impact that use has on the market for the creative work the costume comes from (wearing a *Star Wars* stormtrooper costume does not have even a remotely adverse impact on the box office or other revenue earned by Disney, which owns that franchise), is a strong set of facts militating toward a successful fair-use defense.

Moreover, much of cosplay is transformative in a number of ways. To the extent the costume created by the cosplayer adds elements not found in the original costume, it may be a transformative expression. And if you adapt the "universe as a whole" argument from the *Axanar* case, even an identical costume worn by a person who doesn't look like the original character (e.g., an elderly law professor dressing up as Dr. Strange) may, in those differences, transform how one looks at the character, making the work a transformative one as well.

In addition to running the risk that a copyright infringement case against a cosplayer could backfire in the face of a transformative-doctrine defense, several other factors deter copyright infringement claims—cost and negative publicity. Each of these concerns warrants consideration before one leaps into the litigation arena.

As to the cost factor, a production company considering suing a cosplayer has to consider the economic cost of litigation, particularly given the scale of the infringement. The recent release of *Wonder Woman 1984*, DC's much-awaited sequel to the highly successful *Wonder Woman* movie, featuring Wonder Woman in a number of new costumes, including a winged, golden suit of armor, is likely to be next year's comic convention season's most popular costume for cosplayers.

What purpose would be served, and how much would it cost, for DC to file several thousand lawsuits in federal courts all over the country, seeking damages for infringement, against those cosplayers? How will it prove damages? And even if it can win statutory damage awards under copyright law, how likely is it that it will collect those awards?

Secondly, the negative publicity such suits would garner would likely be an offsetting consideration. Suing cosplayers would yield a boatload of negative press and alienate significant chunks of the fan base for those companies and their products. And given the largely nonprofit nature of cosplay, the production companies would not be able to point to any negative impact on their profits from this activity—on the contrary, some pundits point to the free advertising cosplay generates.

Similar problems plague the consideration of bringing a right-of-publicity claim against a cosplayer whose costume and makeup evoke the image of the actor or actress who plays the character the cosplayer is portraying. I've seen some tall, muscular men with long blond hair dressed as Thor who bear a strong resemblance to Chris Hemsworth, the actor who plays Thor in the Marvel universe films, and some tall, strong brunettes who resemble either Linda Carter (television's Wonder Woman) or Gal Gadot (Wonder Woman in the DC universe films). Do those performers have a right to pursue right-of-publicity claims against those cosplayers?

Likely not, for several reasons. First, to the extent that cosplayers are replicating the performers' look in character, they are appropriating the image of the character, not the actor/actress playing that character. Secondly, most, if not all, right-of-publicity claims, on either common law or statutory grounds, require a showing that the appropriation was done for "commercial advantage"—which is usually not the case with cosplayers. And while some cosplayers do get paid for appearances at events in their costumes, the income generated is far too small to warrant the costs of litigation. And finally, the damaging publicity that will follow a performer who sues a cosplayer who imitates him or her would likely far outweigh any benefit to be gained by such a suit.

So are there any negative consequences to engaging in cosplay? Sadly, yes, but they are not legal in nature. The problem arises out of the various threads of sexually suggestive and sometimes sexually explicit costumes worn by cosplayers and the reaction of fans to those costumes. And in part, the problem is fueled by the fact that cosplayers want fans to pay attention to them and to take pictures of them.

At the San Diego Comic-Con International, for example, the hallways and walkways outside of the exhibit halls and meeting rooms are often where cosplayers walk and pose for crowds of fans who want to photograph them. And while con etiquette suggests that fans should always ask permission before taking a photo, if there is a crowd of photographers, consent is usually not an issue.

Many of these cosplayers are wearing costumes that are sexually suggestive, if not explicitly so. And for some fans, mostly male and mostly young, the message that these attractive cosplayers are willing to stop and pose for them gives rise to the thought that perhaps a greater level of contact, rising to touching or caressing the cosplayer, is also being invited.

After a number of incidents at conventions where female cosplayers were physically assaulted (often on their way to or from the con, but also sometimes in crowds at the con or in similar contexts), convention companies became concerned about their secondary liability exposure. If companies know that sexual predators are around their venues and are attacking cosplayers, they could be secondarily liable if they don't do something about it.

And so they have. Most pop-culture conventions where cosplayers participate have launched one or another version of the "Cosplay Is Not Consent" warning-sign programs. At prominent places throughout the con, and particularly on the days that cosplay competitions draw the most cosplayers, they display Cosplay Is Not Consent signs and advise all cosplayers to report any improper behavior to security personnel, who, if they verify the conduct, will ban the offender from the event.

Concurrent with the concerns about unconsented-to touching and other inappropriate contact with cosplayers are complaints coming from parents who bring their children to conventions where some cosplayers wear costumes that are too revealing for G-rated activities like attending pop-culture conventions. Here again, convention producers have to tread carefully so as not to offend the numbers of their attendees who are children or parents, so as to avoid liability claims from those participants.

One company that has dealt with this issue is the Society for the Promotion of Japanese Animation, which annually presents Anime Expo (AX) in Los Angeles in the first week in July. Billed as the largest anime convention in North America, and drawing in excess of 100,000 attendees, it is a mecca for cosplayers. The year I attended, the convention devoted an entire large ballroom at the Los Angeles Convention Center to a series of sets, including a castle dungeon set, a forest set, a Japanese bridge and pond set, etc., for cosplayers to use as a photo backdrop. The Singer Company brought dozens of new sewing machines to its "cosplay repair booth," giving cosplayers a place to make minor repairs to costumes that saw wear and tear during the convention.

Concerned that cosplayers might dress inappropriately for the many parents and children who attend AX, the Society promulgates a clear set of rules for cosplayers to comply with, in an effort to avoid the kind of problems unregulated cosplay can engender. Here is its set of rules:

COSPLAY GUIDELINES

At Anime Expo ("AX"), we celebrate the creativity of cosplayers and encourage everyone to cosplay whomever they wish–regardless of size, gender, age, religion, shape, color, or even species. Cosplay is all about having fun!

We simply ask that you follow the guidelines below and please keep in mind that AX is an all-ages event.

- Shoes are required at all times.
  - Cosplaying a character that's barefoot? Please check out this tutorial on how to make "invisible shoes."
- Costumes and clothing should not expose the body in such a way as to be deemed indecent exposure by the City of Los Angeles or the State of California. Private parts must be covered in an opaque material that will not slip or have gaps.
- Males wearing tight-fitting costumes are required to wear a dance belt.
- Costumes worn on the convention floor must not obstruct or impede the flow of traffic or entryways. If the costume cannot fit through a standard doorway, it may not be allowed during general convention hours. Exceptions may be made day-of for Masquerade contestants.
- Attendees with bulky costumes, costumes that obscure the vision, or costumes with large extensions such as wings or spikes, should have a designated "handler," to assist them through the hallways and crowds.
- Functioning wheels cannot be used as part of a costume or prop (i.e. anything that you might ride, push, or pull). We love your creativity, but please save the wheeled costumes/props for your photoshoots.
- No costumes may be realistic depictions of American law enforcement, current American military uniforms, first responders, emergency medical personnel, or any official government agent. "Vintage," historical, any non-current uniforms, and any military or police-style costumes may be addressed at the convention's discretion (i.e., Resident Evil, Metal Gear Solid, etc.).[1]

In summary, cosplay has not, for the reasons stated, been a genre of fan-created work that has generated much in the way of IP litigation or policy, except in those cases where cosplayers have attempted to monetize their involvement by selling costumes or props. In the case of the cosplayers who design and exhibit their designs at conventions, the only risk they seem to run is from their own conduct in the appropriateness of the costumes they wear or the inappropriate conduct of fans.

---

1. *Policies: Cosplay Guidelines,* AX, https://www.anime-expo.org/plan/policies (last visited Jan. 27, 2021).

SECTION 4

Winding Up and Heading Home

CHAPTER 11

Fandom, Social Media, and the Law

As noted previously throughout this book, the role of social media in providing a venue and forum for finding, reading, and uploading fan fiction; for displaying fan art and films; and even for offering a location for cosplayers to display pictures of themselves in their costumes is of great importance to fandom. It is not an exaggeration to say that the breadth and scope of fan-created works depend on, and are greatly benefited by, the ability to post materials to social media.

But that benefit is not without cost. One element of that cost is a wholesale surrender of rights over the content posted on social media. In my conference and convention talks, I am always encountering fan creators who are shocked to find out the extent of control they give up to social media companies when they upload to those platforms.

It is not my contention that the social media companies make any inappropriate use of the uploaded content—rather, it is my intention to alert creators and their counsel that the power to do just about anything with the content is a part of the standard terms and conditions these companies impose in exchange for the right to post on their platforms. An illustrative example of the broad scope of permission given to social media companies can be seen in YouTube's Terms of Service, found under its "Uploading Content" tab. These terms are replicated almost identically in the terms of service used by other social media sites like Instagram, Pinterest, etc. Let's take a look:

YouTube Terms of Service

Your Content and Conduct

Uploading Content

If you have a YouTube channel, you may be able to upload Content to the Service. You may use your Content to promote your business or artistic enterprise. If you choose to upload Content, you must not submit to the Service any Content that does not comply with this Agreement (including the YouTube Community Guidelines) or the law. For example, the Content you submit must not include third-party intellectual property (such as copyrighted material) unless you have permission from that party or are otherwise legally entitled to do so. You are legally responsible for the Content you submit to the Service. We may use automated systems that analyze your Content to help detect infringement and abuse, such as spam, malware, and illegal content.

Rights you Grant

You retain ownership rights in your Content. However, we do require you to grant certain rights to YouTube and other users of the Service, as described below.

License to YouTube

By providing Content to the Service, you grant to YouTube a worldwide, non-exclusive, royalty-free, sublicensable and transferable license to use that Content (including to reproduce, distribute, prepare derivative works, display and perform it) in connection with the Service and YouTube's (and its successors' and Affiliates') business, including for the purpose of promoting and redistributing part or all of the Service.

License to Other Users

You also grant each other user of the Service a worldwide, non-exclusive, royalty-free license to access your Content through the Service, and to use that Content, including to reproduce, distribute, prepare derivative works, display, and perform it, only as enabled by a feature of the Service (such as video playback or embeds). For clarity, this license does not grant any rights or permissions for a user to make use of your Content independent of the Service.

Duration of License

The licenses granted by you continue for a commercially reasonable period of time after you remove or delete your Content from the Ser-

> ***vice.*** You understand and agree, however, that YouTube may retain, but not display, distribute, or perform, server copies of your videos that have been removed or deleted.
>
> *Removing Your Content*
>
> You may remove your Content from the Service at any time. You also have the option to make a copy of your Content before removing it. You must remove your Content if you no longer have the rights required by these terms.
>
> *Removal of Content By YouTube*
>
> If we reasonably believe that any Content is in breach of this Agreement or may cause harm to YouTube, our users, or third parties, we may remove or take down that Content in our discretion. We will notify you with the reason for our action unless we reasonably believe that to do so: (a) would breach the law or the direction of a legal enforcement authority or would otherwise risk legal liability for YouTube or our Affiliates; (b) would compromise an investigation or the integrity or operation of the Service; or (c) would cause harm to any user, other third party, YouTube or our Affiliates. You can learn more about reporting and enforcement, including how to appeal on the Troubleshooting page of our Help Center.
>
> *Copyright Protection*
>
> We provide information to help copyright holders manage their intellectual property online in our YouTube Copyright Center. If you believe your copyright has been infringed on the Service, please send us a notice.
>
> We respond to notices of alleged copyright infringement according to the process in our YouTube Copyright Center, where you can also find information about how to resolve a copyright strike. YouTube's policies provide for the termination, in appropriate circumstances, of repeat infringers' access to the Service.[1]

The portions of these terms that I have emphasized make it clear that the act of uploading your fan-created content to YouTube and other social media platforms requires you to surrender a degree of your ownership rights to those platforms. And that surrender includes granting the platform the right to "reproduce, distribute, prepare derivative works, display and perform it) in connection with the Service and YouTube's (and its successors' and Affiliates') business, including for the purpose of promoting and redistributing part or

1. *Terms of Service*, YouTube, https://www.youtube.com/static?template=terms#fb098d3e34 (last visited Jan. 28, 2021) (emphasis added).

all of the Service." This is a broad grant of rights, and by granting the right to the platform to make a derivative use, creators truly surrender creative control over their creations. Working in the arts often requires creators to give up rights to creative control over their work—but that is a bargained-for exchange, where the consideration is usually royalties or some other tangible form of compensation.

In the case of the social media platforms, the consideration they offer in exchange for this broad grant of rights is access—access to their platforms so you can display your work and access to the large audience of users of the site.

Can you also make money putting up content on social media platforms? Yes, but not directly from YouTube or the hosts of other such platforms. Instead, you can earn money from advertisers whose ads appear on your page and from sponsors who pay for your endorsements in your capacity as a social media influencer.

Bottom line—there are benefits, in terms of exposure, participation in a community of like-minded fans, and even possible financial gain from uploading your content to a social media platform. But like any of the opportunities to display your content online, it pays to read the terms of service carefully and make sure you are willing to take the risk that your content may be used or repurposed in ways you are not comfortable with.

CHAPTER 12

Summing Up and a View of the Future

As I noted in the introduction, the scope and range of fandom are large—so much so that as I began research for this book, I abandoned the idea that I could call it a "definitive" guide even to the small subpart of fandom, fan-created work, that I am exploring here. Rather, I have endeavored to explain and guide readers through the major trends in IP law and practice that have an impact, either beneficial or negative, on that creative process, followed by a more in-depth guide to key cases and contracts that have a direct impact on creators of fan fiction, art, film, and cosplay.

Hopefully, a few key concepts are now clear. Fandom, and particularly the subset of fans who are also creators of fan-created works of expression, is bound and supported by the community of creators who work not for money or fame but for the sheer joy of creating works that celebrate programs, be they television, movies, games, etc., that they enjoyed and that have touched and enhanced their lives. And the natural progression for some fan creators is to move from the amateur status of fandom into the realm of professional creatives in pop-culture production companies. And while that is the path for financial success for fan creators, it can sometimes come at the high cost of having to leave the freedom and community spirit that drives the amateur creative community—and for some that may be too high a price to pay; for others the financial rewards may be worth it.

In the work I do at San Diego Comic-Con as a panelist in Michael Lovitz's Comic Book Law School program, and in the many lectures and talks I give to members of the fandom community, I am always struck by the lack of understanding many fan creators have of the legal issues that have an impact on their work. Many creators don't understand how copyright, right of publicity, contract terms, and the workings of the legal process can have a substantial impact on their creative process. I have to also note that many lawyers who encounter and are engaged by these creatives may lack formal training in IP law generally, and how those legal doctrines impact pop-culture creators, and as a consequence are unable to fully meet the legal needs of those clients. It is for both of these constituencies that this book is written.

The future for fan creators looks from my vantage point to be a mixed bag. The two most positive developments are the development and continued growth of sites devoted particularly to fan creations, like AO3 and DevianArt, and more general social media platforms like YouTube, which have vastly increased the potential reading and viewing audience for fan fiction, art, and films; and the adoption of the transformative doctrine in copyright law by federal courts throughout the country—a development that has greatly extended the reach of the fair-use doctrine and allowed many otherwise unauthorized derivative works to be published and to add their contributions to the fandom community and the world at large.

But each of these benefits is balanced by some darker trends in fan-created work. Principal among these are the development and spread of the "guidelines" approach used by major production companies that control key portions of pop culture to limit the content fan creators can express without encountering threats of infringement lawsuits and the use of the "universe" approach by Paramount/CBS in the *Axanar* case to get around the fan creator's argument that his work did not infringe. These legal trends may have the effect of constraining the creativity of fan creators.

Ultimately, I end this journey as an optimist. The power, passion, and depth of the community of fan creators is deep, and their love of these pop-culture programs is so strong that I am confident they will surpass the limitations and continue to offer us their joy and their work. I look forward to years of enjoyment of their efforts.

INDEX

D

I

J

K

L

M

T

U

V

W

X

Y

Z

About the ABA Section of Intellectual Property Law

From its strength within the American Bar Association, the ABA Section of Intellectual Property Law (ABA-IPL) advances the development and improvement of intellectual property laws and their fair and just administration. The Section furthers the goals of its members by sharing knowledge and balanced insight on the full spectrum of intellectual property law and practice, including patents, trademarks, copyright, design, and trade secrets. Providing a forum for rich perspectives and reasoned commentary, ABA-IPL serves as the ABA voice of intellectual property law within the profession, before policy makers, and with the public.

ABA Section of Intellectual Property Law (ABA-IPL)
Order today! Call 800-285-2221
Monday-Friday, 8:00 a.m. – 5:00 p.m., CT
or visit www.ambar.org/iplbooks.

Qty	Title	Regular Price	ABA-IPL Member Price	Total
_____	ADR Advocacy, Strategies, and Practices for Intellectual Property and Technology Cases, 2nd Ed. (5370231)	$149.95	$119.95	$_____
_____	ANDA Litigation, 3rd Ed. (5370243)	$379.00	$295.95	$_____
_____	Antitrust Issues in Intellectual Property Law (5370222)	$149.95	$119.95	$_____
_____	Arbitrating Patent Disputes (5370229)	$89.95	$74.95	$_____
_____	Careers in IP Law (5370204) (The ebook is complimentary with ABA-IPL Section membership)	$24.95	$16.95	$_____
_____	Commercialization of IP Rights in China (5370241)	$119.95	$95.95	$_____
_____	Computer Games and Immersive Entertainment, 2nd Ed. (5370239)	$89.95	$69.95	$_____
_____	Copyright Litigation Strategies (5370228)	$369.00	$285.00	$_____
_____	Copyright Remedies (5370208)	$89.95	$74.95	$_____
_____	Copyright Termination Law (5370226)	$139.95	$109.95	$_____
_____	Crash Course on U.S. Patent Law (5370221)	$39.95	$34.95	$_____
_____	The DMCA Handbook; Second Edition (5370234)	$79.95	$64.95	$_____
_____	The Essential Case Law Guide to PTAB Trials (5370233)	$249.95	$199.95	$_____
_____	The Essentials of Japanese Patent Prosecution (5370245)	$149.95	$119.95	$_____
_____	Fandom and the Law (5370251)	$59.95	$47.95	$_____
_____	Fundamentals of Intellectual Property Law (5370218)	$89.95	$69.95	$_____
_____	Intellectural Property and Technology Due Diligence (5370236)	$219.95	$179.95	$_____
_____	The Intellectual Property Law Handbook, 2nd Ed. (5620154)	$139.95	$109.95	$_____
_____	IP Attorney's Handbook for Insurance Coverage in Intellectual Property Disputes, 2nd Ed. (5370210)	$139.95	$129.95	$_____
_____	IP Protection in China (5370217)	$139.95	$109.95	$_____
_____	IP Strategies for Medical Device Technologies (5370238)	$149.95	$119.95	$_____
_____	IP Valuation for the Future (5370237)	$89.95	$59.95	$_____
_____	The Law of Trade Secret Litigation Under the Uniform Trade Secrets Act, 2nd Ed. (5370242)	$369.95	$295.95	$_____
_____	A Lawyer's Guide to Section 337 Investigations before the U.S. International Trade Commission, 4th Ed. (5370240)	$139.95	$109.95	$_____
_____	Legal Guide to Video Game Development, 2nd Ed. (5370227)	$74.95	$59.95	$_____
_____	A Legal Strategist's Guide to Trademark Trial and Appeal Board Practice, 4th Ed. (5370247)	$179.95	$144.95	$_____
_____	Music & Copyright in America (5370201)	$97.95	$67.95	$_____
_____	New Practitioner's Guide to Intellectual Property (5370198)	$89.95	$69.95	$_____
_____	Patent Freedom to Operate Searches, Opinions, Techniques, and Studies (5370230)	$139.95	$109.95	$_____
_____	Patent Neutral (5370232)	$89.95	$69.95	$_____
_____	Patent Trial Advocacy Casebook, 3rd Ed. (5370124)	$149.95	$119.95	$_____